BUSINESS AND PROFESSIONAL SPEAKING

ERIC W. SKOPEC
Syracuse University

Prentice-Hall, Inc., Englewood Cliffs, New Jersey 07632

Library of Congress Cataloging in Publication Data

Skopec, Eric W., (date)
    Business and professional speaking.

    Includes index.
    1. Oral communication.   I. Title.
PN4121.S4857   1983   001.54′2   82-21520
ISBN 0-13-107532-2

Editorial/production supervision and
  interior design: Andrew Roney
Cover design: 20/20 Services, Inc.
Manufacturing buyer: Ron Chapman

Printed in the United States of America

10 9 8 7 6 5 4 3 2 1

ISBN 0-13-107532-2

Prentice-Hall International, Inc., *London*
Prentice-Hall of Australia Pty. Limited, *Sydney*
Editora Prentice-Hall do Brasil, Ltda., *Rio de Janeiro*
Prentice-Hall Canada Inc., *Toronto*
Prentice-Hall of India Private Limited, *New Delhi*
Prentice-Hall of Japan, Inc., *Tokyo*
Prentice-Hall of Southeast Asia Pte. Ltd., *Singapore*
Whitehall Books Limited, *Wellington, New Zealand*

CONTENTS

PREFACE

As you read this book, you will be sharing my experiences with three groups of people. One very prominent group is composed of college students, those people with whom I have most worked in recent years. This is a very diverse group; the interests of its many members cover the full range of programs offered in three major universities. However, all had one thing in common—the desire to improve the communication skills required for their chosen professions. This group taught me how to adapt my ideas to the needs of students undertaking the systematic study of professional communication.

The second group is composed of the professionals with whom I've worked in my role as a communication consultant. These professionals include engineers, scientists, managers, foremen, production superintendents, plant managers, personnel directors, training specialists, secretaries, salesmen, and teachers. All have shared the demands of their professions with me; in addition, from their descriptions I have learned to recognize opportunities for professional communication; finally, they have shown me how to adapt concepts and principles to everyday situations.

The final group consists of scholars, past and present, who have studied the nature and effects of communication. This group is probably the least familiar to you and deserves a special introduction. Although the study of organizational communication and business and professional speaking seems to be in its infancy, civilized men have always been fascinated by the power of spoken words. The efforts of our remote ancestors to preserve their experiences through primative drawings show their reverence for the magic power of symbolism, and our earliest written records note the accomplishments of skilled speakers. In spite of wars, famines, and natural disasters, we have a nearly unbroken record of speculation about speech-making covering more than twenty-four centuries. This record bridges the gulf from the speculative methods of ancient Greek philosophers to the most sophisticated methods of contemporary behavioral scientists. I was fortunate that my study of this tradition was guided by thoughtful instructors and colleagues who showed me that it provides a nearly inexhaustible source of concepts, materials, and approaches applicable to professional communication. One instructor in particular, Douglas Ehninger, formerly of the University of Iowa, pushed me to see that concepts from earlier centuries could be applied to current concerns; and for his prodding, I will be always grateful.

As you now turn to the study of professional communication, I encourage you to take advantage of contributions from representatives of the same groups. The students with whom you explore the demands of professional communication can help you to experience good and bad features of presentations; the colleagues with whom you work in professional activities can provide suggestions and feedback to help direct your development; and the rhetorical tradition continues to evolve as studies of human interaction provide an ever broader and more substantial foundation for understanding professional communication.

Eric Skopec

CHAPTER ONE
INTRODUCTION

Interest in professional communication has grown rapidly in recent years and it is generally recognized that the ability to communicate effectively is necessary in most professions. A recent survey conducted by the American Management Association asked senior managers to identify those factors that were most likely to interfere with career advancement. Remarkably, "lack of adequate communicative and other interpersonal skills" was second only to "lack of own adequate managerial talents and/or professional skills." Communication ranked ahead of such commonly mentioned factors as "sex, age, race, or matters involving private life or personal habits," "being too closely identified with a particular organizational faction or power group," "inadequate career planning and guidance," and "competition from better-educated managers."[1]

The growing awareness of communication is a direct result of the increasing complexity of organizations on which most professionals depend. Saul W. Gellerman, a management consultant and frequent contributor to *Harvard Business Review,* explains the function of communication in complex organizations:

> Nothing is more central to an organization's effectiveness than its ability to transmit accurate, relevant, understandable information among its members. All the advan-

[1] Robert F. Pearse, *Manager to Manager II: What Managers Think of Their Managerial Careers, An AMA Survey Report* (New York: AMACOM, a division of American Management Associations, 1977), p. 31

tages of organizations—economy of scale, financial and technical resources, diverse talents, and contacts—are of no practical value if the organization's members are unaware of what other members require of them, and why. Awareness enables them to put their resources, talents, and contacts to work in a concerted, responsive way. Thus, the role of communication in an organization is roughly analogous to that of a nervous system in a living organism—it orchestrates what would otherwise be chaotic.[2]

Because communication is central to the functions of any organization, most employers evaluate job applicants' communication skills during screening interviews. Satisfactory communication skills, too, are often required for advancement into managerial ranks. For example, over 800 large companies use assessment centers to identify potential managers, and a glance at the criteria used shows the importance of communication.

Although inadequately developed communication skills can be harmful to your career, you should not be intimidated. You already have developed a substantial number of communication skills, including techniques of receiving information (listening, reading); techniques of making yourself understood (speaking, writing, and nonverbal signalling); and techniques of securing compliance (threatening, begging, and persuading). The number and sophistication of your techniques depend largely on the environment in which you were raised and the emphasis placed on communication by those with whom you associated. But, however broad and sophisticated your existing skills, the best way to enhance your speaking ability is to capitalize on your prior experiences. Many of your existing techniques will work in professional contexts, but some will need to be revised or discarded; and, you will probably need to develop additional skills to cope with the relatively formal nature of presentational speaking. In fact, many people find themselves relatively well equipped to cope with communication situations other than formal presentations.

This introductory chapter is designed to help you make the most of your existing skills and to identify new skills to be developed. In it, the nature of oral communication is discussed, communication in organizations is described, and the role of presentational speaking is highlighted. A final section explains the plan of this book.

THE NATURE OF COMMUNICATION

Communication is the process through which people exchange information. This relatively simple definition avoids a number of fascinating and complex issues,[3] but it is ideal for our purposes because it focuses on elements common to many

[2] From THE MANAGEMENT OF HUMAN RESOURCES by Saul W. Gellerman, p. 54. Copyright © 1976 by the Dryden Press, a division of Holt, Rinehart and Winston. Reprinted by permission of Holt, Rinehart and Winston, CBS College Publishing.

[3] Interest in the study of communication has diffused in recent years and the basic concepts have become blurred as a result. The notion of communication has been applied to situations as diverse as life itself. At one extreme, researchers have found it profitable to study neurological pro-

familiar situations. The common elements are: a message, the source of the message, one or more receivers to whom the message is directed, and the context or setting in which communication takes place. Exploring each of these components provides a background for a discussion of communication in professional contexts.

The Message

Messages are central to the communication process and we normally experience them as the essence or substance of interaction. Whether the message is a casual greeting, a written report, or a formal presentation, it is the focal point of the communication process. Although its concept is relatively simple and commonplace, we should consider several distinctions. First, messages may be either written or oral. Letters, reports, books, and newspapers are all written messages. Speeches, lectures, sermons, conversations, and discussions are common oral messages.

Second, messages can be verbal or nonverbal. Verbal messages are those that use language and consist of spoken or written words. Nonverbal messages include all of the unspoken qualifiers that affect the way in which verbal messages are interpreted. Nonverbal messages include facial expression, posture, gesture, and vocal qualities (volume, rate, and pitch). Both verbal and nonverbal components are present in all messages, and several studies have attempted to describe their relative impact. Albert Mehrabian has argued that only 7 percent of the total impact of a message is attributable to the verbal components—what is said—while 93 percent is attributable to nonverbal components—the way it is said.[4] Less controversial estimates indicate that nonverbal components carry 65 percent of the message and verbal components represent 35 percent in face-to-face interaction.[5]

Third, messages may be intended or accidental. Intended messages are those items of information that the speaker deliberately presents to the other person. Accidental messages are those that a listener observes or infers from the manner, conduct, and appearance of the speaker. The importance of accidental messages is evident to interviewers who frequently ask job candidates stress questions. These interviewers listen to what the applicant says, but they are more interested in signs of discomfort that may betray an applicant's lack of confidence.

Finally, messages may be either primary or secondary. Primary messages

---

cesses as communication, while scholars at the other end of the spectrum characterize entire societies as communication systems. In addition, a variety of theoretical perspectives has emerged and traditional notions about the constituents of the communication process have been challenged. You may want to explore some of the emerging issues and the following books are a good starting point: Philip Emmert and William C. Donaghy, *Human Communication* (Reading, Mass.: Addison-Wesley, 1981); B. Aubrey Fisher, *Perspectives on Human Communication* (New York: Macmillan 1978): and Gerhard J. Hanneman and William J. McEwen, eds., *Communication and Behavior* (Reading, Mass.: Addison-Wesley, 1975).

[4] Albert Mehrabian, "Communication Without Words," *Psychology Today* (1968), 52–55.

[5] John W. Keltner, *Interpersonal Speech Communication* (Belmont, Calif.: Wadsworth, 1970), p. 107.

TABLE 1.1 Comparison of Variables from Selected Programs

AT&T	IBM	SOHIO	IRS	WOLVERINE TUBE DIVISION OF UNIVERSAL OIL PRODUCTS
Organization and planning	*Self-confidence	*Amount of participation	Decision making	Intellectual ability
Decision making	*Written communications	*Oral communication	Decisiveness	*Oral communication skills
Creativity	*Administrative ability	Personal acceptability	Flexibility	*Written communication skills
*Human relations skills	*Interpersonal contact	*Impact	*Leadership	*Leadership
*Behavior flexibility	Energy level	*Quality of participation	*Oral communications	Creativeness
*Personal impact	Decision making	Personal breadth	Organization and planning	Self-objectivity
Tolerance of uncertainty	Resistance to stress	Orientation to detail	*Perception and analytic ability	Behavior flexibility
Resistance to stress	Planning and organizing	Self-direction	*Persuasiveness	Primacy of work
Scholastic aptitude	*Persuasiveness	*Relationship with authority	*Sensitivity to people	Realism of expectations
Range of interests	Aggressiveness	Originality	Stress tolerance	Range of interests
Inner work standards	Risk taking	*Understanding of people		Energy and drive
Primacy of work	*Oral communications	Drive		Acceptance
*Oral communications skills		Potential		Organization and planning
*Perception of social cues				Initiative
Self-objectivity				Decision making
Energy				Motivation
Realism of expectations				
Bell System value orientation				
Social objectivity				
Need advancement				
Ability to delay gratification				
Need for superior approval				
Need for peer approval				
Goal flexibility				
Need for security				
Staff prediction				

From Robert B. Finkle, "Managerial Assessment Centers," in Marvin D. Dunnette, ed., *Handbook of Industrial and Organizational Psychology*, (Chicago: Rand McNally 1976). p. 872. Stars have been added to the criteria that relate most directly to communication.

are the explicit content of the communication, while there are three types of secondary messages. One type of secondary message is called *feedback,* which consists of reactions to the primary message. Feedback shows whether or not the primary message is being received, how it is being interpreted, and whether or not the receiver agrees with it. The second type of secondary message concerns the *relationship* between the participants. All messages include both content and relationship dimensions, and the relative importance of the two varies from situation to situation. In smoothly functioning relationships, elements of the message dealing with the relationship are submerged and assumed. But, in cases of conflict or tension, the relationship dimension becomes so important that explicit content is sacrificed to status or ego games. The final type of secondary message consists of *cues* as to how the primary message should be interpreted. A message may be a request for information or an opinion (question); a statement without behavioral implications (conversation or gossip); a recommendation or suggestion; or an order. For example, a friend who says, "I hear Professor Skopec is teaching Organizational Communication again this fall," may be asking for confirmation or an opinion (a question); passing time (conversation); recommending that you take the course; or—if he is your adviser—encouraging (ordering?) you to take the course. Conflicts often result from confusion at this level and many people have difficulty recognizing secondary messages of this type.

The Source

The source is the second element in communication. The *source* can be defined at the person who creates the message, and this interpretation is satisfactory for many situations. At a lecture, the speaker is the source; in a sales interview, the sales representative is the source; in a church service, the minister is the source. However, in situations where there are high degrees of interaction, there are likely to be a number of messages present. In casual situations, both parties provide substantial portions of the conversation; in meetings, most participants contribute to the discussion; and in many classrooms, the teacher is one source of information, while students contribute their experiences and opinions. The point of the preceding examples is this: In most situations involving high degrees of interaction, there are many sources because everyone present contributes. As a result, it is often more fruitful to think of the source as a function that everyone shares. As the conversation ebbs and flows, each person will be the source of some messages and the reciever of others. And even when one person is acting as the source—for example, the speaker in a formal situation—the reactions of other members contribute to the total interaction. At any time, any member may function as the source by contributing oral or written, verbal and nonverbal, intended and accidental, and primary and secondary messages.

Although it may be difficult or impossible to identify the person who is *the* source in a communication, understanding the function of a source is important because the outcome of any communication event depends in large part on the ability of the individual communicators. When you function as the source, you can influence the outcome of the event by the way in which you generate messages. The extent to which you succeed in accomplishing your objectives through communication depends in large measure on your ability to function as a source. The specific skills you need to exercise in functioning as a source include explaining and proving your ideas, using visual representations when appropriate, choosing an appropriate level of language, organizing the message in a coherent manner, delivering the message in an acceptable way, and adapting to the particular audience you face. These are fundamental skills, which we will examine more closely in Part I of this book.

The Receiver

The difficulties encountered in trying to identifying the source of a communication can also occur when trying to determine the *receiver*. In most communication situations participants are constantly shifting roles, being both source and receiver at different times. And, with the use of active listening techniques, effective receivers are constantly sending secondary messages to show that they are receiving the primary message. It is important to understand, too, the way in which messages are received because it has implications for the way you send them.

Studies of perception show that receiving messages is a more complex process than most people realize. These studies indicate that people actively construct messages from isolated cues rather than receiving them intact. To understand this point, you need to realize that we are constantly bombarded by changes in our environment that have the potential to make an impression on our sensory organs. Changes in temperature and pressure affect our tactile senses, changes in the level and intensity of light affect our eyes, vibrations in the air affect our ears, and so forth. Each of these changes constitutes a cue and could become an object of our attention. However, because so many cues could be overwhelming, we learn to disregard most of them as unimportant. In other words, from the potential cues around us, we select those to which we pay attention. This is a basic perceptual process that affects our reception of a speaker's message as well as our reaction to other elements of the environment.

We construct a picture that fits the isolated cues recorded by our senses into a pattern, which, in turn, helps us make sense out of our environment. For example, when John sits at his desk, he notices these sounds: a continuous buzz and a soft hum in the room he is occupying, a constant hammering in the next room, and occasional, distant blaring noises. Someone who had never been exposed to these patterns of stimuli might find this a terrifying experience, but John recognizes the sounds as coming from the air conditioner, a defective neon bulb, a secretary typing correspondence, and cars honking at pedestrians on a nearby street. In receiving a message, we function in much the same manner. From the sounds, gestures, facial expressions, visual images, and movements of the speaker we construct a message that includes meaning, purpose, attitude, motive, pattern, and many other features of interest.

Finally, the message to which we respond may have little relation to the message the speaker intended to send. We may or may not have attended to cues the speaker generated; we may have interpreted words, gestures, and expressions in a manner other than he or she intended; and, we may have organized the fragmentary cues into a pattern totally unexpected by the speaker. Thus, before a receiver even decides whether or not to agree with the speaker, a thousand things may have happened to distinguish the message sent by the speaker and the message recognized by the receiver.

Understanding the reception process is important because it explains the value of many techniques introduced in this book. Many of them have been developed through trial and error over centuries in which people have communicated with one another. Our knowledge of human information processing has only recently reached the level needed to explain the value of these techniques, but the explanation conforms nicely with the recorded experience of speakers and scholars alike. Some techniques affect the selection of cues by emphasizing some and reducing competition from outside sources; other techniques help receivers structure perceived cues into predictable patterns; and some techniques present ideas in terms most likely to promote agreement.

The Context

The final element in communication is the context or setting in which the event takes place. Every communication event takes place in some context or setting and the importance of context is implicit in what has been said about the other elements. As you can imagine, a detailed analysis of any communication event reveals a startling complexity that we seldom notice. Everyone involved in the event is generating cues that could be joined to form written or oral, verbal or nonverbal, intended or accidental, and primary or secondary messages. Adding to the complexity is the fact that each receiver independently selects cues to pay attention to, organizes the cues into messages that are meaningful to him or her, and reacts to the messages as he or she thinks appropriate. Each of these processes is governed by expectations receivers bring to the event but seldom discuss. The reason that we seldom notice this complexity, and the reason it is possible for us to develop some common meanings, is that the context or setting is a common factor shared by the participants. This common factor helps participants communicate with one another by indicating what expectations are appropriate and how message elements or cues should be processed.

Although it is easy to think about the context as a common factor, it is more accurate to say "relatively common factor." This correction is necessary because we know that no two people view a situation in quite the same way and because two people from very different cultures are likely to see any situation in very different ways. However, for the overwhelming majority of people raised in our culture, most settings call up some common expectations. For example, think about the expectations most people share when they attend a college lecture: the verbal and nonverbal cues of the lecturer constitute a message; cues from other sources—traffic noises, room temperature, audience reactions, and movement outside the room—are "distractions" and should be ignored; accidental messages showing that the lecturer is unsure of herself may be recognized, but should not diminish the worth of her intended message; the "principal points" listed on the blackboard should be remembered and may be used to organize notes; and, those who disagree with the lecturer should not interrupt her until she pauses for questions or comments. Of course, these are only a few of the expectations we bring to a lecture, but they make it possible for participants to communicate with one another by indicating which cues deserve attention, how they are to be organized, what evaluations are appropriate, and what behavior is proper. When one or more of these expectations is not shared by members of the audience, chaos is likely to result and little information will be exchanged.[6]

COMMUNICATION IN ORGANIZATIONS

Organizations are groups of people working together to achieve a common purpose within a defined structure. Understanding organizations is important to your development as a speaker because they are the dominant feature of contemporary professional activity. Virtually all of your professional communication will take place in situations defined by one or more organizations. As a professional, you will communicate both within and outside of organizations. *Within* the organization to which you belong, you will communicate with people defined as your superiors, peers, and/or subordinates; *outside* of your organization, you will represent the group in dealings with members of other organizations. In both internal and external communication, the nature of the organization will influence the kind of communication in which you engage. It will affect who you communicate with, how you address them, what subjects you discuss, how the subjects are handled, and a host of other factors regulating your communicative behavior.

The study of communication in organizations has expanded dramatically in recent years and several volumes could be consumed merely listing relevant research.[7] This research has demonstrated the effects of two elements, hierarchy and climate, on communication within and between organizations.

Hierarchy in Organizations

To coordinate the activities of individuals in order to accomplish common objectives, organizations have evolved structures specifying each individual's relationship to other members. These relationships are defined according to duties

---

[6] Of course, participants may choose to disrupt a lecture or other gathering as a means of "sending a message" to someone else, and this was frequently the case during the protests of the late 1960s. However, once that happens, little information is likely to be communicated between participants in the setting.

[7] For example, see Howard H. Greenbaum, Raymond L. Falcione, et al., eds., *Organizational Communication Abstracts,* published by Sage Publications in cooperation with the American Business Communication Association and the International Communication Association (1974–1982).

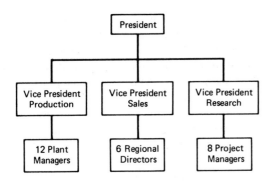

FIGURE 1.1.

and responsibilities, and they are recorded in organizational charts describing official communication patterns. The hypothetical example in Figure 1.1 is fairly typical, demonstrating most of the important features of organizational hierarchies.

In this hypothetical organization, the company president is responsible for overall coordination of the organization, while the vice presidents are responsible for more specific activities roughly described as production, sales, and research. Below the vice presidents, plant managers, regional directors, and project managers have more limited responsibilities; people under the supervision of these three groups have even more specific responsibilities. The pattern described here is characteristic of all organizations: members at higher levels have broader, less clearly defined responsibilities than members at lower levels; those at lower levels have narrower, more clearly defined responsibilities than those above them. Thus, the company president is likely to be concerned with broad policy matters and may become involved in specific problems only when they cannot be resolved at lower levels. Conversely, employees at lower levels of the organization are rarely concerned with policy matters and are likely to perform their duties in a relatively unambiguous environment created by specific directives from higher levels.

Individuals at any level are usually given sufficient authority to carry out their assigned duties. This distribution of power gives rise to the vocabulary commonly used to describe positions within organizations. Each person has more authority than those below him or her and is *superior* with respect to them. Each person has less power than those above and is *subordinate* with respect to them. People at the same level have the same amount of authority and are said to be *peers*.[8]

The existence of divisions and levels within organizations gives rise to

---

[8] Of course, there are some important exceptions to the principle that power or authority corresponds to level. Within most organizations, some functions are seen to be less important than others. People occupying positions in less important functional areas have less authority and less power than their peers in other areas. For example, the personnel function is often seen to be less important than production and a personnel director is likely to be less influential than peers in other divisions. Similarly, the manager of a small project is less powerful than a peer directing a larger project.

clearly defined channels and patterns of communication. People in each division are expected to communicate *up* to their superior and *down* to their subordinates. Going "over your superior's head" to talk to his or her superior or bypassing an immediate subordinate to talk to someone lower in the hierarchy is considered to be bad manners by most professionals. Talking with peers is an accepted practice when the conversation relates to shared problems and responsibilities. Communication that does not correspond to this pattern is frowned upon, but most experienced professionals recognize the existence of unofficial communication networks ("grapevines") and occasionally use them to their own advantage.

In addition to established channels and patterns, organizational hierarchies regulate the type of communication that takes place between participants at different levels. Although new theories of management deemphasize these structured types of communication, they remain the practice in most organizations. Superiors give instructions to subordinates and occasionally pass information "down the line." Subordinates report to their superiors and occasionally make requests. Power relationships between peers are ambiguous, so they may cooperate or compete with one another and often engage in negotiation.

The hypothetical organization used in the preceding discussion consists of a relatively simple hierarchy. More complex structures, called *project* or *matrix* organizations, have emerged in recent years. The essence of these organizations is the use of multiple hierarchies within the organization. For example, matrix organizations use one line or hierarchy for all personnel functions and another line for project functions. The effect of this type of structure is a substantial increase in the number of people who are peers to one another and a reduction in the number of traditional superior-subordinate patterns. However, even in this environment, participants in superior-subordinate relationships recognize one another and engage in appropriate forms of communication.

Organizational Climate

Organizational climate is a characteristic of organizations that is roughly equivalent to personality in individuals. Just as individuals differ in the way they react to situations, organizations have characteristic behavior patterns that are more or less uniformly employed by their members. The extremes are easy to visualize and most people recognize them quickly. Some organizations are warm and accepting, they welcome outsiders, and participants at all levels appreciate contributions from nonmembers. Other organizations are cold and rigid, they distrust strangers, and members from the chairperson of the board to the receptionist behave in a distant manner structured by formal conventions. Of course, real organizations fill nearly every spot between these extremes. The number of different factors involved has made it difficult for researchers to identify the dimensions of organizational climate, and a formal definition that includes all of the phenomena that have been studied is not easy to formulate. Some scholars have suggested dropping the concept, but it is useful to think of the climate in an organization as the work-related attitudes shared by its members. It also helps to clarify "unwritten rules" of conduct, which include at least three elements of communication.

One of the most important effects of climate is the extent to which hierarchy limits communication between members. Some organizations are extremely conscious of their hierarchical structure and communication patterns are strictly enforced. Subordinate behavior includes a great deal of deference expressed in a variety of ways: at meetings nobody sits down until the top person does, seating may be arranged by level, subordinates speak only when addressed, and subordinates use formal titles when speaking, while superiors use first names. Conversely, other organizations function as if the hierarchy were merely an administrative convenience: members sit where they wish at meetings, individuals speak without regard to title or seniority, and friendships are likely to be more important than formal relationships.

The second element of communication related to climate is the willingness of participants to deal with personal or emotional issues. Emotions are involved whenever people work together and they may be a dominant factor in some relationships. However, some organizations refuse to recognize emotional issues and function as if they did not exist. Members of these organizations suppress personal feelings and try to function in a totally objective manner. Other organizations recognize the effect of emotions on work-related behavior and legitimize their expression. In these organizations, superiors encourage expression of emotions and they deal with subjective matters as they would with any other feature of the work environment.

The third communication element affected by climate is the manner in which members deal with mistakes or failures. Some organizations impose severe penalities for even minor errors and anyone calling attention to a mistake is likely to be punished as well. The result of these practices is a norm of secrecy in which subordinates withhold damaging information from their superiors, and peers are likely to use information as a weapon in their dealings with one another. Other organizations develop policies such that neither the person making an error nor the person reporting it is punished. The result of such nonpunitive behavior is an open, supportive climate in which mistakes are discussed in order to avoid further difficulties.

PRESENTATIONAL SPEAKING

As a professional, you will be called upon to communicate in a variety of settings. These settings include casual conversations with coworkers, at one end of the spectrum, and formal presentations, at the other end. Scholars studying human communication have found it convenient to divide settings into three broad categories: interpersonal communication, small group communication, and public communication. These categories differ from one another in the size of the audience, but all three include casual and formal varieties.

Interpersonal communication is face-to-face communication between two people. The most common form is casual conversation in which participants employ interaction patterns reflecting their personalities and their relationship. Both parties contribute roughly equal amounts to conversations called "symmetrical exchanges," but one person may do most or even all of the talking in "complementary exchanges." Formal kinds of interpersonal communication are called interviews and they are often distinguished from conversations by the fact that one of the parties—or perhaps both—is trying to accomplish something as a result of the interaction. The fact that interviews are conducted for a purpose gives rise to the convention of naming them according to the purpose the interviewer. Selection interviews, sales interviews, appraisal interviews, and information gathering interviews are common forms.

Small group communication includes all forms of face-to-face communication involving three to fifteen people. The upper limit is arbitrary, but it reflects the fact that in groups that are larger than fifteen it is nearly impossible for everyone to participate without the imposition of parliamentary rules. Such rules change a discussion into a series of short speeches, and situations employing such rules are commonly studied as instances of public communication. Casual forms of small group communication are called discussions and are characterized by a relatively relaxed atmosphere. Formal types are called meetings and usually employ agendas that list purposes, topics, and time limits.

When groups grow beyond fifteen, the resulting communication is generally considered to be public communication. Because of the size, participants must take turns in addressing the group. This creates a restrictive environment in which each contribution becomes a longer, more carefully prepared statement. Our vocabulary does not provide a name for casual types, but the term *presentational speaking* is used to refer to the formal variety. The manner in which interruptions from the audience are handled makes it easy to distinguish presentational from casual settings. In relatively informal public communication, the speaker may pause to answer questions from the audience, may engage in a dialogue with members of the audience, and may even relinquish the floor during the presentation to give others the opportunity to comment. In presentational speaking, interruptions from the audience are ignored and discussion or comment is postponed until after the speaker has completed the presentation.

While reading the descriptions of common communication settings, you probably realized that you have the least experience in situations calling for formal presentations. In fact, formal presentations may be the most difficult for you because you have relatively little experience making them and because they differ from other forms of interaction in two respects. First, in a formal presentation, you are the focal point of the interaction and all attention should be focused on you and your message. Any deviation from this norm is a sign of trouble. Second, the fact that other people are not free to interrupt you—to contribute ideas or to ask questions—means that you must carry the entire presentation without the interaction that normally provides direction in other settings. In other words, in all of the other settings, remarks by other participants contribute to the interaction and provide direction for your own statements. But, in the formal presentation, you alone provide the content and direct the flow of ideas.

Because formal presentations make special demands on communicators, this text introduces a refined approach to professional communication, emphasizing the skills most needed in formal presentations. These skills are related to those used in other forms of communication and may be adapted to less formal varieties, but the primary focus is on the formal presentation.

PLAN OF THIS BOOK

Taken as a whole, the text is a nearly comprehensive discussion of presentational activities in modern organizations; virtually every type of formal presentation you are likely to encounter is described. The amount of material covered could be a barrier to the beginning student, but the order of presentation has been designed to reduce difficulty. Part I introduces the essential skills used in presentational speaking and beginners are expected to start by learning the concepts and skills introduced in this section.

Part II describes common professional presentations. The chapters in this section furnish relatively specific directions for presentations that you are most likely to encounter. Beginning students should master the material in Part II before progressing to these speeches, while speakers of intermediate ability may use Part II for review and begin with Part III.

Finally, the chapters in Part III explain the application of presentational skills to dyadic and small group communication. These chapters are not intended to survey the extensive and rapidly growing literature on organizational communication, and they are not adequate substitutes for specialized training in interpersonal communication, group discussion, and conference leadership. However, by adapting presentational skills to less formal contexts, they expand the range of situations in which you can function effectively.

SUMMARY

Communication is vital to organizations and many companies regularly evaluate the skills of job applicants and current personnel. You have already developed a variety of communication skills and expanding your abilities requires attention to the nature of communication, factors affecting communication in organizations, and the character of presentational speaking. Communication is the process through which people exchange information, and common elements of communication include message, source, receiver(s), and context. As a professional, your communication will be within an organization when you interact with superiors, peers, and subordinates, and outside the organization when you interact with representatives of other organizations. Organizational hierarchy and climate affect the communicative behavior of most members. Your professional activities will include formal and informal varieties of interpersonal, small group, and public communication, and presentational speaking is the formal variety of public communication.

LEARNING ACTIVITIES

1. Ask your instructor, campus placement officer, academic adviser, or friends to help you identify several professionals who now hold the kind of position that you would like to have. Arrange appointments with some of the professionals and ask each to talk about the role of communication in his or her field. What types of communication are important? With whom do they communicate? How much time do they spend communicating? What can you do to prepare yourself for the kinds of communication they encounter?

2. Interview several people who hold positions at different levels in the same organization. Ask each to describe the kinds of communication in which they participate, the importance of communication to them, and the amount of time they spend communicating. How do their experiences differ? To what extent are these differences the result of their positions in the organization? How would you explain these differences to the people involved?

3. Generate a list of topics you might use for classroom presentations. Begin by making a chart with five columns to record potential topics in the following areas: (1) national and international affairs, (2) state and local news, (3) campus events and activities, (4) classes and academic responsibilities, and (5) hobbies and personal experiences. Keep the list in your notebook and add to it whenever you encounter a topic that might be interesting.

4. Watch the reactions of other students to a particularly boring lecture. How can you tell that they are bored? What kinds of verbal and nonverbal feedback are they sending? Is the lecturer adapting to the feedback? How would you react if you were the lecturer?

PART ONE
BASIC SKILLS

Making a presentation is a complex process, and Chapter 1 has shown you some of the factors involved. The total message you present includes written and oral components, verbal and nonverbal elements, intended and accidental cues, and primary and secondary messages. Each receiver reconstructs your message according to individual expectations and the context only partially reduces chances for misunderstanding. You need to be sensitive to the effects of hierarchy and climate in the organization, and the nature of presentational speaking makes novel demands on you. You are the focal point and the audience is not free to interact with you as they would in other settings.

This complexity can be a real barrier to learning because there appears to be no easy starting point. Some students conclude that they just don't have it—whatever "it" is—and give up. Too often it seems that some people are good speakers, other people are poor speakers, and there is no way to move from the second group into the first. Such pessimism is unfortunate because those most in need of instruction in presentational speaking avoid it, and more skilled speakers overlook opportunities for improvement.

The easiest way to overcome pessimism and frustration is to break the presentational speaking process into smaller parts and introduce them one at a time. This procedure is used here because it allows you to develop your skills one at a time and provides a good foundation for further learning. In the following chapters, you will learn how to make your ideas meaningful to an audience, use visual representations for best advantage, organize a coherent presentation, employ appropriate language, deliver your message without distraction, and adapt to specific audiences. These divisions are logical breaking points in the process, but you should remember that they are arbitrary. Audiences react to the whole presentation and seldom recognize elements that contributed to good or bad impressions. Finished presentations succeed or fail as a unit, but studying them a piece at a time makes it easier to recognize the good and bad in each.

CHAPTER TWO
VERBAL DEVELOPING MATERIALS

The first step in mastering presentational speaking is learning how to make your ideas meaningful to an audience. Here you can benefit from the practice of experienced speakers who have learned to prepare speeches a piece at a time. They draft a number of small units, which are eventually combined to form the speech. This is the easiest way to write a speech because the fundamental process of composition is making a statement and then developing it. In this context, the word *develop* means to expand on the statement in order to make it more understandable or acceptable to the audience. In fact, the process of making a statement and expanding upon it is so basic that entire speeches may consist of nothing more than a single statement and its associated developing materials. For example, a complete speech might be written around the statement, "communication skills are essential to success in business." Someone composing such a speech would probably develop the statement by defining the phrase "communication skills," adding an example or two, introducing some statistics, and concluding with a humorous anecdote. Here is what this basic speech would look like in outline form:

I.   Communication skills are essential for success in business.
    A.   These skills include dealing with others on a one-to-one basis, participating in group discussions, and making formal presentations.
    B.   A friend of mine has been told that his company has "big things" planned for him, but he must first improve his formal speaking skills.

    C.   Company X uses "oral communication ability" as a criterion in selecting managers for promotion.

    D.   A recent study conducted by Robert F. Pearse for the American Management Association asked executives to identify three factors most likely to impede career advancement. Nearly two-thirds of the respondents selected only two items, and "lack of adequate communicative or other interpersonal skills" was indicated by over 25 percent of the managers. Among top-level managers, lack of communication skills was the second most frequently chosen item, and it ranked ahead of such factors as competition, identification with political factions, retirement practices, and reduction in the number of managerial jobs.[1]

    E.   It has been said that half of the world is composed of people who have something to say and cannot, and the other half is composed of people who have nothing to say and keep on saying it. The object lesson to remember is that if you want to be a success, you must avoid both of these halves.[2]

The process of making a statement and developing it is fundamentally important. It is vital first to be able to successfully prepare simple presentations because longer speeches employ the same process, but take the additional step of developing several statements in an orderly manner. For example, to the statement, "Communication skills are essential to success in business," you might add the statements, "Communication skills can be acquired in several ways" and "Corporations should support their employees' efforts to acquire communication skills." Developing each of these statements in turn produces the following speech:

I.   Communication skills are essential for success in business.

    A.   These skills include dealing with others on a one-to-one basis, participating in group discussions, and making formal presentations.

    B.   A friend of mine has been told that his company has "big things" planned for him, but he must first improve his formal speaking skills.

    C.   Company X uses "oral communication ability" as a criterion in selecting managers for promotion.

    D.   A recent study conducted by Robert F. Pearse for the American Management Association asked executives to identify three factors most likely to impede career advancement. Nearly two-thirds of the respondents selected only two items and "lack of adequate communicative or other interpersonal skills" was indicated by over 25 percent of the managers. Among top-level managers, lack of communication skills was the second most frequently chosen item, and it ranked ahead of such factors as competition, identification with political factions, retirement practices, and reduction in the number of managerial jobs.[3]

---

[1] Robert F. Pearse, *Manager to Manager II: What Managers Think of Their Managerial Careers,* An AMA Survey Report (New York: AMACOM, a division of American Management Association, 1977), p. 31.

[2] This example looks somewhat sketchy because I have omitted much of the verbal embellishment that would be provided by the speaker. As a general rule, full sentence outlines should include about one third as many words as the finished speech. This leaves the speaker freedom to adapt to the responses of the audience while providing a clear plan for the speech as a whole. Other forms may better suit your needs and some alternatives are explained in Chapter 6, "Delivery Fundamentals."

[3] Pearse, *Manager to Manager II,* p. 31.

    E. It has been said that half of the world is composed of people who have something to say and cannot, and the other half is composed of people who have nothing to say and keep on saying it. The object lesson to remember is that if you want to be a success, you must avoid both of these halves.

II. Communication skills can be acquired in several ways.
    A. For example, Syracuse University offers five Speech Communication courses designed to build professional communication competence.
    B. Toastmasters, International gives its members many opportunities to learn and practice communication skills.
    C. Professional trainers offer many programs in Effective Managerial Communication.
    D. Professor Lisa L. Smith of Syracuse University says that "one of the best ways of learning to give speeches is by studying the speeches of accomplished speakers. If you want to see how a speech should be given, pick up a copy of *Vital Speeches of the Day* and model your presentation after one which has been given by someone who is an experienced speaker."

III. Corporations should support their employees' efforts to acquire communication skills.
    A. Companies can provide many forms of support: they can pay for all or part of the cost of training programs, they can provide time off during the day and furnish transportation to classes, and they can use bonuses and promotions to encourage employees who participate.
    B. Company Y found that production increased by nearly 15 percent after their supervisors were trained in communicating performance appraisals.
    C. John Smith of Logos, Inc., says that his "employees were interested in a communication training program, but none took advantage of it until the company volunteered to pay half of the cost. Once the announcement was made, so many people signed up that we had to double the number of classes offered."
    D. One study shows that nearly 80 percent of the top executives in American companies believe corporations should take responsibility for developing their most promising employees.

This speech is a little rough because it lacks an introduction and conclusion, and because the transitions from one idea to the next are rather abrupt. However, it is structurally sound and would be acceptable in many speaking environments. You may find it easiest to learn to use developing materials by looking at three subordinate processes: finding materials, identifying usable materials, and selecting materials used in finished presentations.

FINDING MATERIALS

It isn't difficult to find materials for a presentation, but too many novice speakers stop searching before they have accumulated enough. A handy rule of thumb is that you should gather about three times as much material as you plan to use *before* starting to write. The surplus material allows you to choose the particular items that will be most meaningful to your audience. In addition, the materials not used in the finished speech are often useful in answering questions.

    Professionals often find accumulating materials to be one of the easiest tasks associated with composing a speech because they are usually called upon to speak about projects or other activities with which they have been working for some time. It is not uncommon to have a speaker summarize a year-long research project in a written report and a relatively brief, twenty-minute oral presentation. However, most students lack the advantage of such extended preparation, and even if you are involved in an ongoing project, you will need to find supplementary materials. Supplementary materials may add to your knowledge of the subject, but their primary function is to provide a bridge between your knowledge and the interests and abilities of the audience. Some common bibliographic aids and a few reference works will help you locate materials, and you can choose those with which you are most comfortable. However, you should be acquainted with some works in each category.

Bibliographic Aids

Bibliographic aids are used to locate articles, books, and other materials related to specific subjects. Some routinely index a broad range of materials appearing in popular sources, while others are more restrictive and list only specific types of material or material dealing only with specific subjects. Reference librarians can help you identify the aids most appropriate for particular tasks, and some of the most commonly used aids are described below.

The Readers' Guide to Periodical Literature is the most frequently used and widely available guide. It includes both author and subject listings in a single alphabetical index. Although it indexes articles appearing in nearly 200 magazines, its value is limited by the popular character of the periodicals surveyed. Articles indexed tend to be relatively brief and often lack detailed or technical information.

The Public Affairs Information Service Bulletin, abbreviated PAIS, provides an alphabetical subject index to articles appearing in more than 1,400 periodicals, selected books, and a variety of federal, state, and local government publications. The PAIS is more useful than the *Readers' Guide* because it 'aims to identify the public affairs information likely to be most useful and interesting to legislators, administrators, the business and financial community, policy researchers and students. The PAIS indexes list publications on all subjects that bear on contemporary public issues and the making and evaluation of public policy, irrespective of source or traditional disciplinary boundaries. This includes the policy-oriented literature of the academic social sciences—economics, political science, public administration, international law and relations, sociology and demography; professional publications in the fields such as business, finance, law, education, and social work; and reports and commentary on public issues from the serious general press.' A fifteen-volume, cumulative subject index covering the years 1915 to 1974 merges more than 1 million entries from the first sixty years of publication.

Finally, the *Business Periodicals Index* covers articles appearing in a diverse group of nearly 300 publications ranging from the *American Federationist* to the *University of Michigan Business Review.* The unique feature of this index is that 'selection of periodicals for indexing . . . is accomplished by subscriber vote. In voting their preferences, subscribers are asked to place primary emphasis on the reference value of the periodicals under consideration. They are also asked to give consideration to subject balance in order to insure that no particular field be overlooked in proportion to overall index coverage.'[4]

Reference Works

The bibliographic aids described above will help you locate a great deal of information. It will also help you to keep a supply of reference works at hand while preparing presentations. These works provide a ready source of up-to-date information and may even answer questions that inevitably arise in the process of composition. Reference works range from popular almanacs prepared annually by several publishers to highly specialized handbooks designed for use by professionals. You are probably familiar with several in each category and may use the ones you find most helpful. There is also a group of reference works specifically designed for the speaker. These works can help you by providing a large supply of attractive and interesting illustrative material. The materials provided include humorous anecdotes, inspirational quotations, and amusing parables. In most works of this type, the materials are arranged by subject in alphabetical order, and several works include thorough indexes and cross references. The following list includes some of the best.

JACOB M. BRAUDE, *The Complete Speaker's Index to Selected Stories for Every Occasion* (Englewood Cliffs, New Jersey: Prentice-Hall, 1966), lists 1,953 stories on a variety of subjects.

EUGENE E. BRUSSEL, *Dictionary of Quotable Quotations* (Englewood Cliffs, New Jersey: Prentice-Hall, 1970), includes more than 22,000 quotations listed by subject in alphabetical order.

EDWARD L. FRIEDMAN, *The Speaker's Handy Reference* (New York: Harper & Row, Pub., 1967), is divided into chapters by subject, but the index makes it possible to find materials quickly.

HERBERT V. PROCHNOW, *The Speaker's Treasury of Wit and Wisdom* (New York: Harper & Row, Pub., 1958), is one of the most comprehensive works of this type, with subject headings arranged alphabetically from "ability" to "zeal."

HERBERT V. PROCHNOW, *A Speaker's Treasury* (Grand Rapids, Michigan: Baker House Books, 1973), is a little difficult to use because the subject headings are not arranged alphabetically, but the six parts form logical divisions, including excerpts from speeches, illustrations of interesting lives, and inspiring observations.

Although these works furnish a great deal of material, the quality is uneven and you should exercise care in selecting items. Some of the humor is dated, and the circumstances surrounding some of the stories may be offensive to an audience.

---

[4] 'Prefatory Note," *Business Periodicals Index,* August 1980—July 1981 (New York: The H.W. Wilson Company, 1981). The two quotes within this passage came from "PAIS Selection Policy," *Public Affairs Information Service Bulletin Annual Cumulation* (New York: Public Affairs Information Service), and they are reproduced in every issue of that bulletin.

IDENTIFYING USABLE MATERIAL

Once you have discovered a supply of material, the next step is to identify specific items for use. This process is not as easy as it might appear because many forms of material are not suitable for oral presentation. Highly detailed or technical data are difficult to use, and audiences soon tire of hearing mere "facts."

However, the most useful types of material are easily identified, and the following list is the product of centuries of experimentation. As a general rule, specific pieces of information are likely to be usable if, and only if, they represent one of the types described below. Items that do not correspond to any of the following categories may be interesting reading, but ought to be avoided in oral presentations.

Examples

Examples are probably the most widely used type of developing material. There are several commonly recognized types, but they have one thing in common. All examples are particular cases of general phenomena. The following instances show the relationship between particular cases and general phenomena:

GENERAL PHENOMENON: Cars are expensive.
PARTICULAR CASE: My car cost $8,500.
GENERAL PHENOMENON: Martin Luther King, Jr. presented some excellent speeches.
PARTICULAR CASE: He presented the speech titled, "I Have A Dream."
GENERAL PHENOMENON: Some U.S. presidents have been accomplished speakers.
PARTICULAR CASES: Abraham Lincoln and John F. Kennedy were accomplished speakers.

Examples are valuable because they give audiences concrete references for general statements. However, they are effective only when the particular cases are familiar to the audience or when they are described in sufficient detail to bring them within the experiences of the audience. Theorists have developed several ways of classifying examples, but two characteristics are sufficient for deciding between types commonly encountered.

Short or long   One way of classifying examples is according to their length and the amount of detail employed in presenting them. Very short examples are known as *specific instances* and may be as brief as a name or phrase. Such instances function by reminding audiences of well-known cases and are much like "name dropping." The principal value of specific instances is that several can be used in a relatively brief period of time. However, because they lack detailed information, they are ineffective as a means of developing materials with which an audience is unfamiliar.

Very long examples are known as *illustrations* and may occupy as much as half of an entire presentation. Illustrations are stories used to make a point and they are most effective when an audience is relatively unfamiliar with the subject matter. Moreover, the inclusion of details that are not directly relevant to the point being illustrated adds realism to the presentation and may help to maintain interest—particularly if the incidental details are interesting in and of themselves. The obvious limitation to the use of illustrations is the amount of time consumed in their presentation. In addition, when they are extensive, audiences may drift away from the discussion.

Midway in length between specific instances and illustrations are *examples proper.* Examples proper include more detail than specific instances, but, unlike illustrations, they include only the details relevant to the point being developed. Specifying the point at which an example proper becomes an illustration is difficult, but it is convenient to say that an example proper may be as long as 10 percent of the presentation. However, the distinguishing characteristic is that all of the details presented are directly relevant to the point developed. The following illustration may help to clarify the distinctions among specific instances, examples proper, and illustrations.

In a speech, "Managing Conflict," James P. McFarland explains that the best means of dealing with conflict is to "avoid isolation—seek reality." He illustrates this rule with the following description of the YAMA method:

> One of the better methods I've encountered for keeping in touch and avoiding isolation is the "YAMA" technique, which was originally devised by Henry Ford, Sr. He felt that many industrialists were not properly engaging themselves in matters beyond their immediate objective of running their businesses. He called a meeting of what he considered to be the 25 most prominent businessmen of the day, and established some ground rules. Ford had observed that in groups of 25 or more, three or four people usually dominated the conversation and consequently, many brilliant, unique and ingenious ideas were not presented, due to the mildness, humbleness or humility on the part of their creators. For this reason, Ford asked each man to bring an eight-minute talk on any topic he felt would be relevant to the assembled group. All of the names were put into a hat and drawn randomly—so there would always be one presenter and one man "on deck." At the end of seven minutes, a warning bell was rung, and at the end of eight minutes, two bells were rung. The man speaking had to end his talk with that sentence, whether he was finished or not. If another speaker had by chance selected a similar topic, he was allowed to take his time immediately following the first presentation. The conference leader, in this case Ford

himself, would then engage all of the conferees in a discussion of the subject matter which had been presented.

During my tenure at General Mills, we used the "YAMA" technique as part of an ongoing program called Inter-Relations Management Encounters, with various managerial representatives, in our organization. We never failed to get remarkably good suggestions for action, and we were frequently able to dispel misunderstandings which were expressed in a very sincere way and thus avoid potential conflict.

The "YAMA" technique is fairly simple to put into operation and should be used regularly to bring together various disciplines, different levels of people, and different interests in order for management to understand their fundamental thinking.[5]

This illustration occupies nearly 20 percent of McFarland's text, but it could be reduced to the following example.

During my tenure at General Mills, we used the "YAMA" technique as part of a management development program. Each member of an executive group of twenty was asked to bring to the meeting a prepared eight-minute speech. All names were placed in a hat and drawn at random. After each speech, the conference leader would engage all of the conferees in a discussion of the subject which had been presented. We never failed to get remarkably good suggestions for action, and we were frequently able to dispel misunderstandings and thus avoid the potential for conflict.

Finally, even this example could be reduced to a specific instance by merely saying, "at General Mills we used the 'YAMA' technique to dispel misunderstandings." Of course, the instance would not be as interesting as the illustration, and it would lack the explanatory value of the example. But for an audience that already knew the details, it would be sufficient to prove the speaker's point.

Real or hypothetical   The second way of classifying examples is according to whether the particular cases have actually happened or are typical of something that might happen. Cases that have actually happened serve as *real* examples, while cases that might happen provide *hypothetical* examples. The value of real examples should be clear from the preceding discussion. However, it is often difficult to find an example involving people or places that are familiar to your audience. No doubt real examples could be found, but the search may not be worth the time or effort required. Hypothetical examples may be composed rapidly and have the virtue of being adapted to the particular audience addressed. They allow audiences to see themselves in the kind of situation described by the speaker and serve to make presentations more immediate and personal.

Although hypothetical examples are a valuable means of explanation, two problems may arise if they are misused. First, it is inexcusable to use a hypothetical example as if it were a real one. To avoid this danger, you should always indicate that hypothetical examples are fictitious when you introduce

[5] Mr. McFarland is Director and retired Board Chairman of General Mills. The illustration is quoted from *Vital Speeches,* XLV (November 15, 1979), 79.

them. Useful phrases for this purpose include ''Imagine that . . . .''; ''Think what it would be like if . . . .''; and ''Consider the possibility that . . . .'' You can invent more attractive phrasing, but the hypothetical character of such examples must be made clear to the audience.

The second danger is that hypothetical examples may be deceptive. Remember, hypothetical examples represent the kind of thing that might actually happen or is expected to happen. Fantasies are fine in literature, but they have little place in serious business and professional speaking.

Restatements

Restatements are repetitions of the statement developed and serve to focus audience attention. Although they do not add to the content of a speech, restatements provide convenient points of reference when an audience is momentarily distracted.

Literal restatements repeat the statement developed in exactly the same language used initially. Their principal advantage is that they provide the clearest possible focus, thereby avoiding the danger of confusion. In spite of this advantage, literal restatements sound harshly mechanical and most audiences will react negatively if they are used excessively. You may limit the use of literal restatements to internal summaries and transitions, or add them during presentations when the audience appears confused or distracted.

You can also capitalize on the value of repetition by using a slightly more sophisticated device: the *synonymous restatement*. English has an abundant vocabulary, and it is possible to find several different expressions for most ideas. The range of vocabulary used depends on the subject and audience, but the number of possible variations is almost endless. For example, all of the following express about the same idea as ''Communication skills are essential for success in business'':

Discursive ability is required for professional advancement.
Facility in communication is necessary for economic security.
The ability to talk to people is the foundation of prosperity.
Profits depend on effective communication.

You can probably think of variations that I have not listed, especially if you use a good thesaurus. *The Original Roget's Thesaurus*[6] is standard, but there are several other good dictionaries of synonyms and antonyms.

Both literal and synonymous restatements are effective because they help you highlight principal ideas. In addition, they may be used to smooth transitions from the development of one statement to the next. For example, you might use restatements as effective transitions in the model speech developed above.

---

[6] *The Original Roget's Thesaurus,* rev. ed. (New York: St. Martins Press, 1965).

The point I have been trying to make is that communication skills are essential for success in business. Now I'll explain how they can be learned.

I've been trying to show that communication skills can be acquired in several ways. Let's conclude by talking about who should pay for the training.

Comparisons and Contrasts

Comparisons and *contrasts* are especially effective for describing unfamiliar things. Whether the things described are objects, people, or events, comparisons and contrasts relate qualities of the thing described to qualities of things with which audiences are familiar. They help audiences visualize unfamiliar objects. Composing them is not difficult, but you should set aside time to work systematically. Begin by isolating the qualities you want to emphasize and then find familiar objects that display the same qualities in different degrees. State differences of magnitude in roughly mathematical terms, and then compose an orderly paragraph including both similarities and differences. For example, some of my clients work with extremely sophisticated microelectronic circuits and popular audiences have difficulty visualizing the computing power packed into a small chip. Two important qualities of the chips are size and complexity, and comparisons and contrasts are particularly helpful in describing them. The following shows these qualities isolated for analysis and then a paragraph as it would be presented.

Object Described: Motorola 68,000 Chip

Quality: size: one-half inch square
Similarity: the surface of a sugar cube
Difference: you could easily hold twenty-five in the palm of your hand

Quality: complexity: equivalent to 68,000 transistors
Similarity: enough to manufacture sixty-eight color television sets
Difference: more than enough to give four to every student at Syracuse University

The Motorola 68,000 chip measures one-half inch on a side; that is about the size of a sugar cube and you could easily hold twenty-five in the palm of your hand. The chip has the complexity of 68,000 transistors: that is enough to build sixty-eight color television sets and more than enough to give four to each student at Syracuse University.

Definitions

Definitions are useful for clarifying statements and should be used whenever you introduce a word or phrase that may be unfamiliar to your audience. They should also be used to clarify words or phrases that have several meanings. The easiest type of definition to use is called a *stipulated definition*. This type of definition merely indicates your intention to use a given word in a certain manner. For example, ''I use the phrase 'stipulated definition' to identify a definition constructed by the speaker.'' To avoid confusion, stipulated definitions should always be stated to show that they are the product of the speaker and are not necessarily generally accepted. Phrases that serve this purpose include, "I mean . . . ."; "I use . . . ."; "for the purpose of this speech, I define . . . ."; and "I define . . . ."

Authoritative definitions are preferable when the audience is expected to use the materials presented in a context other than the immediate speaking situation. Authoritative definitions are the accepted, proper descriptions of words and phrases, and are typically taken from dictionaries, encyclopedias, and other reference works. The easiest way to distinguish authoritative from stipulated definitions is to cite their source. This can be accomplished quickly by using such phrases as "According to *Webster's New World Dictionary* . . . ."; "*The Oxford English Dictionary* defines . . . ."; and ". . . is defined by the *Handbook of Social Psychology* as . . . ."

Although they are primarily intended to clarify statements, definitions may also help to avoid controversy by distinguishing ideas from those that are less acceptable. For example, a speech favoring "socialism" may produce considerable conflict unless the speaker stipulates that he means "sharing of social responsibility." However, there are limits to such stipulations, especially when the subject is emotionally charged. Pseudo definitions such as, "For 'abortion' we can substitute 'murder'," and "By 'national health insurance' I mean 'communism'," are of little value. They deliberately confuse concepts that most sophisticated audiences hold distinct.

Quotations/Testimony

Quotations serve to support ideas because they show that respected authorities share the point of view presented. Not all speakers or writers are worth quoting, and the following criteria are important in selecting quotable material.

First, the person quoted should be an authority on the subject. The reason for this requirement is obvious, but observing it may be difficult. Many people who are authorities in one area make public pronouncements about subjects of which they know little. Some recent examples include an actor discussing social welfare policies, a nuclear physicist commenting on instructional techniques, a sales representative teaching psychology, and an accountant reviewing movies.

Second, the person quoted should have firsthand knowledge of the material that is being discussed. The term "firsthand" is used to distinguish between what people learn by working on a project or observing an event from what they learn by listening to or reading about the accounts of others. This requirement is important because information is often distorted as it passes from one person to the next, and the speaker should strive to present material that is as complete and accurate as possible.

Third, the person quoted should have no personal interest or bias that might affect his or her testimony. Audiences are sensitive to the effects of bias and are likely to react negatively to speakers employing suspect testimony. Examples of people whose quotations might be shaded due to personal interest or bias include political candidates arguing for changes in election laws, elected officials requesting salary increases, union leaders opposing inflation controls, and corporate officials testifying about antitrust legislation. There is one very important exception to the rule that a person quoted should have no personal interest. A source who testifies *against* a personal interest often seems to be more credible. A speaker using such testimony should take pains to highlight it and to capitalize on its added believability.

Finally, the person quoted should be respected by the audience. It is easiest to quote someone who is known by members of the audience, but that is not always possible. When the source is not widely known, it is advisable to include the person's credentials in the citation. The introduction need not be detailed, but it should include enough information so that the audience appreciates the expertise of the source. For example, a speaker quoting from this book might precede the quotation by saying, ''According to Dr. Eric Skopec, Associate Professor of Speech Communication and Faculty Coordinator in the Center for Management Services at Syracuse University . . . .''

Statistics

Statistics are a very powerful form of developing material and are used more frequently than any other kind in some environments. Their power results from the fact that they summarize the results of hundreds or even thousands of separate observations. For example, the Dow Jones average summarizes changes in the value of sixty-five stocks, the NASDAQ composite index summarizes the performance of roughly 3,300 over-the-counter stocks, your grade-point average summarizes your performance in many different courses, and Census Bureau reports summarize the characteristics of over 220 million people living in this country. Of course, the value of these summaries depends on the measure employed, and only knowledge of the subject will indicate if the measure is relevant to a presentation. Also, only measures and statistics that are meaningful to the audience should be used. Most readers probably recognize the Dow Jones average, but few understand the NASDAQ composite index; students and teachers appreciate the values and limitations of grade-point averages, while others may not; and, most people understand Census Bureau reports without knowing how they are compiled.

A chart or graph showing distribution is the best way to present statistical data, and there are many measures summarizing different distributions. A speaker may use very sophisticated measures in addressing some audiences, but one of two types should be used when addressing popular audiences. The first type, *averages,* measures central tendencies, and includes mean, median, and mode. The mean is the arithmetic average compiled by dividing the total value of a set of observations by the number of observations. The median is the value above which half of the observations with the largest values falls and below which the half with the smallest values falls. The mode is the most common value observed in a set of observations. Each of these measures may be called an ''average,'' and speakers should be cautious in using the term. For example, real estate transactions reported in a local paper showed the following values: $100,000; $45,000; $45,000; $45,000; $40,000; $30,000; $28,000; $25,000;

$20,000; and $20,000. The "average" price is $39,800 (mean), $45,000 (mode), or $35,000 (median) depending on which measure is used. The mean is the preferred form, but you should be careful because your sources may report the median or mode on some occasions.

The second type of statistic that may be used measures a spread or distribution. Distributions show how well the average of a set represents the group as a whole, and one measure of distribution is the range (high and low points). Other statistics can provide a more precise image of the distribution. You can appreciate the importance of these statistics by comparing the value of homes in this group with those in the first group: $100,000; $100,000; $100,000; $20,000; $15,000; $15,000; $12,000; $12,000; $12,000; and $12,000. The average (mean) price of both groups is $39,800, and there is very little difference in the range, but it is obvious that the average is far more typical of the first group than of the second. One statistic that shows this difference is the standard deviation, and understanding it will help to distinguish between cases where the average is meaningful and where it is not.[7] With a normal population, the standard deviation reports the range of scores by showing how far from the mean one must move in either direction to include one-third of the total observations. The larger the standard deviation, the less characteristic the mean is. For example, the standard deviation for the first group of homes is $23,436.91 and for the second group it is $41,614.10.

Even if you limit yourself to the statistics described here, you should use some care in oral presentation. It is a good idea to use as few novel statistics as possible, and pause briefly after each to allow the audience time to digest them. In addition, the following techniques should be employed in presenting them. First, simplify or round-off complex numbers. Thus, 0.745821 is "approximately three-fourths" and 40,729 is "nearly forty-one thousand." Second, use comparisons and contrasts to help audiences visualize magnitude. For instance, a town with a population of 41,000 might be described by saying that the number of people living there is almost twice the enrollment of a given university. Or, the fact that over 20 percent of the U.S. population lives in poverty might be explained by observing that the percentage is equivalent to five members of a class of twenty-five. Finally, statistical data can often be presented most effectively by using visual representations. Specific types are described in the next chapter, but remember that visual portrayal is always valuable in presenting statistical material.

SELECTING MATERIAL FOR USE

The final subordinate process in developing statements is selecting the materials to be used in the oral presentation. When you reach this point in the composition process, you should have discovered a variety of materials and sifted out items that

---

[7] I don't recommend that you learn to compute standard deviations because it is usually reported by those who compile statistics and several inexpensive calculators are available that compute it automatically.

do not conform to the types listed in the preceding section. Remember, this final stage of composition requires about three times as much material as time allows for presentation.

Making knowledgeable selections from the materials discovered requires attention to your purpose, the demands of the audience, and the principle of variety. Your purpose identifies the condition you wish to produce by giving your speech. Specific purposes range from merely promoting understanding, at one extreme, to producing a predetermined action at the other. If you are unsure of the nature of your purpose, you may test yourself with the following question: "What do I want the audience to do as a result of hearing my speech?" If you are unable to answer this question, you are not prepared to make a presentation. However, when you are satisfied if the audience learns something and remembers some or all of the material presented, you are engaged in informative speaking. When you want the audience to do something more than merely remember the message, when you want them to take some action as a result of hearing the speech, you are engaged in persuasive speaking. Of course, there are many gradations between purely informative and purely persuasive presentations, and some authors have argued that neither extreme is possible. However, understanding these limits is sufficient for use in selecting materials. For informative speeches, you should choose materials which *clarify* or *explain* the statements presented. Briefly examine Table 2.1.

Reading down the first column, notice that the materials that serve to clarify ideas are hypothetical examples (of any length), literal and synonymous restatements, comparisons and contrasts, and definitions. All informative speeches should rely on materials of these types. Real examples and a few statistics or quotations might be added for an "air of realism," but the bulk of the presentation should be composed of materials from the first column.

When your purpose goes beyond informing, you need to consider a second factor: the demands of the audience. "Audience demand" is a technical concept, and is discussed with reference to persuasive and sales presentations. However, audiences that don't understand the action to be taken or the reason for it are unlikely to respond favorably. As a result, when you try to motivate an audience to act, you may need to start by simply informing them. That is, an audience is likely to demand explanations of actions or purposes that they do not understand, and you should respond to that demand by employing materials that clarify.

Audiences already familiar with the subject are less likely to need explanations, but they may demand proof. That is, they may understand the action requested, but they may require you to prove that the action is necessary or desirable. When you face such audiences, you should use materials that prove. These materials are listed in the third column of Table 2.1. Notice also that real examples and illustrations in the second column of the table are capable of both proving and clarifying. This fact makes them particularly valuable when audience demands are unclear, and when different members of the audience make different demands.

TABLE 2.1 Developing Materials

CLARIFY	CLARIFY AND PROVE	PROVE
Hypothetical Instances, Examples, and Illustrations	Real Examples and Illustrations	Real Instances
Literal and Synonymous Restatements		Statistics
Comparisons and Contrasts*		Quotations
Stipulated and Authoritative Definitions		

* Some theorists believe a particular form of comparison, the analogy, has the ability to prove. You may wish to examine some of the theoretical literature on this point, but it is safest to assume that the value of comparisons is limited to clarification.

It is important not to overlook the fact that an audience may demand different forms of development for the individual statements in a complex speech. When several statements are presented in a single speech, the audience may need clarification of some, proof of others, and both proof and clarification of still others. Briefly review the complex speech described above. Some audiences might require clarification of all three statements, other audiences might need proof of all three, while still others might accept all three statements without demanding either proof or clarification—in which case there would probably be no reason to give the speech. However, a moderately sophisticated audience might require clarification of one or two statements and proof of the others. Many employers accept the first statement ("Communication skills are essential to success in business") without question, ask for clarification of the second ("Communication skills can be acquired in several ways"), and demand proof for the third ("Corporations should support their employees efforts to acquire communication skills").

The final factor to consider in selecting developing materials is the principle of variety. The principle of variety means that speakers should avoid unnecessary repetition in the kinds of material employed. This principle is of less importance than either purpose or audience demand, but it is necessary to consider it. Moreover, variety is especially significant in longer presentations and in situations where maintaining audience interest may be a problem. This chapter describes fourteen different forms of developing material, nine of which are limited to clarifying statements, and five of which either clarify and prove, or merely prove. These numbers are sufficient to offer you an almost limitless number of combinations. Above all, you should avoid mechanical sequences that allow the audience to anticipate subsequent items. Variety in developing materials creates an element of suspense, which helps to hold audience interest and attention.

SUMMARY

The basic process of composition is making a statement and developing it. Finding developing material is relatively easy for most professionals and you can simplify the process by using appropriate bibliographic aids and reference works. Usable materials include examples (long and short, real and hypothetical), restatements, comparisons and contrasts, definitions, testimony/quotations, and statistics. You should consider the needs of the audience when deciding which form to use and you may clarify, prove, or prove and clarify the statements you present.

LEARNING ACTIVITIES

1. Select a short story or fable that develops a single object lesson and think of the story as an extended illustration. Which elements of the story would you retain if you had to reduce the illustration to an example? How would the impression created by the example differ from the one created by the illustration? Which would be most persuasive? Which would be most entertaining? Could you reduce the fable to a specific instance in speaking to your classroom audience?

2. Read a presentation from *Vital Speeches* or another source and underline the principal ideas presented. Circle developing materials used and identify each by type, such as illustration. Which ideas are proved? Which ideas are clarified? Which are both proved and clarified? Can you see a pattern in the speaker's choice of supporting materials? What does the pattern tell you about the speaker's understanding of the audience? If you were presenting the speech analyzed to your classroom audience, how would you change the selection of materials? Why?

3. Practice selecting materials by taking a statement from a textbook and deciding what kinds of materials you would use in presenting it to your classroom audience, a group of your parents' friends, a group of high-school students, or a group of professionals in positions you would like to hold.

CHAPTER THREE
VISUAL DEVELOPING
MATERIALS

Anything that gives visual representation to ideas may be called a visual aid. Gestures indicating size, shape, or location are among the most commonly used forms, but there are many other types that may be employed. Charts and graphs are excellent for some displays; physical objects and models may be used selectively; photographs, movies, and slides are effective in various settings; and recent technological developments have made it possible to use video monitors controlled by microcomputers. This variety can be confusing, but difficulties are minimized by the fact that the functions of visual aids are more important than the format employed. Visual aids provide a visible image of ideas and may both clarify them and make them more appealing to an audience.

You probably recognize that these effects are identical to the functions of developing materials explained in the last chapter. Just as statements may clarify, prove, or both prove and clarify, so visual aids may help in explaining an idea, demonstrating its truth, or both. Because of this similarity, visual aids can be thought of as specialized forms of developing material closely related to the types discussed in the last chapter. The principal difference between them is that the types of material described in the last chapter are presented orally and reach the audience through auditory channels, while visual aids are presented visually and reach the audience through visual channels.

Comparing visual aids to oral forms of developing material is important not only as a means of defining them, but also as a means of illustrating their potential value in a speech. When they are used appropriately, visual aids either complement the oral channels so that the same message reaches the listener through two

channels, or they are used to introduce material that is best suited to visual presentation. Unfortunately, relatively few speakers derive maximum value from the use of visual aids and many use them in a manner that actually weakens the presentation. When too few visual aids are used, concepts that could be most effectively displayed visually are deprived of adequate support. When too many are used, the presentation becomes a blur of charts, graphs, transparencies, and so forth, reducing the impact of each. And, when visual aids are used at inappropriate times, competition between visual and oral channels reduces the impact of the message. In addition, a careless introduction of visual aids gives undue emphasis to incidental ideas, while the principal ones get lost among other materials.

To make effective use of visual aids and to avoid these pitfalls, you need to understand the purposes for which they are best used, some means for selecting from the kinds available, the fundamentals of constructing them, and some procedures for displaying them in the speech. The first three items will be discussed in this chapter and procedures for displaying them will be covered in Chapter 6.

In this chapter only those types of visual aids that can be represented in two-dimensional drawings will be discussed. This includes lists, pictures, diagrams, charts, and graphs. Imposing this limitation does not mean that other types (objects, models, and so forth) are inappropriate or ineffective. However, effective use of other forms makes special demands on the speaker and you should avoid them until you have mastered more conventional forms.

PURPOSE OF USING VISUAL AIDS

We have already observed that properly used visual aids have the same effects as other forms of developing material. They prove, clarify, or both prove and clarify the ideas of the speaker. In spite of this similarity, you will soon learn that designing and using visual aids requires more time and attention than presenting the same material with oral forms alone. Why, you may ask, should people take the time to prepare visual aids when they have the same functions as oral forms of developing material? The question is a good one and many different answers have been offered. If you look at several books on public speaking, you will find that visual aids are said to serve many unique purposes. Those frequently mentioned include: (1) making the speech interesting and attractive; (2) providing a "change of pace" to maintain attention; (3) compressing material that would require lengthy oral presentation; (4) displaying the artistic ability or serious intentions of the speaker; (5) providing a tangible record of the speech; and (6) relieving the speaker's anxiety by providing physical support. I agree that visual aids may do all of these things, but I believe that they are secondary or incidental to the special functions of visual representation in a speech.

The special functions of visual aids are *making ideas memorable* and *displaying complex relationships*. The key to effective use of visual materials is introducing them only when their use is dictated by one of these functions. Use them when you wish to make an idea particularly memorable or when the substance of your presentation includes complex materials that would be difficult for the audience to comprehend on the basis of oral statements alone. These functions are so important in deciding whether or not to use visual aids that we will look at each of them in greater detail.

Making Ideas Memorable

Most speakers present far more information than their audience is likely to remember. This is true in even brief presentations, and most of us realize that parts of a message are quickly forgotten. The full extent of the problem was first disclosed by a series of pioneering experiments conducted by Ralph Nichols at the University of Minnesota. He found that immediately after a lecture students remembered less than half of what they had heard and that after two months they could recall less than one-quarter of the information presented.[1] In a later chapter we will discuss ways of improving your own listening ability, but for the time being it is important to remember that members of your audience are likely to forget large portions of the material you present. This appears to be an inevitable consequence of the way people receive and process information. You cannot prevent it, but, as a speaker, you can use visual aids to increase the chances of certain ideas being remembered.

Visual aids make ideas memorable by associating them with specific images and by making them stand out from other parts of the speech. To take advantage of this fact, you must decide before your presentation which ideas you believe are worthy of special attention. One way of doing this is to sit down with a completed draft or outline of the speech and ask yourself, "If my audience remembers only four things, what do I want them to be?" This is a question only you can answer, but answering it prior to your speech is essential because the items you identify should be given some form of visual representation to help insure that they are retained.

Displaying Complex Relationships

The bulk of material in your speeches should be relatively easy for the audience to understand. However, some types may pose particular difficulties and presenting them effectively may require extra effort on your part. Those that most often cause problems involve relationships between two or more items, each of which must be understood before the relationship between them is meaningful. When your audience already understands the individual items, visual representation may be unnecessary, but when both the items and the relationship between them must be explained there is a real danger of presenting more data than your audience is able to master in the time available. This condition is known as *information overload,* and the fact that visual aids display large amounts of data in easily recognized forms is particularly valuable in preventing overload. The relationships you may want to display in a speech involve *ideas, steps in a process, physical*

---

[1] Ralph G. Nichols and Leonard A. Stevens, "Listening to People," *Harvard Business Review,* 35 (September-October 1957), 85–92.

locations or *spaces,* and *quantity* or *number.* Whenever you break a complex subject into its parts, compare your ideas to others, or present a series of topics, you are dealing with relationships between ideas. Describing systematic ways of doing something and explaining a sequence of events are situations in which you must work with steps in a process. Relationships between physical locations are involved in describing a place or object, directing someone to an unfamiliar location, and in comparing designs. Finally, statistics always represent relationships between quantities or numbers. This is so because all statistics are compiled by comparing particular measurements to base figures.

Visual aids may be appropriate whenever materials in a speech involve one or more of these relationships. Of course, the specific materials you introduce are determined by your subject and purpose, and the extent to which they cause difficulty depends on your audience. However, materials involving any one of the four relationships are potential trouble spots and good candidates for the use of visual aids. Deciding when to use a visual aid requires identifying portions of the speech including materials expressing a relationship; determining whether or not the audience will need assistance in understanding it; and selecting an appropriate form. The last few pages should help you to identify complex relationships, and you can use your own experiences in deciding whether or not the audience needs assistance. Selecting visual forms is the subject of the next section.

SELECTING VISUAL FORMS

Even though this chapter is limited to the discussion of visual developing materials that can be reproduced by two-dimensional drawings, there is still a great number of types from which you can choose. Selecting an appropriate type is almost as important as deciding whether or not to use a visual aid because use of an inappropriate type generates confusion and distracts the audience.

Your purpose is the surest guide in selecting forms for use. If you want to make an idea memorable, any visual aid will make it stand out, but the most memorable form is a picture associating the idea with an image. When your purpose is to aid the audience in comprehending complex materials, you should use forms uniquely adapted to each type of relationship. Relationships between ideas are best displayed by lists, semantic trees, and organization charts; relationships between steps in a process by flow charts, time lines, and competition brackets; relationships between locations by maps, diagrams, and cutaways; and relationships between quantity and number by tables, bar graphs, pictographs, pie graphs, and line graphs. These applications are summarized in Exhibit 3.1, and each type is illustrated in the following pages.

Pictures used to make ideas memorable do not have to be elaborate, and commercial ones from magazines are seldom large enough to be used effectively. Simple ones are the best means of establishing an association between your ideas and an image, and you can probably draw most of the pictures you use. The examples below show what you can do with relatively primitive art work, and both are com-

EXHIBIT 3-1   TYPES OF VISUAL REPRESENTATION

To make ideas memorable, use *pictures*. To display complex relationships between _____, use:

IDEAS	**STEPS IN A PROCESS**
Lists	Flow Charts
Semantic Trees	Time Lines
Organization Charts	Competition Brackets

LOCATIONS	**QUANTITIES**
Maps	Tables
Diagrams	Bar Graphs
Cutaways	Picture Graphs
	Pie Graphs
	Line Graphs

mendable because they establish a clear association between the speaker's idea and the visible image. In Figure 3.1 the speaker summarizes the advantages of a new site for a company's distribution center, and in Figure 3.2 the speaker emphasizes some unsafe boating habits.

Photographs can have considerable persuasive value when they are large enough to be seen and when they provide visual illustrations. Properly used, they help an audience visualize unfamiliar events and they force the audience to consider ones that they prefer to ignore. Both of the following photographs (Figures 3.3 and 3.4) have been used in relatively successful persuasive campaigns. The

FIGURE 3.1

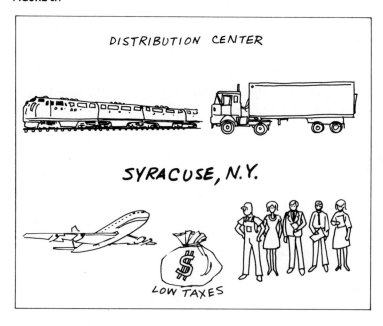

DISTRIBUTION CENTER

SYRACUSE, N.Y.

LOW TAXES

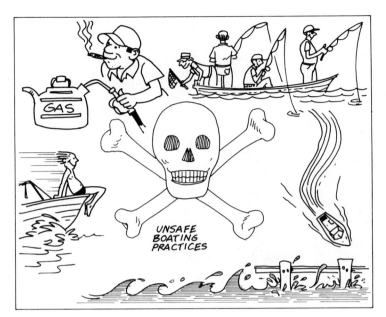

FIGURE 3.2

FIGURE 3.3

Small Size, Big Power   © Western Electric

FIGURE 3.4

**COMMUNICATION
CLIMATE**

1   Superior/Subordinate Communication
2   Quality of Information
3   Superior Openness
4   Upward Communication Opportunity
5   Reliability of Information

FIGURE 3.5

danger of using pictures in this manner is that they may be too distressing and the audience may withdraw or refuse to deal with the subject.

Lists show a series of ideas in order and should present a clean, uncluttered appearance. In preparing them you should avoid use of ornate lettering that calls attention to itself and that may be difficult to read from a distance. Items included should be relatively brief and key words should be identical to those used in your oral presentation. The example in Figure 3.5 is acceptable, but the one in Figure

3.6 has the advantage of using key words and phrases that are more likely to be recalled.

Semantic trees are used to show how separate ideas or concepts combine to produce a distinctive unit. They use words to represent individual components and arrows or lines to show how the units are combined. They may be used either to build a new concept from familiar materials or to break a complex concept into smaller parts. Figure 3.7 was developed to explain the unique Speech Com-

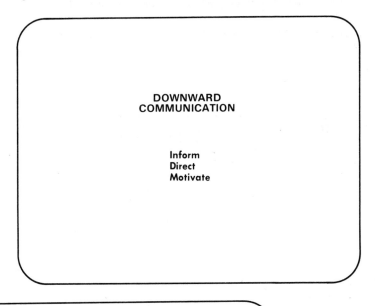

FIGURE 3.6

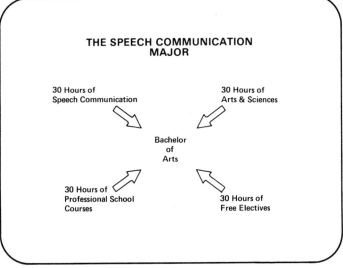

FIGURE 3.7

munication major at Syracuse University and Figure 3.8 reduces the concept
''professional responsibility'' to more familiar components.

Organization charts are used to display the administrative structure of formal
groups and may be modified to describe the position of any individual member in
the hierarchy. Boxes commonly represent each individual and lines connecting
the boxes display accepted patterns of command and report. Figure 3.9 shows the
structure of a hypothetical organization and Figure 3.10 shows the same structure
in a modified form to emphasize the role of a particular individual.

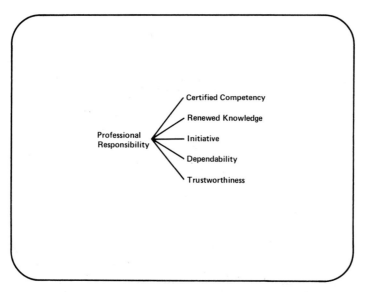

FIGURE 3.8

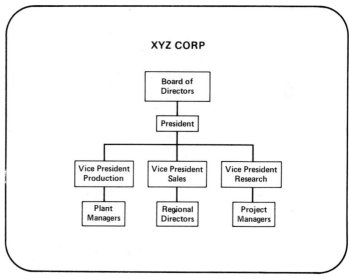

FIGURE 3.9

Flow charts are used most commonly for displaying the steps in a process. Each step is represented by an image and arrows show the progression from each step to the next. In simple flow charts, images are nothing more than rectangles with labels identifying the step represented (see Figure 3.11). More sophisticated flow charts take advantage of pictures and use them to display each step (see Figure 3.12).

Flow charts display the steps in a process by emphasizing the activity at each step. *Time lines* also display the steps in a process, but they focus attention on the

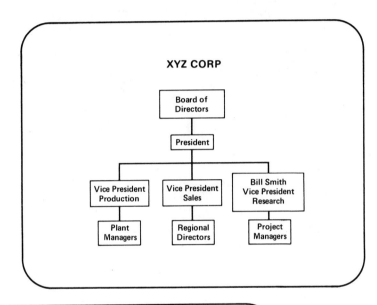

FIGURE 3.10

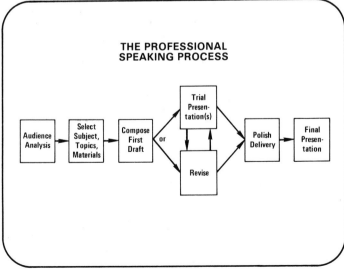

FIGURE 3.11

amount of time required for the completion of each step. Individual steps are noted, but the organizing feature of the image is a horizontal line divided into units representing periods of time. Figure 3.13 shows a commonly used type and Figure 3.14 reproduces one displaying two concurrent sets of activity.

Processes in which each step results in the elimination of alternatives can be displayed by *competition brackets*. The alternatives at each step are displayed on parallel lines and the result of each step is indicated by the emergence of the chosen

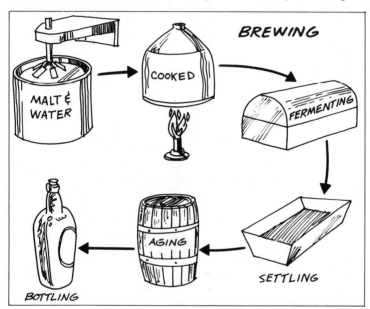

FIGURE 3.12

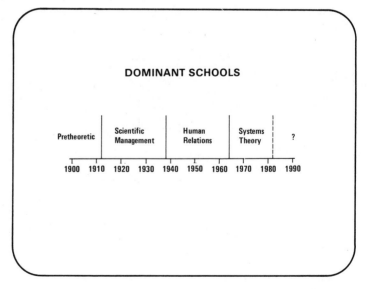

FIGURE 3.13

alternative. Figure 3.15 shows a common application of competition brackets to athletic competition and Figure 3.16 displays a paired comparison testing procedure.

Maps are regularly used to display relationships between objects and locations, and colors or symbols may be used to identify distinctive characteristics of each area. Commercial maps are seldom suited for use in a speech because they include a great deal of unnecessary information. Maps used as visual aids should in-

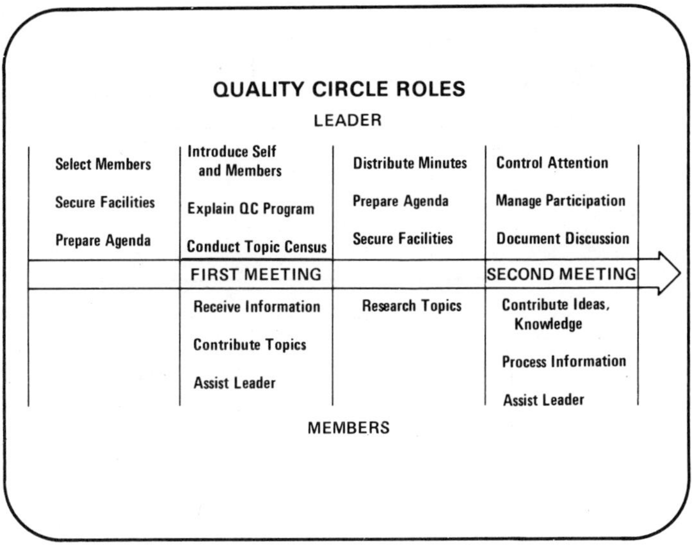

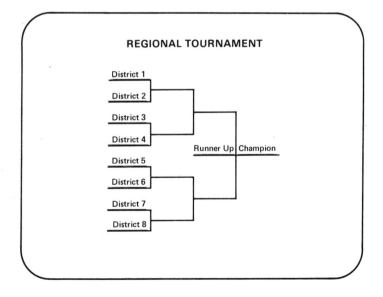

FIGURE 3.14

FIGURE 3.15

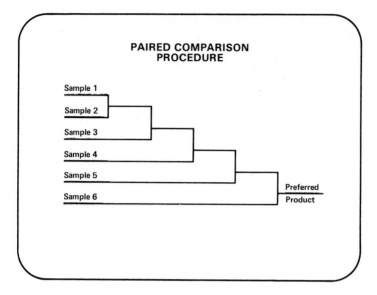

FIGURE 3.16

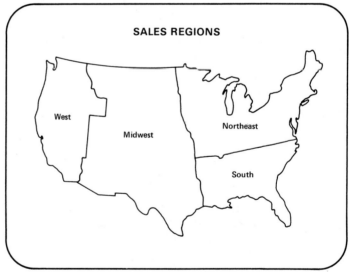

FIGURE 3.17

clude only essential features and a few other items to provide points of reference. Figure 3.17 is a good visual aid because it includes all necessary points, but it excludes many items found on commercial maps.

Features that would be found on commercial maps, but that have been excluded from this one, include most rivers, mountains, transportation lines, and topographic indicators. A few cities and some geographic features that are not essential for the speech itself have been included to provide points of reference for the audience. Points of reference are essential when the audience is unacquainted

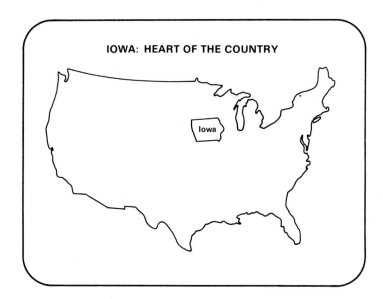

FIGURE 3.18

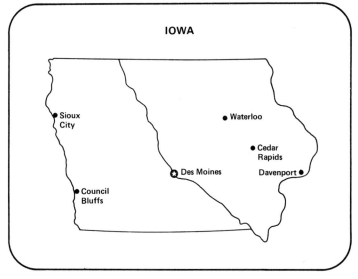

FIGURE 3.19

with the area displayed, and it may be necessary to use two maps in sequence. Such a sequence is displayed in Figures 3.18 and 3.19: The first is drawn to a large scale so that the audience can locate the area, and the second shows part of the region in detail.

A *diagram* is a line drawing that presents spatial relationships by displaying an outline of the objects included. Blueprints and perspective drawings are specialized diagrams, but they include so many details that they are unserviceable in presentations to nonspecialist audiences. However, much of the essential infor-

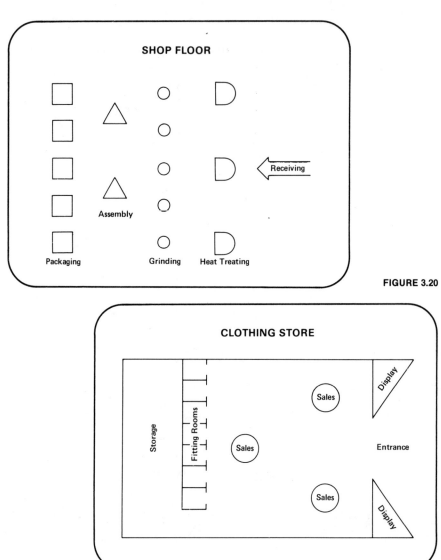

FIGURE 3.20

FIGURE 3.21

mation can be conveyed by using simplified shapes to outline components, and even stick figures can be used to represent people. Figures 3.20 and 3.21 are good examples of simplified diagrams based on complicated commercial renderings.

Cutaways are important forms of visual representation because they do something no other type can: they show relationships between parts or sections within an object. Cutaways display the interior of an object as if a slice has been taken from it to expose the hidden parts within. They are frequently used to explain geologic formations (Figure 3.22), construction techniques (Figure 3.23),

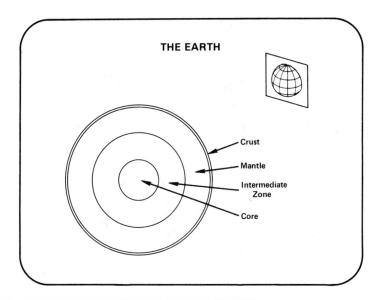

FIGURE 3.22

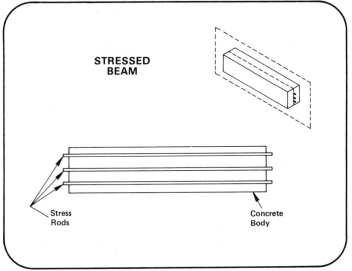

FIGURE 3.23

and mechanical systems (Figure 3.24). Other applications abound, and in all, it is important to explain the relationship between the slice displayed and the resulting image. In the three examples shown, small figures in the upper right corner show how the slice was taken.

Statistics are particularly difficult for audiences to master because they represent large amounts of data at high levels of abstraction. Several means of displaying statistical data are available and *tables* are the least acceptable. Tables are used in written reports because a lot of material can be compressed into a small

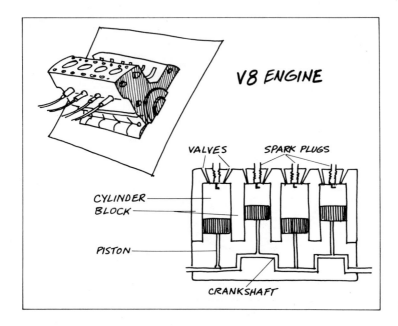

VALVES   SPARK PLUGS

CYLINDER
BLOCK

PISTON

CRANKSHAFT

V8 ENGINE

FIGURE 3.24

amount of space, but the quantity of information displayed is a serious disadvantage in an oral presentation. The fact that much information is presented deprives the audience of a clear focal point, and more time may be consumed explaining the table than working with the material presented. One solution is to exclude unnecessary columns and rows to produce a partial table. Figure 3.25 shows a table that would be unacceptable in oral presentation, and Figure 3.26 shows a partial table that would have a better chance of conveying meaningful information to an audience.

It is better still to take one specific relationship from a table and express it in some type of visual form. This is the preferred approach because most tables include two or more relationships, each of which could be represented by a distinct visual form. The relationships that may be contained in a table are the relative size or magnitude of items, the relative contribution of different sources to a final figure, and changes over time in any one category.

Relative sizes or magnitudes may be displayed with either *bar graphs* or *picture graphs*. Bar graphs use vertical columns to represent the entries and the relative height of the bars corresponds to the size of each. Picture graphs use separate pictures for numbers of units and the number of pictures displayed corresponds to the total number of units present. Figures 3.27 and 3.28 compare defense and nondefense spending by the federal government in 1979 using the two techniques.

Pie graphs are used to display the breakdown when a single total is derived from several sources. The size of each slice corresponds to the portion of the total represented. For example, Figure 3.29 displays the components of the gross national product in 1979.

FIGURE 3.25 Economic Indicators (Billions of current dollars; quarterly data at seasonally adjusted annual rates)

PERIOD	GROSS NATIONAL PRODUCT	PERSONAL CONSUMPTION EXPEND-ITURES	GROSS PRIVATE DOMESTIC INVEST-MENT	EXPORTS AND IMPORTS OF GOODS AND SERVICES		
				NET EXPORTS	EXPORTS	IMPORTS
1969----	935.5	579.7	146.2	1.8	54.7	52.9
1970----	982.4	618.8	140.8	3.9	62.5	58.5
1971----	1,063.4	668.2	160.0	1.6	65.6	64.0
1972----	1,171.1	733.0	188.3	—3.3	72.7	75.9
1973----	1,306.6	809.9	220.0	7.1	101.6	94.4
1974----	1,412.9	889.6	214.6	6.0	137.9	131.9
1975----	1,528.8	979.1	190.9	20.4	147.3	126.9
1976----	1,702.2	1.089.9	243.0	8.0	163.3	155.4
1977----	1,899.5	1,210.0	303.3	—9.9	175.9	185.8
1978----	2,127.6	1,350.8	351.5	—10.3	207.2	217.5
1979----	2,368.8	1,509.8	387.2	—4.6	257.5	262.1

Council of Economic Advisors, *Economic Indicators* (June, 1980), 1.

GOVERNMENT PURCHASES OF GOODS AND SERVICES

TOTAL	TOTAL	FEDERAL NATIONAL DEFENSE [1]	NONDEFENSE	STATE AND LOCAL	FINAL SALES
207.9	97.5	76.3	21.2	110.4	926.2
218.9	95.6	73.5	22.1	123.2	978.6
233.7	96.2	70.2	26.0	137.5	1,057.1
253.1	102.1	73.5	28.6	151.0	1,161.7
269.5	102.2	73.5	28.7	167.3	1,288.6
302.7	111.1	77.0	34.1	191.5	1,404.0
338.4	123.1	83.7	39.4	215.4	1,539.6
361.3	129.7	86.4	43.3	231.6	1,692.1
396.2	144.4	93.7	50.6	251.8	1,877.6
435.6	152.6	99.0	53.6	283.0	2,105.2
476.4	166.6	108.3	58.4	309.8	2,350.6

FIGURE 3.26 Economic Indicators (Billions of current dollars)

PERIOD	GROSS NATIONAL PRODUCT	PERSONAL CONSUMPTION	GROSS PRIVATE INVESTMENT	NET EXPORTS	GOVERNMENT PURCHASES
1969	935.5				
1970	982.4				
1971	1,063.4				
1972	1,171.1				
1973	1,306.6				
1974	1,412.9				
1975	1,528.8				
1976	1,702.2				
1977	1,899.5				
1978	2,127.6				
1979	2,368.8	1,509.8	387.2	—4.6	476.4

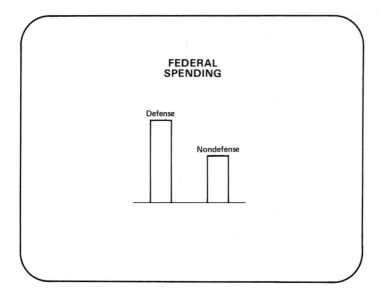

FEDERAL
SPENDING

Defense

Nondefense

FIGURE 3.27

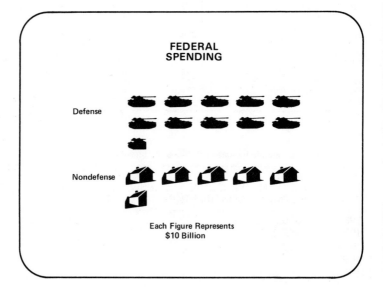

FEDERAL
SPENDING

Defense

Nondefense

Each Figure Represents
$10 Billion

FIGURE 3.28

Finally, changes in a single category can be displayed with simple *line graphs.*
By convention, the horizontal axis represents the passage of time from left to right,
and the vertical axis represents the quantity recorded. Complex line graphs are
composed according to the same conventions, but several lines are used on a field

FIGURE 3.29

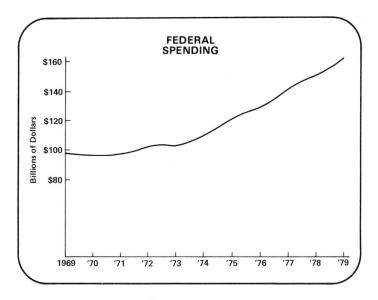

FIGURE 3.30

to represent changes in two or more categories. Figure 3.30 shows the growth in federal spending during the period 1969–1979, and Figure 3.31 divides federal spending into defense and nondefense categories while showing state and local expenditures as well.

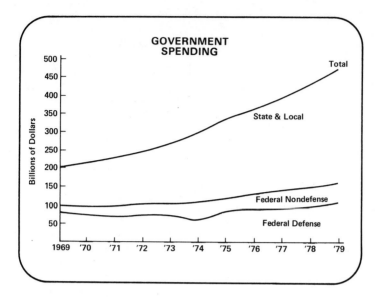

GOVERNMENT
SPENDING

FIGURE 3.31

CONSTRUCTING VISUAL AIDS

Constructing visual aids that enhance your speech requires some care and attention, but neither great skill nor special tools are necessary. You may approach the task in the way that you feel most comfortable and the suggestions presented here are intended to be general guides for your work. The end product is the important consideration and the visual aids that you use should be neat and attractive, legible to all members of the audience, clearly related to your oral presentation, and composed in a manner that does not confuse the audience. Producing aids that meet these criteria is relatively easy if you consider the audience, use appropriate materials, and work systematically.

Audience Consideration

As you construct your visual aids, it is important to keep the needs of the audience in mind. One of the most critical factors is the size of the audience, because the more people present, the larger your visuals will have to be. Precise figures are arbitrary, but remember that with a large group it is often necessary for some people to sit further from you. In a typical classroom with people as far as twenty feet away, the smallest lettering used should be about one inch high with lines one-eighth inch wide. Block letters are easy to read and are preferred to more elaborate styles. The size of the lettering and the content of your visual will determine the size of the other components and the minimum dimensions necessary for the entire visual aid. As a general rule, the size of the components should double for each ten feet beyond the initial figure. Thus, lettering 1 × ⅛ inch is suitable when the farthest member is up to twenty feet away. With audience members thirty feet away, you should use lettering 2 × ¼ inch, and so forth.

Because visual acuity declines rapidly with age, the average age of your audience should also be considered in determining the size of your visuals. The figures suggested above are representative of the needs of an audience that is about twenty years of age. If the average age is forty, your visuals should be about 10 percent larger; if sixty, about 35 percent larger; and if eighty, just over twice as large.

Your concern for the audience should also direct your attention to the use of labels and colors. All of your visual aids should be clearly labelled to help the audience identify critical items. In particular, all components should be labelled and the visual aid should have a general heading indicating its role in the presentation. These requirements can be softened a bit when the components are pictures with which the audience is already familiar, but it is usually better to use too many labels than too few.

Use of color becomes increasingly important as the distance between you and the audience increases and as the visual aids with which you work become increasingly complex. It is especially important that all components and lettering stand out clearly against the background and that light shades and soft hues never be used. Strong, bold colors should be used to present a clear contrast to the background. The color wheel can offer some assistance in choosing colors—especially for items that are adjacent to one another and that need to be kept distinct. (See Figure 3.32.)

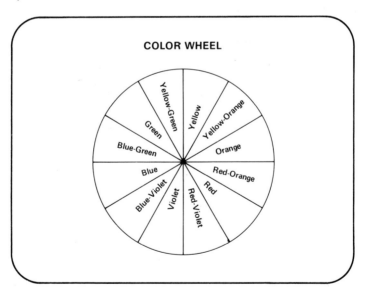

FIGURE 3.32

Colors that are directly opposite from one another on the color wheel are called "complements" and provide the strongest contrasts. Thus, red and green are complements and could be used beside one another in a visual aid to produce an image in which the components remain distinct, even at long distances. When several items must be presented in close proximity to one another, as in a bar

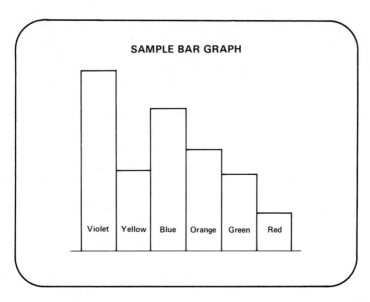

FIGURE 3.33

graph with several bars, contrasts can be maintained by using complements and near complements in succession. For example, the first bar in the Figure 3.33 would be violet, the second one yellow, the third one blue, the fourth bar orange, and the fifth and sixth bars green and red.

Use Appropriate Materials

The materials needed to construct visual aids are poster board, a pencil, and a supply of colored marking pens. You may also need a few sheets of colored paper and some glue. Markings pens are not very good for coloring in solid masses such as the bars in bar graphs or the slices in pie graphs. You can produce a neater visual aid by using pieces of colored paper cut to shape for these components.

Use of visual aids will add some expense to preparing your speech, but this is not a good time to worry about economy. Shortcuts in time or material are likely to produce inferior visual aids that distract your audience. Three specific cautions should be noted.

Do not use the blackboard   One way speakers try to economize is by using a blackboard. Unfortunately, blackboards are not very useful and efforts to use them will cause you considerable difficulty. Because few are portable, you seldom have adequate time to prepare visuals on them in advance. The common results are hastily drawn figures and efforts to draw the figures while speaking. Few students have escaped instructors who turn their backs on the class and talk to the board. If you have experienced this, you know how distracting it can be, and you should also realize that you lose your ability to control audience reaction when you no longer face the group.

In some cases, you may have access to the blackboard prior to your speech and have time to prepare finished visuals. Even in these cases, use of the blackboard is undesirable because you are less able to control your audience's attention. Visual channels usually command more attention than oral ones and the sight of prepared charts and diagrams on the board will cause your audience to concentrate on them at the expense of other portions of your presentation. Even a movie screen lowered to hide the board is a distraction that can be avoided by using other forms.

The only case in which use of the blackboard is justified is when you want to add to or modify the visual representation while your speech is in progress. This is a useful technique when you are explaining complex systems and want to display the minimum features initially and add other components as the speech progresses. It is also helpful when you want to make sure that the audience understands a situation as it existed in the past and then demonstrate the effects of subsequent developments. Both of these cases invite use of visual representations that can be altered in the course of your presentation.

Do not use inferior materials   Both poster board and marking pens are available in several grades. Lighter grades of board, white-coated cardboard, and paper tablets can save you some money. However, they usually lack the rigidity of higher quality board, and this will cause you problems if you choose any of them. In general, rigid boards should be used to prevent visuals from folding and buckling during a presentation. The board should be substantial enough so that it can be held on one edge without having to worry that it will twist or wrinkle.

Cheaper grades of marking pen may be satisfactory for some purposes, but most produce uneven lines. Quality pens produce lines of uniform width and intensity, and this fact will save you many headaches in producing your visuals.

Do not economize on space   Occasionally speakers try to economize by producing more than one visual aid on a single board. This can be done either by putting two or more visuals on one side or, when the surface is finished, putting visuals on both sides. Neither approach is desirable. Placing two visuals on one side makes it difficult to control the audience's attention and may produce a cluttered, unattractive image. Using both sides makes it difficult to keep track of the order of presentation during a speech and—as we will see in the section on presenting visual aids—there are better uses for the back side.

Work Systematically

Visual aids display your work habits more directly than any other part of the speech. Sloppy or carelessly prepared visual aids are serious liabilities and suggest a lack of concern on your part. Even though your drafting skills may be limited, you can prepare clean and neat visual aids by taking the time to work systematically. Working through the following steps may help in preparing visual aids:

1. Prepare a preliminary sketch using pen or pencil on scratch paper. Great detail is not necessary, but you should try to work to approximate scale and include all major elements and labels. Done carefully, the preliminary sketch should show how the image will appear to your audience. You may wish to try several preliminary sketches, discarding those that are unsatisfactory, or you may prepare just one and modify it until you are satisfied.

2. Select a piece of poster board in the proper size and shape, and use a pencil to outline the visual aid. Draw lightly so that errors can be erased without leaving permanent marks. The outline should include all features to be displayed, the labels to be used, and the colors to be used should be noted.

3. Following the pencilled sketch, use marking pens to permanently enter outlines and labels. Make sure that the lines are broad and dark enough to be seen easily, and that appropriate colors are used.

4. Finally, use marking pens, paint, or colored paper to fill in areas that are to be solid masses of color. Colored paper is the preferred alternative because it is possible to cut it to the precise shape without worrying about uniform intensity or smudging.

SUMMARY

A visual aid is anything that gives visual representation to an idea, but images that clarify, prove, or prove and clarify statements are most useful. The special functions of visual aids are making ideas memorable and displaying complex relationships between ideas, steps in a process, physical locations, and quantity or number. Visual forms should be selected according to their ability to fulfill these functions, and in constructing visual aids you should consider the audience, use appropriate materials, and work systematically.

LEARNING ACTIVITIES

1. Return to the speech you analyzed after reading the last chapter and determine where you could use visual aids. Which of the ideas presented require visual supporting materials? What types of visual display would be most helpful in presenting these materials? How could you adapt the visual representations to your classroom audience? Make a rough sketch of the visuals you would use and ask your instructor to comment on your plan.

2. Find a table in a textbook or other source and identify the relationships displayed in rows and columns. Plan a separate visual representation to display each of the relationships and make a sketch of the visual you would use. Ask your instructor or another student to comment on your plan.

3. Select a textbook, article, or other written report that makes extensive use of visual materials. Decide which of the visual materials could be

used in making a presentation and how you would adapt them to the oral setting. If you were to make the presentation to your classroom audience, how large would the visuals have to be? What colors would you use to represent the elements? What labels would you use? What kinds of lettering would you use? Make a sketch of your proposed visuals and ask your instructor or another student to comment on your plan.

CHAPTER FOUR
ORGANIZATION
The Structure of a Presentation

Organization is the one quality that will most clearly distinguish your work from that of less skilled speakers. This does not mean that organizing a speech is especially difficult, but it does emphasize the unique role of structure in formal presentations. Of course, organization is important in other forms of communication, but the demands are not as great as in formal speeches. For example, reading a poorly organized written report is unpleasant, but the reader is able to put the submitted material in a more suitable order. Similarly, receiving disorganized oral reports in conversation is difficult, but the receiver is usually free to ask questions, which may force the reporter to offer further information in a coherent sequence. Contrary to these situations, the audience for a formal presentation seldom has the speaker's text and almost never feels free to interrupt with questions. As a result, you should anticipate the order that will be most meaningful to your audiences, and arrange presentations accordingly.

Because audiences differ in knowledge, interests, and ability, no single structure will work well in all situations. However, certain general sequences have been found to work well on most occasions. You can learn to use these sequences most effectively if you divide the complex process of organization into its three elements. *Format* refers to the overall structure of a presentation; *pattern* describes the order of ideas in the main part or "body" of a speech; and *transitions* are devices that tell the audience how one part of a presentation relates to the others.

This chapter introduces you to each of these elements and concludes with some directions for composing a finished speech.

FORMAT

When you look at the outline of a well-planned speech, its most noticeable feature is its division into three distinct units. These units are the introduction, body, and conclusion. Each of these units has a distinct function, and you can think of the entire speech as a pair of funnels placed end to end. (See Figure 4–1.)

An introduction usually begins with a discussion about the subject in very broad terms, and it is aimed at attracting as much interest as possible; it then focuses on the particular topics discussed in the body. The body is a sequential discussion of the topics introduced, using standard patterns discussed later in this chapter. The conclusion summarizes the body and then expands the focus to discuss implications of the presentation.

Introduction

The purpose of the introduction is to prepare the audience for the material that follows. To achieve this task, you should secure your audience's attention, provide necessary background or orientation, state your purpose, and preview the topics in the body. The amount of time and effort required for these steps varies with the audience and subject, but more speakers err by doing too little than by doing too much. A handy rule of thumb is to use roughly 20 percent of your allotted time for the introduction. This time can be reduced when your audience knows the subject, already is interested in what you have to say, or when your speech is longer than usual.

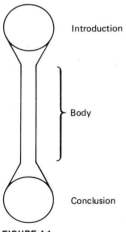

Introduction

Body

Conclusion

FIGURE 4.1

"My fellow Americans. . .welcome. . .opening joke. . .personal
anecdote. . .straight party line. . .second joke. . .presidential en-
dorsement. . .final joke. . .closing remarks. . .thank you."

Attention material   The first portion of your introduction should be
designed specifically to gain your audience's attention. This is an important step
because a good first impression will work to your advantage throughout the
presentation. And, a poor first impression will damage your chances of success no
matter how well the rest of the speech is prepared.

The material you use to gain attention should be clearly related to the subject of your presentation, and it should be both interesting and understandable.
The most common techniques are familiar reference, striking example, striking
quotation, and humorous anecdote. For example, any one of them could be used
to gain attention for a speech on the importance of communication in business.

Familiar Reference

If you could stand where I am and look around the room, you would realize that
we've gotten to be pretty good friends over the last few years. John Smith on my left
has been coming to these meetings for over ten years; Janet Spurrier on my right has
been coming for almost as long—nine and a half years, isn't it Janet? If you stood
here, you would see quite a few familiar faces. You might also notice that a few of our
old friends aren't here. The one I have in mind is Susan Carter. Susan had been with
us for almost five years as regional transportation manager, and most of you know

why she isn't here today. If you haven't heard, I'm pleased to announce that Susan has been promoted to vice-president for transportation systems. I had a chance to talk to her before she left and I asked what she thought was responsible for her promotion. You might be surprised by her answer. The one thing that she thinks made her stand out is her ability to talk to people—to communicate in a variety of situations.

Striking Example

We hear a lot about the importance of communication and the serious problems caused by communication breakdowns. One really striking example caught my eye the other day and I'd like to share it with you. Some of our friends at a local company—I can't tell you which one, but I think you'll recognize it when you hear the story—have been working on an improved temperature sensor. It is designed to monitor production of corrosion-resistant alloys used in the space program and it promises to be the best thing on the market. Anyway, they've been working on it for a year and a half. Yesterday they had their "launch meeting" and ran into some real surprises. The engineer responsible for design announced that his team had solved earlier problems and would be able to meet 80 percent of the original specifications. The production engineer exploded because the production line would be done in three weeks—only six weeks behind schedule—but the changed design would require an additional three months. Finally the marketing manager explained that he couldn't accept design changes or delays because his representatives had already sold over 500 units based on the original specifications, with promised delivery dates as early as next month. The last I heard, the project director was on his way to a new assignment in Greenland and the other folks are trying to figure out what to do next.

Striking Quotation

As I was getting ready for this presentation, I realized that the one thing we have in common is the organization we work for. With that in mind I started looking for information about the importance of communciation in organizations and I found a passage that summarizes things far better than I can. The author is Saul W. Gellerman, a management consultant and contributor to the *Harvard Business Review.* Here is what he says about communication:

> Nothing is more central to an organization's effectiveness than its ability to transmit accurate, relevant, understandable information among its members. All the advantages of organizations—economy of scale, financial and technical resources, diverse talents, and contacts—are of no practical value if the organization's members are unaware of what other members require of them and why. Awareness enables them to put their resources, talents, and contacts to work in a concerted, responsive way. Thus the role of communication in an organization is roughly analogous to that of a nervous system in a living organism—it orchestrates what would otherwise be chaotic. Nevertheless, despite its overwhelming and acknowledged importance, the process of communication is frequently misunderstood and mismanaged.[1]

Humorous Anecdote

Most of us think about communication only when something goes wrong. Well, I have a friend named Eric who is thinking about communication a lot these days. Eric teaches at a local university and his car stalled while driving to school. He tried to

[1] Saul W. Gellerman, *The Management of Human Resources* (Hinsdale, Illinois: The Dryden Press, 1976), p. 54.

restart it but the battery was too weak. He was just about to give up when a young man stopped and volunteered to help. He said he had never pushed a car before, but would be glad to give it a try. Eric told him how to line up the car bumpers and explained that he had an automatic transmission. To get the car started, he said, they would have to be going about 35 mph. The young man said he understood and they both got back into their cars. Eric waited for the expected bump and turned around when it didn't come. That's when he realized how important communication can be. There about 20 feet behind him was the young man coming to give him a push—going exactly 35 mph.

Orientation material   The second part of your introduction is called orientation material. It should provide your audience with whatever background information they need to appreciate the significance of your speech, and you can think of it as a bridge between attention material and the detailed materials that follow.

Audience needs change from situation to situation, but people usually require an explanation of one or more of the following: division of the subject, historical background, or basic definitions.

When the audience is familiar with your subject in very general terms, you may divide the subject to focus their attention on a specific part that you want to discuss. For example, if your attention material introduced the concept "communication breakdown," you divide it to get your audience thinking about interpersonal communication skills.

> There are all kinds of communication breakdowns. Some are caused by factors over which we have little control. Solar flares interfere with radio and television, causing communication breakdowns. Mechanical equipment can malfunction, causing communication breakdowns. And messages get confused and distorted when they pass through several hands, causing still different communication breakdowns. All of these kinds of breakdown are important, but I want you to think about just those that occur when two people are talking face to face.

The orientation is also a convenient place to provide historical background that may help your audience understand the subject. Someone giving a speech about the importance of communication skills might provide the following bit of history.

> Interest in communication isn't something that has just happened. People have been worrying about effective communication for some time. It may interest you to know that the oldest textbook we know of is on communication. It is almost 4,000 years old and was designed to teach a young Egyptian Pharaoh how to talk his way into the underworld. However, until recently public speaking was the only kind of communication studied seriously. People only started studying interpersonal communication a few years ago and courses in organizational communication are an even more recent development.

Finally, the orientation material is a good place to define any terms or phrases that you use throughout your speech. This is particularly important when you are using terms in a slightly different way from usual or when you want to make sure there is no confusion. For example, someone giving a speech about communication in business might want to make sure his audience knew what he meant by "effective communication."

> We're surrounded by communication, but not much of the noise is what I call effective communication. So we don't go off on different tracks, I want you to know precisely what I mean by effective communication. When I say communication is effective, I mean that four things have happened. First, the speaker said what he meant; second, the receiver clearly heard what was said; third, the receiver interpreted the message the way the speaker intended; and, fourth, the receiver reacted to the message the way the speaker intended. I call communication effective only when all four of these things happen.

Compose the orientation material after everything else is done so that you can anticipate the needs of your audience and make a smooth transition from the attention material to what follows.

Purpose statement   The third component of your introduction should be a statement of your purpose. This statement indicates what you hope to accomplish by presenting the speech and it will help you focus your material if you restrict the purpose to a single, simple sentence. This grammatical concern is important because some speeches include too many distinct topics and too few pieces of developing material for each. By restricting yourself to a simple sentence, you can insure a clear focus for your presentation. Of the statements listed below, only the third is suitable for use as a purpose statement.

1.   The purpose of this speech is to talk about communication skills in business.
2.   The purpose of this speech is to explain communication skills and show how they can be acquired.
3.   The purpose of this speech is to show that corporations should give greater attention to the communication skills of their employees.

The phrase "talk about" in the first is ambiguous, while the second is a compound sentence and sets forth two distinct objectives.

Although it is rather mechanical, a purpose statement should be introduced with a phrase like "the purpose of this presentation is" or "I intend to show that." Either of these phrases is acceptable and you can probably think of others that will work as well. However, two cautions should be observed in stating your purpose. First, the statement should be clearly marked to insure that your audience recognizes it. Second, your statement should avoid references to persuasion because they may make the audience defensive. Specific cases in which you should be particularly cautious about stating your purpose involve persuasion and are discussed in Part II of this book.

Preview   The final component of an introduction is the preview, or forecasting summary. This statement completes the introduction by listing the topics discussed in the body of a presentation. It marks an extremely important juncture in the speech because it announces the pattern employed in the body and establishes a set of audience expectations.

It is easiest to compose the preview after the body has been completely outlined because the preview can be compiled by simply listing the major ideas from the body in the order in which they are to be presented. For example, if the body of a speech uses the following topics; the preview might be presented in simple list form:

1. Communication skills are essential for success in business.
2. Communication skills can be acquired in several ways.
3. Corporations should support their employees' efforts to acquire communication skills.

However, it can be polished by adding an introductory phrase and by adding numerical labels. The polished preview might appear as follows:

> In this speech, I will first show that communication skills are essential for success in business; second, that they can be acquired in several ways; and third, that corporations should support their employees' efforts to become better communicators.

You can probably think of more attractive phrasing, but be sure that it clearly identifies the preview and distinguishes it from surrounding statements.

Conclusion

The final unit of your speech should be the conclusion. Careful planning is essential because the conclusion has two specific functions, which are better executed here than anywhere else. These functions are (1) drawing the materials together to form a single coherent impression of the whole speech, and (2) capitalizing on favorable audience reactions. The first is achieved through the *summary* and the second through the *final appeal.* Like the introduction, the conclusion may be as much as 20 percent of the finished speech.

Summary   The summary is your best opportunity to see that an audience has a clear view of the whole presentation. Audiences may become involved with specific materials and this may cause them to lose sight of the overall structure of the speech, give undue emphasis to subordinate materials, or to draw conclusions different from those intended by the speaker.

To avoid this danger, start the conclusion with a summary that emphasizes the principal ideas. The easiest way to do this is by simply restating the purpose and preview in the past tense. For example, the purpose and preview created above could be restated to form the following summary:

> The purpose of this speech was to show that communication skills should be given greater attention. I showed first that communication skills are essential for success in business; second, that they can be acquired in many ways; and third, that corporations should support their employees' efforts to become better communicators.

In addition, you may want to refer briefly to some of the more striking developing materials, and you may wish to vary the phrasing. However, be sure that the summary focuses attention on the principal ideas, and that it emphasizes the overall impression you want the audience to retain.

Final appeal   The ideal way to finish a presentation is by capitalizing on favorable reactions of the audience. Both your purpose in speaking and the extent of audience reaction affect the results for which you can aim, but three basic techniques are always available.

The least ambitious final appeal merely reminds the audience of the importance of the subject and of the manner in which it may affect them. These factors should parallel the materials with which you secured initial attention, and an example is often the most effective means of displaying potential impact of the subject.

> No matter what your job is, your ability to communicate with others determines your chances for success. If you have any doubts, remember how rapidly Mike Bradbury advanced. There is another side of the coin to remember as well: Every time a Mike Bradbury takes a step up, he takes an opportunity that could have been yours.

A slightly more ambitious technique may be used when the audience appears to side with you, but is not ready to act: Explain to the audience where additional information about the subject can be found. Also, questions can be solicited from the audience at this point in a presentation. Other sources of information to which you may refer your audience include written reports, journal articles, books, and publications prepared by professional groups and public interest organizations.

Finally, there are some situations in which the speaker's purpose calls for specific action and audience response indicates that they are ready to act. When both of these conditions exist, you may use the most ambitious final appeal technique. This consists of giving your audience specific, step-by-step directions for the action desired. For example, a sales representative may conclude a presentation by explaining the process used to place an order, a civil engineer by showing how environmental clearance can be obtained, and a public relations spokesperson by explaining how the audience should respond to critics.

PATTERNS OF ORGANIZATION

With minor variations, the format explained above should be used for all oral presentations. However, there are several ways in which the body of a speech can be organized and the choice of pattern should reflect the particular features of the subject you want to emphasize.

The body of a presentation consists of a few major statements and the materials used to develop each. The way in which you state the major ideas and the order in which they are presented are determined by the pattern chosen. Some textbooks list as many as twelve distinct patterns, but the three most common ones are sufficient to deal with most situations that can be encountered. These three are *chronological, spatial,* and *topical patterns.*

Chronological Pattern

A chronological pattern is used when each of the major statements in the body refers to a period of time and the materials used to develop each statement describe characteristics of the period. The sequence of major ideas is determined by the order in which the events actually happen, and you may begin at either end of the time sequence. That is, your pattern may start from the earliest period and work to the most recent, or begin with the most recent and work back to the earliest. Whichever order you elect to use, be sure that you follow the natural sequence and do not discuss events out of order.

The most common error speakers make in using a chronological pattern is phrasing their major ideas so that they refer to specific dates rather than to periods. Remember, specific dates should be used as part of the developing material when they define the period described. However, the major statements should refer to the entire period. Also, the sequence of periods should represent the entire time covered by the speech, and no period should be omitted.

Public relations speakers often use time order to describe the organizations they represent. Such "historical" presentations help to build the confidence of potential investors by displaying the growth and development of the corporation. The following three sets of statements all use a time pattern to describe a particular company.

SAMPLE 1

    I. The J. C. Lambret company was founded in 1914.
    II. The J. C. Lambret company acquired a controlling interest in Mildred Pharmaceuticals in 1957.
    III. The corporate name was changed to the Lambret Holding Company in 1967.

SAMPLE 2

    I. In the most recent period, the corporate name was changed to the Lambret Holding Company.
    II. The J. C. Lambret company was founded in 1914.
    III. The J. C. Lambret company acquired a controlling interest in Mildred Pharmaceuticals in 1957.

SAMPLE 3

    I. The early years were marked by slow growth.
    II. The company expanded rapidly during the middle years.
    III. The company has now become a major holding company.

Of these three, only the final one makes optimum use of the time pattern. The first is limited to particular dates and appears to exclude large portions of material, while the second follows an unnatural order. The third, however, is acceptable on all counts.

Spatial Pattern

Spatial patterns are used to emphasize the physical distribution of a subject. For example, a corporate representative might explain her company's operations in the East, South, Midwest, and West. Or, a training officer might explain a plant to new employees by starting at one end of a building, describing each area in the order encountered while walking the length of the work space.

Each of the principal statements in a spatial pattern should refer to a specific area, and the order should be the order a person would normally encounter in moving across the space described. However, these requirements provide considerable latitude and you should feel free to choose the divisions that best reflect your view of the subject and the path through the material that best displays your interests. The following samples show how spatial patterns might be used to describe a building, a workshop, and an industrial site.

SAMPLE 1

I. The first floor is occupied by the accounting department.
II. The second floor houses the marketing research group.
III. The third floor consists of unassigned training and seminar rooms.

SAMPLE 2

I. The western third of the workshop is the receiving area for raw materials.
II. The central third of the workshop is the initial fabrication area.
III. The eastern third of the workshop is the final assembly area.

SAMPLE 3

I. The northeastern quadrant includes modern transportation facilities.
II. The southeastern quadrant consists of undeveloped marshland.
III. The southwestern quadrant provides locations for several small shops.
IV. The northwestern quadrant has been developed for heavy manufacturing.

Topical Pattern

Topical patterns are used when neither chronological nor spatial patterns highlight the features a speaker believes are important. The following examples illustrate a student describing a course to a friend, an executive arguing that a proposal should be adopted, and a sales representative introducing a new product to a potential consumer.

SAMPLE 1

    I. The work is about what you would expect for a 400-level course.

    II. The instructor is an interesting teacher.

    III. The textbooks are difficult to get through, but very informative.

SAMPLE 2

    I. The proposal should be adopted because it will help us maintain technological leadership.

    II. The proposal should be adopted because it will help us recruit talented personnel.

    III. The proposal should be adopted because it will help us regulate investment expenditures.

SAMPLE 3

    I. This machine is similar to several that you use now.

    II. This machine will reduce the amount of time you spend in processing.

    III. This machine has a number of features that competitors' machines lack.

    IV. We offer several alternatives to high-interest financing.

The topical pattern allows great flexibility and often is used because it gives speakers freedom to emphasize the points of greatest importance. However, it should not be used as a ''catchall'' pattern or as an excuse for talking about whatever the speaker happens to be thinking about at a particular moment. The rule of thumb is that the topics discussed should appear to the audience to be a logical division of the subject. The divisions that fulfill this rule vary considerably with the subject matter and with the background of the audience. The speaker should organize and present material in anticipation of questions the audience might have and in the order they would arise. However, the best guide in selecting a division is to find out what an audience thinks is important. Some presentations are very strictly defined; a speaker presenting the annual financial report has little choice about the topics covered. Other subjects give the speaker greater discretion, but the expectations of the audience are always determining factors.

TRANSITIONS

Even when you employ the format recommended here and choose a pattern that accurately reflects the subject, audiences may have difficulty in understanding the order employed and in seeing how specific pieces of information relate to other factors. These dangers are always present, but they are greatest when presenting highly detailed information to audiences with relatively little background.

You can reduce the frequency of misunderstandings and lessen their severity by using devices known as transitions. Transitions tell audiences how one part of a speech relates to another and they mark the end of one unit or the start of another. Transitions describe the speech itself—not the subject discussed—and some authors say that as much as 25 percent of a finished speech should consist of remarks of this type. That figure seems high because the format carries part of the load, but transitions are essential at many points. In shorter presentations, they should be used after the development of each idea. In longer presentations, they should be used after the discussion of each principal idea *and* at the end of each long piece of developing material. They may also be used to direct audience attention to visual aids. The three most widely used types of transition are *labels, directive statements,* and *internal summaries.*

Labels

Labels are used to show how a particular statement relates to the speech as a whole. You may use both numerical and verbal labels, and the two are often combined.

A numerical label designates the position of an item in a sequence. If you are introducing three arguments, you can number them and use the number to introduce each. For example:

> Professional speakers address four types of audience: first, fellow professionals; second, superiors; third, subordinates; and fourth, nonprofessionals.

Such numerical labels keep the order clear and they are especially valuable when used in conjunction with verbal labels. Verbal labels identify materials by specifying their role in a speech. Some examples follow:

> For example
> For instance
> The main point is
> The claim I want to emphasize is
> In summary

Each of these phrases helps a listener to appreciate the function of the material that follows by indicating its role in the presentation. They are particularly effective when used in conjunction with numerical labels:

> My first principal idea is . . . .
> The second instance is . . . .
> A third illustration is . . . .
> My fourth claim is . . . .

Directive Statements

Directive statements reveal the purpose of a speaker's remarks, but they sound rather harsh and should be used sparingly. Such statements are particularly valuable in instructional presentations and may be used whenever you want to minimize chances of confusion. Some examples follow:

That finishes my remarks about the first case.
I will now consider the second problem area.
The next topic I will discuss is . . . .
I want you to remember that . . . .
The point I have been illustrating is . . . .

Internal Summaries

Internal summaries are used to collect a speaker's remarks about one topic and point the way to the next. Their function is identical to that of the summary in a conclusion, but on a smaller scale. They are particularly useful in showing how several pieces of developing material relate to the topic. For example, a speaker using three examples to show that his company is concerned about environmental protection might use the following internal summary:

> These examples show how much we are concerned about protecting the environment. We have reduced toxic emissions, we have built dikes to prevent ground water seepage, and we have removed accumulated debris.

OUTLINING: PUTTING IT ALL TOGETHER

The distinction between format and pattern not only clarifies the common sequences, but it also has an important implication for your subsequent speaking career. In many professions, you may be required to speak with relatively little preparation. In these situations, the format recommended gives you a somewhat rigid way of ordering your presentation, while the patterns described previously give you flexibility to adapt your materials to the interests of the particular audience. This combination of rigidity and flexibility allows for the organization of clear presentations on the spur of the moment. And, by adding transitions, you can be sure that the audience will understand the sequence used. Memorizing the format, standard patterns, and common transitions will help you overcome problems in composition.

One point at which many speakers feel uncomfortable is when they begin writing a speech. Surrounded by the materials gathered through research and accumulated from personal experience, they may lose sight of the particular demands of speech organization. Their composition process is slow and erratic—often marked by false starts and jangled nerves.

You can avoid this unpleasantness by using the format described here to direct your composition. The format prescribes the units of the presentation, and the location and contents of each. Relying on this format, you can compile a blank or open-cell outline consisting of the unit labels, allowing space below each label. An open-cell outline is reproduced in Exhibit 4.1.

As you prepare to fill in the outline, keep in mind that there are many different preferences regarding the form of each entry, but that a full sentence outline

EXHIBIT 4.1   *ORGANIZATION: THE STRUCTURE OF A PRESENTATION*

INTRODUCTION

ATTENTION MATERIAL

ORIENTATION MATERIAL

PURPOSE STATEMENT

PREVIEW

BODY

CONCLUSION

SUMMARY

FINAL APPEAL

is particularly helpful in planning a presentation. By leaving out verbal embellishment, you can reduce the outline to about one-third as many words as would be presented orally. Since the normal rate of speech is approximately 145 words per minute, your outline should include approximately 50 words for each minute of speaking time. Student speakers often complain when required to compile outlines and many speakers have difficulty using full sentence outlines during an actual presentation. Full sentence outlines are often less than ideal texts from which to speak, and some alternatives are considered in the chapter on delivery.

However, full sentence outlines are the best means of composing speeches because they have a number of advantages over the alternatives. The physical structure of an outline makes it easy to distinguish developing materials from the ideas developed. This makes it possible to check for the logical relationships between statements and to insure that all statements are adequately developed. It also makes it possible to anticipate the amount of time to be spent on each idea, and to insure a balanced presentation of the material. Key word outlines share these advantages over manuscripts, but they have one great liability. Key words or phrases do not present complete ideas and may be interpreted in different ways. As a result, sequences that seem to be logical when represented by key words may appear illogical and disorganized when presented orally in full sentences.

The first entry you should make in the blank outline is the purpose sentence. The grammatical requirements for this entry help to insure that your presentation is well focused, and a clear statement here makes it easy to see if your speech will fulfill your assignment.

After the purpose has been stated, you are ready to select the body pattern. If you have a strong preference for a particular pattern, this will be an easy choice. If not, you can quickly sketch several alternatives and see which you like best. Remember, any subject can be divided according to time, space, or special topic, and you should choose the pattern that emphasizes the topics you believe to be most important or which best meets the expectations of your audience.

Once you have selected a pattern, quickly state each of the principal ideas and sketch the developing materials to be used with each. Following the completion of these items, you can write both the preview and summary. With this sketch of the presentation before you, it is time to select attention material and compose the final appeal. Both require attention to the needs and interests of your specific audience, and they can be written simultaneously. Finally, compose the orientation material. Remember, it should bridge the gap between attention material and purpose statement while providing any background information necessary for your audience to appreciate the significance of your presentation.

Once the orientation material is prepared, the outline will be complete and editing should begin. The length of time required for editing depends on a number of factors: the skill and care with which the first draft was composed, the time available, and your feelings about the finished product. Some speakers like to compose carefully and edit quickly. Others prefer to write quickly and edit carefully. Whichever approach you prefer, editing is an essential part of the composition process and is often as important as the initial writing. As you edit your presentation, check to see that each unit fulfills its proper function, and observe the amount of time required to present each. The introduction may be as much as 20 percent of the whole, the conclusion, 20 percent, and the body 60 percent. Within the body, each major statement should receive approximately equal amounts of time. At this point, you should also make any stylistic corrections necessary and revise any materials with which you are uncomfortable. Several changes may be made while editing and you may want to rewrite the speech several times before you are satisfied. The final step in composition is preparing the finished text from which you will speak. It is often easiest to simply make a finished copy of the full sentence outline, but you may prefer to use one of the other forms described in Chapter 6.

SUMMARY

The nature of oral presentations requires special care in organization and the quality of your organization will distinguish your efforts from those of less-skilled speakers. Format refers to the overall structure of a presentation, pattern describes the sequence of ideas in the main part or body of a presentation, and transitions show the audience how one part of a presentation relates to the others. The speech format divides a presentation into three parts: introduction, body, and conclusion. The introduction consists of attention material, orientation material, purpose, and preview, and the conclusion includes a summary and a final appeal. The body may use a chronological pattern, spatial pattern, or topical pattern, and transitions include labels, directive statements, and internal summaries. Although they may not be the best form to use in delivering presentations, full sentence outlines are particularly helpful in composing presentations.

LEARNING ACTIVITIES

1. Analyze the structure of a speech from a recent issue of *Vital Speeches.* Begin by underlining the principal ideas presented, circling the developing materials, and crossing out statements designed to establish a rapport with the audience. The remaining portions of the speech are elements intended to establish its structure. You may be surprised to see how few structural elements are present. After this preliminary analysis, rewrite the speech as if you were going to present it. Add structural features including purpose and preview, transitions, and a formal conclusion.

2. Focus on the body of a presentation by underlining the principal ideas developed and circling the developing materials. What pattern is used? Is thè pattern used properly? What errors do you find in sequence or statement? Make any corrections necessary and ask yourself why the speaker chose the pattern. Answering this question will be difficult, but it may give you some insight if you think about how the overall impression would change if a different pattern were used.

3. Select any subject with which you are familiar and think about the materials you would want to include if you presented the subject to your class. Then, outline the body of a presentation on this subject using each of the patterns described in this chapter. Your outlines need not be elaborate, but you should sketch a presentation using each. Compare the

presentations and decide which one you would prefer. Which is most consistent with your view of the subject? Which allows you to use most of the information you would like to present? Which would be most familiar to the audience?

4. Compare several newspaper accounts of the same event. How does the order of presentation employed in each differ from the others? How does the difference affect the overall impression created by each of the stories? To what extent are authors' assumptions, biases, or expectations evident in the patterns?

CHAPTER FIVE
STYLE
The Language
of Presentations

Style is a term commonly used to refer to the way someone does something. For example, "clothing style" refers to the way someone dresses, "personal style" refers to the way someone interacts with other people, and "leadership style" refers to the way someone conducts business. The term is used in much the same way in this book, but with specific reference to the way someone uses language. The important elements of style are word choices and sentence structures, and both must be adapted to the speaking situation before the resulting style can be called "good." Unfortunately, the way we learn to use language makes it difficult for most people to consciously do this.

As children, we expend tremendous amounts of energy learning to use language, and adults give us much help and encouragement. Most children manage to speak their first words some time during their second year and their vocabularies expand at a rapid rate during the following years. By the time a child enters school, his or her total vocabulary probably exceeds 3,000 words, and the average adult has a reading vocabulary of 25,000 words. However, once a person sufficiently masters language for daily use, there is little subsequent learning. In fact, most people become so confident in their use of language that they seldom think about it. They may search for "just the right word" when writing an important letter or report, and they may open a dictionary occasionally to assist them in completing a crossword puzzle or to check spelling. But, for the most part, use of language becomes a habit that requires no conscious effort.

This aspect of speaking offers advantages and disadvantages. One advantage of using language freely and without thought is that it saves us a great deal of time and energy. The English language includes more than 500,000 words, but the average person would have to consult a massive dictionary like the thirteen-volume *Oxford English Dictionary* to find many of them. More common dictionaries, such as the college edition of *Webster's New World Dictionary of the American Language,* include roughly 140,000 entries. Having to search through so many words whenever we wanted to say something would be an exhaustive, almost impossible task, which is why the majority of people rely on a much smaller set of words. Most adults have a "passive" vocabulary of approximately 25,000 words. They understand these words when someone else uses them, but they would not use them without special attention. Our "active" vocabularies, the sets of words we actually use, are smaller still. An active vocabulary of 5,000 to 6,000 words serves most people. Although this number is small compared to the total number of words available, it still gives us considerable latitude in selecting words for our communicative needs. Scholars trying to develop a version of the English language that is suitable for use as an easily learned international language have found that a much smaller vocabulary is sufficient for most purposes. They have demonstrated that a basic vocabulary of 850 words is adequate for general use and that additional vocabularies of 100 words each are sufficient for business and scientific communication.[1]

Although the habitual use of language makes our daily activities easier by reducing the number of choices we have to make before saying something, it also reduces our ability to use language in the most effective way possible. Few people are aware of the full resources of the language, and fewer still take time to find words or expressions that will convey their meaning most accurately to their audience.

Although presentational speakers seldom need to use all of the resources of language, most can make better use of them. Recognizing the disparity between the resources available and the materials actually used, authors of textbooks frequently give three pieces of advice:

1. Observe the way others speak and write.
2. Be conscious of your own use of language.
3. Search for ways of varying your habitual style by consulting a thesaurus and composing alternate expressions.

This advice is sound, but you may want more precise guidance. The breadth of language and the variety of situations in which you are likely to speak make it difficult to present a list of simple formulas or prescriptions for improving your

[1] C. K. Ogden, *Basic English International Second Language* (New York: Harcourt Brace Jovanovich, Inc., 1968).

style. However, it is useful to recognize the differences between oral and written styles, to identify the functions of language in a presentation, and to describe the qualities of good style.

DIFFERENCES BETWEEN ORAL AND WRITTEN STYLES

Research based on the practices of skilled speakers and on speculation about the nature of writing and speaking show that there are substantial differences between good oral style and good written style. As a speaker, the first difference you are likely to notice is that it is almost impossible to be as polished in speaking as you are in writing. In preparing a written communication, you can spend large amounts of time searching for exact expressions and polishing the form of your message. In extreme cases, you may write and rewrite your message several times in the search for perfection. As a speaker, you usually do not have time for such extensive polishing. Faced with an audience, you must speak, and efforts to postpone the presentation may weaken your credibility or cost you the opportunity. Even when the speech is written out, momentary lapses in attention will cause you to depart from the prepared text and audience reactions may solicit unplanned comments and digressions.

Although the factors affecting you as a speaker are most noticeable, they do not explain the difference between oral and written styles. Even if you were able to prepare a manuscript with great care and deliver it without departing from the prepared text, there is a good chance that it would be far from perfect orally. This is because the real foundations for the distinction between oral and written styles are the nature of the speaking situation and the needs of the audience.

Differences Founded on the Nature of the Situation

The nature of the speaking situation gives the speaker several advantages over the writer. First, and perhaps foremost, the speaker is confronted with a real, tangible audience. Whereas the writer must often address an unknown audience, or one that is limited only by matters of general interest and age, the speaker comes face to face with an audience and can adapt to the specific interests and abilities of the group. Style reflects this direct contact when it becomes direct and personal. Skilled speakers use personal pronouns, direct references to the audience, and rhetorical questions to capitalize on their contact with the audience.

As a consequence of this direct contact, a speaker has far more immediate feedback from the audience than a writer can ever hope to receive. A writer must select a level of verbal sophistication that he or she thinks is consistent with the abilities of the anticipated audience and maintain it throughout. A writer may learn later that he or she missed the mark, and then has to adapt subsequent messages, but in each the writer is locked into a level of language based on some

initial assumptions. Writers receive no feedback to cue them to the need for altera-
tion. In contrast, a speaker begins receiving feedback at once. Like a writer, he or
she must make some initial assumptions about the abilities of the audience, but
unlike the writer, changes can be made before material is presented. Thus, a good
oral style is dynamic, constantly changing in response to the reactions of the audience, while a written style is static, locked into a pattern set by the initial expectations of the author.

A third advantage of the speaking situation is that the oral presentation is far
less permanent than a written message. As a result, the speaker is free to respond
to the particular needs and interests of the moment with relatively little fear that
statements made will haunt him or her in the future. Of course, political candidates must exercise some care when reporters are present, and digging out press
clippings of opponents' past remarks has become a popular means of embarrassing them. However, details of most speeches are quickly forgotten. In contrast,
the permanence of the written message requires writers to observe caution and
make frequent use of qualifiers:

> On the basis of what we know now. . . .
> Current studies indicate. . . .
> From such-and-such point of view. . . .

These qualifiers are necessary because the written record may surface at any
time and may be circulated to hostile or unexpected audiences.

Finally, the spoken message has the advantage of nonverbal qualifiers that
take the place of grammatical conventions. In fact, many grammatical conventions have developed because written language lacks the inflections, pauses, and
gestures accompanying oral presentations. For example, periods, semicolons, and
commas are used to mark separations between parts of a message that would be
registered by pauses in oral presentation; question marks and quotation marks
record changes in meaning that would be registered by changes in tone or volume
during an oral presentation; and, parentheses and dashes designate in writing
digressions that would be marked by changes in rate and by various gestures in an
oral message. A good oral style capitalizes on the advantages of nonverbal accom-
paniments and abandons the grammatical conventions that substitute for them in
written records. As a result, an accurate transcription of good oral style is likely to
be a grammarian's nightmare: Sentences, clauses, and phrases are not distinguished from one another; many ideas are expressed in fragments; and contrac-
tions are used far more frequently than would be acceptable in a written report.

Differences Founded on the Needs of the Audience

Although differences based on the nature of the situation work to the
speaker's advantage, those founded on the needs of the audience make special
demands on him or her. Whereas readers may read and reread a passage at their
leisure, listeners have only one opportunity to get the message from a speech. As a

result, a good oral style is one that is immediately intelligible. Good written style—or at least good literary style—invites the reader to read a passage again and again. Each rereading reveals new meaning and the reader derives pleasure with the discovery of each new interpretation.

Because the listener lacks the opportunity of rehearing a speech, levels of meaning must be reduced to the fewest possible and the number of interpretations limited to the one or two that are consistent with the speaker's purpose. Inferences must be drawn explicitly and the pleasure of discovery (and rediscovery) replaced by appreciation for the clarity of the speech. Research indicates that skilled speakers respond to the needs of the audience by reducing the complexity of their message. Some stylistic techniques employed to simplify messages are listed below:

1. Use of short, direct sentences
2. Use of short, familiar words drawn primarily from the listener's active vocabulary
3. Avoidance of indefinite pronouns—"which," "whose," and "that"—because they force the audience to recall a noun to complete the meaning
4. Increased frequency of repetition to keep major ideas prominent in the minds of the listeners.

THE FUNCTIONS OF LANGUAGE

The way a speaker uses language has three distinct functions in communicating a message to the audience. First and most commonly recognized is presenting the content or intended message. Language is the primary medium through which the speaker's thoughts, ideas, and inferences about the subject of discourse are conveyed to the audience. Nonverbal cues supplement language, but language remains the principal vehicle for transmitting the substance of a speech.

In addition to packaging the materials of a speech, language also displays the speaker's attitude toward the subject. No matter how hard you try to be objective, the language you use includes evaluative components that show approval and disapproval, praise and blame, and affection and animosity. This fact is so fundamental to understanding the role of language in a speech that it may be helpful to turn to an authority on rhetoric for a more complete statement. W. Ross Winterowd explains "the myth of neutral language" in the following passage:

> There is no such thing as neutral language. This proposition demands a bit of analysis, for currently we are laboring under the myth that some language is loaded, whereas some is objective, fair, and neutral. We continually hear about the objectivity of wire-service reports; scientists assure us that their reports are only reports, not inferences; and the mass-circulation news magazines piously disclaim their own implied judgments. One of the common misconceptions about language is that the mathematical "language" of science is not loaded—that it is purely objective and that it carries no emotional overtones. The intimidated college freshman looking at a page in the text for his required course in math would certainly not agree that the precise language of mathematics is "unloaded," and that the simple equation

$E = MC^2$ is not perhaps one of the mose portentous utterances of our era. . . . In short, no language—not even the language of mathematics . . . is neutral.[2]

Language is not neutral. The numerous possibilities available to us in choosing words to describe an object or event require us to make judgments about the object when we select what we think is the most appropriate vocabulary.

Finally, the way a speaker uses language exhibits an understanding of his or her relationship to the audience. Variations in language indicate that a speaker thinks an audience is more or less knowledgeable about the subject; favorably or unfavorably disposed to the proposals being made; sympathetic friends or distant strangers; more or less influential; and so forth.

Thus, the speaker's style expresses a message, displays an attitude toward the subject, and exhibits an understanding of his or her relationship to the audience. Each of these functions is unavoidable in the use of language and each may have a decisive influence on the reactions of the audience. Moreover, these functions make special demands on the speaker and each provides a different point of view to consider in deciding what constitutes good style.

Language and the Message

Viewing style as a means of expressing ideas, your primary concern should be using language that gives the audience the same meaning you intended. This is not as easy as you might suspect because words have more than one meaning. Many of the words that will become parts of your professional vocabulary have precise technical meanings and numerous imprecise popular meanings. For example, the *Oxford English Dictionary* lists twelve different meanings for "communication," but specialists recognize more than twice that many.[3] The context often helps to reduce the number of possible meanings associated with each use of a word, but the variety of meanings makes possible a communication breakdown known as *bypassing.*

Bypassing occurs whenever one person uses a word to mean one thing and another person interprets it to mean something else. For example, representatives of two firms agreed to meet for lunch to finalize a major contract. The meeting was never held and the contract was jeopardized because neither realized that "lunch" is an ambiguous word: One representative customarily eats lunch at noon, while the other lunches at one o'clock. Bypassing may also occur when two people use different words to describe the same thing and neither realizes it.

The opportunities for bypassing are increased by the fact that two distinct sorts of meaning are associated with each word. The commonly recognized meaning is the conventional association between a word and the object(s) to which it refers. This is called the *denotative* meaning and is the type of meaning recorded in dictionaries. In addition, each word has a more personal meaning consisting of

[2] W. Ross Winterowd, *Rhetoric: A Synthesis* (New York: Holt, Rinehart & Winston, 1976), pp. 1–2.

[3] See Thomas R. Nilsen, "On Defining Communication," *Speech Teacher,* 6 (1957), 10–17.

THE WIZARD OF ID   by Brant parker and Johnny hart

By permission of Johnny Hart and Field Enterprises, Inc.

emotions that its use arouses. This is called the *connotative* meaning, and its strength depends on the situations in which the speaker learned to use the word. For example, a denotative meaning of "dog" is "any of a large and varied group of domesticated animals related to the fox, wolf, and jackal."[4] However, someone whose pet has died recently is less likely to respond to the denotative meaning than to their own sense of loss, the connotative meaning.

There are three distinct types of bypassing that cause a message to fall short of the ideal. An ideal style is one that conveys to the audience the same denotative and connotative meaning intended by the speaker. Style is faulty whenever the receiver gets a different denotative meaning, a different connotative meaning, or different denotative and connotative meanings.

Language and the Speaker's Attitudes

Your attitude toward a subject is evidenced by the language you use to discuss it. Systematic studies of this phenomenon focus on a variable called *language intensity,* which is defined as "the quality of language which indicates the degree to which the speaker's attitude toward a concept departs from neutrality."[5] Research to date is incomplete, but it points to three conclusions relevant to presentational speaking:

1. Use of intense language does not make a presentation more persuasive, and in some cases it reduces the willingness of an audience to accept the message.
2. Use of intense language is likely to reduce the audience's estimate of the speaker's trustworthiness and competence.
3. Use of intense language reduces a presentation's aesthetic appeal.

Because use of intense language can be a serious disadvantage in presentational speaking, it should be avoided whenever possible. It is particularly impor-

---

[4] *Webster's New World Dictionary of the American Language* College Edition (Cleveland: The World Publishing Company, 1964), p. 430.

[5] John Waite Bowers, "Language Intensity, Social Introversion, and Attitude Change," *Speech Monographs,* 30 (1963), 345. For a helpful summary of research, see James J. Bradac, John Waite Bowers, and John A. Courtright, "Three Language Variables in Communication Research: Intensity, Immediacy, and Diversity," *Human Communication Research,* 5 (1979), 257–269.

tant that you avoid the use of three stylistic features commonly associated with intense language. They are *profanity/obscenity, metaphoric* or *obscure terms,* and *rigidity.*

Use of profanity or obscenity in a presentation is almost certain to work to your disadvantage. The shock of hearing profanity may temporarily increase the audience's attention level, but the end result is a lowered estimate of the speaker and a reduced appreciation for the quality of the speech.[6] Although audience attitudes may vary from time to time and from place to place, the relative impact of various types of profanity/obscenity are well established. Terms with religious references are the least offensive, those suggesting excretory functions are more offensive, and those suggesting sexual functions are most offensive.[7]

The intensity of metaphoric language is generally recognized by authors of speech textbooks, and recent study has identified the same effect for obscure language. John Waite Bowers found that obscure terms are regarded as being more intense than familiar words, words qualified by adverbs and adjectives are more intense than those without qualification, and use of metaphoric language is more intense than literal expression. In fact, there is a perfect correlation between intensity and use of metaphors based on death and sex.[8]

Finally, language suggesting rigidity is usually taken to be intense. Support for this generalization comes from a study in which several phrases were systematically altered to produce messages of high and low intensity.[9] A comparison of the terms used in constructing the messages shows the kinds of phrasing that is likely to appear intense.

In general, style that employs profanity/obscenity, metaphoric and obscure language, and rigidity suggests high intensity and should be avoided. However, this generalization is not absolute and you may encounter a few cases in which intense language would work to your advantage. These cases arise when (1) the audience has a high regard for you, (2) the audience shares your feeling about the subject, and (3) your purpose is to move the audience to immediate action. You may benefit from the use of intense language when all three of these conditions exist, but you should avoid intense language if you are unsure about any of them.

Language and the Speaker-Audience Relationship

Recent studies show that most people change their language usage as they deal with different groups of people. Different vocabularies are used when talking to friends, to parents, to instructors, and to employers. It is interesting to note that changes in language usage are so characteristic of native-born speakers that they

[6] Anthony Mulac, "Effects of Obscene Language Upon Three Dimensions of Listener Attitude," *Communication Monographs,* 43 (1976), 300–307.

[7] Robert N. Bostrom, John R. Baseheart, and Charles M. Rossiter, Jr., "The Effects of Three Types of Profane Language in Persuasive Messages," *Journal of Communication,* 23 (1973), 461–475.

[8] "Some Correlates of Language Intensity," *Quarterly Journal of Speech,* 20 (1964), 415–420.

[9] William J. McEwen and Bradley S. Greenberg, "The Effects of Message Intensity of Receiver Evaluations of Source, Message, and Topic," *Journal of Communication,* 20 (1970), 340–350.

TABLE 5.1   Rigid Language

HIGH RIGIDITY	LOW RIGIDITY
Positively	Perhaps
Certainly	Possibly
Most	Some
Definitely	Slightly
Extremely	Somewhat
Is	Seems to be
Causes	May cause
Must	Could

Adapted from William J. McEwen and Bradley S. Greenberg, "The Effects Of Message Intensity on Receiver Evaluations Of Source, Message, And Topic," *Journal Of Communication*, 20 (1970), 340–350.

constitute systematic variations in style. Martin Joos describes the various styles in a book called *The Five Clocks,* and the point behind his title is worth considering.[10] For many years, people have been taught to speak English as if there was one correct style to be used for all purposes. Departures from this style were seen to be errors, just as a clock telling nonstandard time was said to be "off." However, Joos argues, we properly use different styles in different situations just as we use different clocks in different time zones.

Joos identifies five different styles, which are summarized in Table 5.2 and described in the following passages. Of these five, the style is appropriate for presentations, and you should note its characteristics with particular care.

The *frozen* style is the preferred style for literature and it is subject to the most rigid grammatical rules. Since it is intended for use in written messages, grammatical conventions are substituted for the intonations a speaker would use and they are essential elements of the message. The audience is assumed to be absent and the writer uses two stylistic variations to respond to this assumption. First, since the audience has no opportunity to ask questions, the writer provides far more background information than is needed. This technique insures that all possible questions about the message can be answered on the basis of the written text, but it also produces a ponderous text with numerous digressions. Second, the author employs an impersonal style and presents his or her message as if it existed independently. A speaker employing a conversational style becomes associated directly with the message through phrases like "I think," "I believe," and "I said," but a writer using a frozen style becomes dissociated from the message through phrases like "It is thought," "It is believed," and "It was said."

Formal style is the style of presentational speaking. It differs from the frozen style in that nonverbal cues are substituted for some grammatical conventions,

[10] Martin Joos, *The Five Clocks* (Bloomington, Indiana; Indiana University Research Center in Anthropology, Folklore, and Linguistics, 1962).

TABLE 5.2   Five Common Styles

STYLE	COMMON USES
Frozen	Literature and Declamation
Formal	Reports, Speeches, Briefings, and Presentations
Consultative	Business conversations, Meetings, and Dealing with strangers
Casual	Routine conversations with friends and professional associates
Intimate	Interactions with close friends and most family members

but it is still more nearly "correct" than the remaining styles. It is characterized by the presentation of sufficient background information to build coherent messages without trying to answer all possible questions. The speaker using a formal style envisions a particular audience and addresses them directly. He or she uses a personal style, but does not solicit immediate reactions from the audience because they would interfere with the continuity of the presentation.

The *consultative* style is the one that most people use for serious conversations, interviews, and conducting business in small groups. It differs from the formal style in that the listeners participate actively by using verbal interjections (yes, I see, um-hum, and so forth), and nonverbal cues (such as smiles and nods) to indicate whether or not they understand the message. Far less preparation is required for use of the consultative style than either the frozen or formal styles because the reactions of the listener indicate areas of interest and suggest points for elaboration. However, background is provided on the assumption that the listener has little knowledge of the subject and will benefit from it.

Casual and *intimate* styles are very informal and are seldom used in professional contexts. The casual style treats the listener as an acquaintance who is "in the know." Background material is omitted, and grammar is less important than intonation. Weak words and connectives are replaced by nonverbal cues, and both slang and professional vocabularies are used with increasing frequency because the other participant is assumed to be familiar with their specialized meanings. The intimate style is the opposite of the frozen style, and virtually all features of formal models are absent from intimate conversations. Grammar effectively ceases to exist and vocal qualities convey large portions of meaning. Jargon—words with meanings shared by relatively small groups of people—is used and the intimate style assumes a close, continuous relationship with the other person.

After reviewing the five styles, you should be able to see why the formal style is best for presentational activities. The rigidity of the frozen model is ponderous and unnecessary when facing an audience. Conversely, the demand for constant respondent participation in the consultative style and the increasing familiarity of the casual and informal styles are inappropriate in presentational settings.

QUALITIES OF GOOD STYLE

As a practical matter, your oral style should be governed by a single dominant concern: the need for *clarity*. The need for clarity has a dominant role because most audiences will hear a speech just once and will have no written record to guide them through obscure, vague, or ambiguous portions. The presentation must be instantly intelligible to insure that it is understood and to maintain audience attention.

The specific language that will produce a clear message varies from subject to subject, occasion to occasion, and audience to audience. Fortunately, the general characteristics of clarity are well understood and as a speaker you should direct your efforts toward producing messages marked by four qualities: accuracy, propriety, specificity, and simplicity.

Accuracy

Accuracy is achieved in a presentation by selecting words whose denotative meanings most nearly represent the objects, events, activities, and ideas that you intend. Accuracy is important in all communication, but securing it in formal presentations is far more difficult than in other settings because there are fewer ways to compare meanings. Much of what we say in casual conversation is vague, ambiguous, and imprecise. A brief glimpse at an ordinary conversation demonstrates the inaccuracy commonly encountered.

ALAN: We all have car, an- and s-stuff like that. Uh, what I would *like* to do is get some time to uh, get tuhgether with ya becuz, I have to go to summer camp.
PETE: Oh you're in the reserves.
ALAN: Yeah.
PETE: Oh.
ALAN: An that's, fer two weeks, in uh, y'know for the nex' two weeks. Actually tuh go into it tonight, I like to be able to s'down an'prepare something specific'ly *for* a person I talk to.
ALAN: Umm, in thinking about it in that terms—er in those terms preparing something specific'ly for you do you have any, *amount* of money, thet you could set aside monthly, that would not, y'know cramp your style so much you can enjoy life while you live—hehhehhehhh Y'know.
PETE: Well, it's really—that's a difficult question it would depend on what kinds of benefits I would get forrit.
ALAN: Yeah.[11]

Presumably, this exchange was meaningful to the participants because they continued with it. When engaged in conversation, we often fail to notice its potential problems because the setting provides a context in which nonverbal cues and

[11] Adapted from Jim Schenkein, "Identity Negotiations in conversation," in Jim Schenkein, ed., *Studies in the Organization of Conversational Interaction* (New York: Academic Press, 1978), p. 60.

other sources of information limit the danger of misunderstanding. However, in a presentation these advantages are reduced and the spoken language must be used with much greater care. The greatest barriers to accuracy in a presentation are unclear ideas and word substitutions.

Inaccuracy can result when you have only a vague notion of what you want to express. Fuzzy ideas are evident in careless phrasing like "thing-a-ma-jig," "what-cha-ma-callit," and "y'know what." These phrases lack a clear referent and the audience may or may not derive a meaning related to that which the speaker intended.

Inaccuracy may also result when you misuse a word. This often happens when someone tries to find a more impressive word and selects a term without examining its meaning. For example, Edwin Newman notes that several witnesses at the Watergate hearings used the word "subsequent" to mean "before," which is the opposite of its recognized meaning.[12] I have heard professionals make similar errors in formal presentations. Frequent errors occur when a word is substituted for one with a related sound or meaning. Common substitutions include "mean" for "mode," "average" for "median," "comprised" for "composed," "parameter" for "perimeter," and "bounty" for "booty." Of course, some audiences will fail to notice the substitution. That fact may save you some embarrassment, but it also indicates that the audience members have no clear idea of what you intended to say or that they failed to understand the meaning expressed.

Propriety

Propriety can be achieved by adapting language to the abilities of the audience addressed. Whenever multiple expressions are available, you should choose ones that are most meaningful to the particular audience. While you are speaking to audiences with backgrounds similar to your own, this is not likely to be very difficult because the words that are most meaningful to you are likely to be most meaningful to them. However, as your career advances and you become more sophisticated in your field, adapting language to audiences who lack your expertise will become increasingly difficult. Most professionals have difficulty addressing lay audiences, and the points at which they have problems are worth noting.

Acronyms are formed from the first letters of words in a title or phrase, and are frequently used to simplify communication among knowledgeable members of a group. For example, "radar" is now a recognized word, but it began as an acronym for "radio detecting and ranging." Radar has become a commonly used word because of the dramatic impact it has had on our lives. Other abbreviated titles that would be familiar to audiences include UNESCO, AFL-CIO, USOC, and CIA. However, most acronyms have far less appeal and many remain unknown to members of the general public. For example, the following acronyms, which are the titles of divisions and program offices in a specific company, would

---

[12] Edwin Newman, *Strictly Speaking* (New York: Warner Books, Inc., 1975), p. 21.

Reprinted by permission of Tribune Company Syndicate, Inc.

be familiar to only those people directly involved with the firm and its activities: MESO, OSD, SCSD, ESBDO, and ESLO.

A closely related problem is posed by the use of *professional jargon.* Its denotative meaning is a specialized vocabulary employed by members of a group engaged in a particular activity. Thus, members of a profession share a jargon, members of a social organization may use unique labels for offices, and people with similar ethnic origins may communicate with a special vocabulary that only they understand. Properly used, jargon saves time because it allows people with shared meanings of words and ideas to express complex notions without laboriously retracing common information. However, problems arise when jargon is used in addressing an audience that does not share the specialized meanings. For example, instructions given to graduate students engaged in rhetorical criticism sometimes sound like this:

> The accepted paradigm implies that interpretive critics should identify the controlling exigence and enumerate situational constraints before assessing motives.

A rough translation of these directions reads, ''If you want to figure out what ideas a speaker is presenting, you should identify the problem he or she is trying to resolve and the limitations that may be encountered.'' This translation is technically inaccurate because it leaves out references to appropriate theories and concepts, but a lay audience would find it far more meaningful than the original.

Another problem with specialized vocabularies is that the words included often have less specific popular meanings. This greatly increases the chance of bypassing when professional jargon is used because the speaker may intend the professional meaning while the audience receives the popular meaning, and neither is aware of the error. Some words that have both precise jargon meanings and imprecise popular meanings are displayed in the Table 5.3.

Specificity

Specificity is achieved by using specific and concrete words while avoiding those which are general or abstract. To appreciate the importance of specificity, you should understand that most words refer to a group of objects and that only

TABLE 5.3   Common and Jargon Meanings

POPULAR MEANING	WORD	JARGON MEANING
Any inaccurate or untruthful statement	Rhetoric	A theory of informative or persuasive discourse
Any gathering of two or more people	Meeting	A scheduled gathering of two or more qualified people for the purpose of making decisions
Any disagreement	Argument	A series of statements structured to make inferences based on accepted principles
A guess about how or why something happened	Theory	Descriptive statements about phenomena that integrate several generalizations, and that conform to rules for conducting and interpreting appropriate tests

proper names refer to particular individuals. For example, although there are very few people called "Eric Skopec," the word "home" refers to a large number of buildings in which one or more people live. It is even possible to refer to the nests of animals as "homes."

Words can be used to refer to large numbers of distinct objects because they do not name particular objects, but rather the features or qualities that the objects have in common. This characteristic creates the possibility for considerable confusion, and the following situations indicate the importance of specificity. Most organizations use production programs that require managers to submit periodic statements about their employees' performance. It is common practice for managers to ask subordinates to compile preliminary reports. One new employee was routinely asked to "give me a list of your accomplishments for the past year as soon as convenient." She didn't recognize the ambiguities in this request until she returned to her desk. How detailed should the list be? Should it merely list items or should it describe each? What constitutes an "accomplishment"? Should she include activities initiated during the year or only those completed? Does "year" mean calendar year, fiscal year, or employment year? What does "convenient" mean? Does the request have priority over other special assignments? Should it take priority over routine work?

The fact that words refer to relatively large categories makes it possible to communicate without having to name every individual object. This saves a great deal of time, but there is a price to be paid. The more general, abstract terms include large numbers of individuals, but they say less and less about each. This tradeoff between number of objects and information about each is displayed in the *abstraction ladder,* which is illustrated in Figure 5.1.

With the exception of proper names, most words can be placed on the ladder of abstraction with more concrete, specific words on the lower rungs, and more

ABSTRACTION LADDER

Start reading from the bottom *UP*

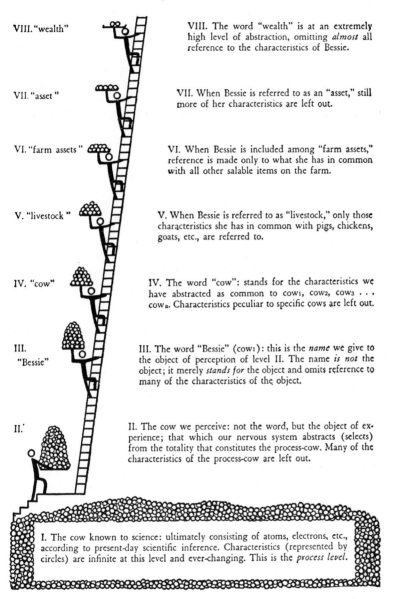

VIII. "wealth"

VIII. The word "wealth" is at an extremely high level of abstraction, omitting *almost* all reference to the characteristics of Bessie.

VII. "asset"

VII. When Bessie is referred to as an "asset," still more of her characteristics are left out.

VI. "farm assets"

VI. When Bessie is included among "farm assets," reference is made only to what she has in common with all other salable items on the farm.

V. "livestock"

V. When Bessie is referred to as "livestock," only those characteristics she has in common with pigs, chickens, goats, etc., are referred to.

IV. "cow"

IV. The word "cow": stands for the characteristics we have abstracted as common to cow$_1$, cow$_2$, cow$_3$ . . . cow$_n$. Characteristics peculiar to specific cows are left out.

III. "Bessie"

III. The word "Bessie" (cow$_1$): this is the *name* we give to the object of perception of level II. The name *is not* the object; it merely *stands for* the object and omits reference to many of the characteristics of the object.

II.

II. The cow we perceive: not the word, but the object of experience; that which our nervous system abstracts (selects) from the totality that constitutes the process-cow. Many of the characteristics of the process-cow are left out.

I. The cow known to science: ultimately consisting of atoms, electrons, etc., according to present-day scientific inference. Characteristics (represented by circles) are infinite at this level and ever-changing. This is the *process level.*

FIGURE 5.1 Abstraction Ladder

Slightly adapted from LANGUAGE IN THOUGHT AND ACTION, Fourth Edition by S. I. Hayakawa. Copyright © 1978 by Harcourt Brace Jovanovich, Inc. Reproduced by permission of the publisher.

general, abstract words on the higher rungs. This fact is important because the more concrete, specific words say more about the object described than the general, abstract words do. If words from lower levels of the ladder are used, the danger of bypassing is reduced and the impact of oral presentations is greater.

Simplicity

You can produce simplicity by using the shortest phrases, most precise sentences, and the most common words consistent with your meanings. Do not include words that leave the meaning of an expression unaltered. Compare the phrases in the columns below:

subject matter	subject
equally as costly	as costly
serious crisis	crisis
unplanned accident	accident
important priority	priority
yearly annual report	annual report
at this point in time	now

A related problem is the use of unnecessarily complex sentences. The passages below show what can happen to common expressions when stated in complex forms.

Do not, however disadvantageous the circumstances, permit yourselves to be forced into a position in which you must acquiesce in the transfer of ownership of this vessel to persons owing allegiance to a country whose interests are inimical to those of ours. I must be given maximum latitude to enjoy the benefits of our country, unfettered by degrading restrictions on my activities; if I am denied this privilege I would prefer to be permanently deprived of the exercise of my viable functions.

"Don't give up the ship" and "give me liberty, or give me death" would be very satisfactory substitutes.[13]

Finally, use of common words helps to simplify your presentations. The uncommon words in the left column could be replaced by the more common ones on the right with little loss in meaning.

exhortation	warning
cajolery	coaxing
posterity	future
subsequent	after
mutable	changeable
abode	home

[13] Quoted from William V. Haney, *Communication and Interpersonal Relations* 4th ed. (Homewood, Illinois: Richard D. Irwin, 1979), pp. 314–315.

SUMMARY

Style refers to the way a speaker uses language, and word choice and sentence structure are the important elements. Good oral style differs from good written style because of the nature of the presentational situation and the needs of the audience. The language in a presentation constitutes the message, displays the speaker's attitudes, and establishes the relationship between speaker and audience. The qualities of good style are accuracy, propriety, specificity, and simplicity.

LEARNING ACTIVITIES

1. Build on your experiences as a writer by translating written prose into a form suitable for oral presentation. Select an essay and convert it into a manuscript for oral presentation. Be sure to divide long, complex sentences into several short, direct sentences; use words drawn primarily from your intended audience's active vocabulary; avoid indefinite pronouns such as "which," "whose," and "that"; and increase redundancy by repeating the major ideas or themes before or after each series of developing materials. Review the discussion of differences between oral and written style to make sure you have done a thorough revision.

2. Select a brief speech or essay and circle words and phrases that are central to the theme. Try to focus on those that reflect the author's attitude toward the subject. Then consult a thesaurus and choose a few words or phrases that you could substitute for those circled. Even limiting yourself to words or phrases with which your audience is familiar, you will find several alternatives for those circled. Using the alternates, rewrite the original and consider the options available. Explore the different moods you can create by varying the language used.

3. Select an oral presentation from *Vital Speeches* and focus on elements of style that exemplify the speaker's understanding of the speaker-audience relationship. What style has the speaker used? Is it consistent with your view of the speaker-audience relationship in the situation? What changes would you make to alter the relationship?

4. Use the word "official" in ten sentences. Compare the sentences and ask yourself what "official" means in each. How many different denotative meanings do you recognize? How many different connotative meanings are apparent? How do these differences affect the total meaning of each sentence? What chances for misunderstanding result from the different meanings?

5. Ask several people what the word "authority" means. Record their remarks and compare the definitions that they offer. How do the definitions differ in denotative meaning? In connotative meaning? In total impression? What chances for bypassing result from the differing meanings?

CHAPTER SIX
DELIVERY

Delivery is a general term that refers to all aspects of a speaker's behavior while he or she is making a presentation. The most noticeable elements are posture and stance, gesture, and vocal qualities, including volume, rate, and pitch. Each of these elements can be varied to produce an almost endless number of patterns and the beginning speaker may be overwhelmed by the number of possibilities. No single pattern is ideal for all situations and you should try several to find the pattern that best suits your natural talents. If you have a relatively weak voice, you may compensate through greater use of gestures and less stationary postures. Conversely, if you are blessed with a particularly strong, dynamic voice, you may make greater use of the vocal variations available to you.

Regardless of the pattern best suited to your abilities, your objective is to deliver a message in a manner that makes it attractive to the audience. As your skill increases, you can use variations in delivery to develop and maintain audience interest, create favorable personal impressions, and predispose audiences to accept your messages. Developing advanced skills takes considerable practice and your initial efforts should be directed toward acquiring a mechanically adequate delivery. A mechanically adequate delivery is one in which nothing in your behavior distracts the audience from the substance of your message. Your delivery should not call attention to itself, and both you and your audience should be free to concentrate on the message presented. A classic expression of this principle is by Donald C. Bryant and Karl R. Wallace:

> The psychology of delivery is grounded on a single basic principle: conceptions and meanings dominate utterance and bodily behavior. Meanings dominate the listener. They dominate the speaker. In delivery that is judged good, listener and speaker fully attend to meanings during moments of utterance. In delivery that is less than good, some competing stimulus—an irrelevant idea, for example—prevents the speaker or audience from concentrating on the relevant idea.[1]

Anything that causes the audience to notice delivery creates a competing stimulus. The list of possible distractions includes numerous habits such as playing with your hands or stroking your hair; vocal qualities including unusual rates or harsh sounds; clothing or physical appearance inconsistent with audience expectations; and use of distracting visual aids or awkward textual materials. Learning to avoid or compensate for potential distractions can be a time-consuming process, but everyone can acquire skills sufficient for most presentations. First steps normally include learning to control anxiety, observing the rudiments of platform behavior, choosing an appropriate delivery form, and displaying visual aids correctly.

CONTROLLING ANXIETY

For many people, the prospect of giving a speech produces anxiety, which prevents them from doing their best in the presentational situation. No matter how gifted they are in other capacities, the tension that results from the speaking situation interferes, and their knowledge and ability is not displayed to the audience. Such tension is doubly unfortunate: it robs the speaker of deserved recognition, and it denies the audience access to the resources of the speaker. There is no easy way to overcome the fears associated with public speaking. The best solution for most people is to understand the physiological processes involved and to confront their fears directly.[2]

Surprisingly, few people realize how widespread the fear of speaking is, and the resulting feeling of being alone often complicates the problem. In 1973, the Speech Communication Association reported the results of a survey conducted by R. H. Bruskin Associates, and the findings may help to put you at ease. In this study, 2,500 adults were asked to identify things that they feared, and the single most frequent response was fear of speaking in public. In fact, slightly more than

---

[1] Donald C. Bryant and Karl R. Wallace, *Fundamentals of Public Speaking,* 5th ed. (Englewood Cliffs, New Jersey: Prentice-Hall, 1976), pp. 349–350.

[2] Current research indicates that there are some people for whom these measures are insufficient. Specialized techniques are available and you may wish to consult with your instructor if you do not become more comfortable as you gain familiarity with basic speaking skills.

40 percent of the participants reported such fear, while fear of going to dentists (17 percent) and fear of high places (3 percent) were distant runners-up.

You have learned that many people fear public speaking, which should help you also understand that the tension you may feel is an entirely natural reaction to a novel and challenging situation. The novelty of the speaking situation is easy to understand. Most of us spend much of our lives engaged in communication, and estimates run as high as 85 percent. However, formal presentations represent a different sort of communication in which most people participate far less often. The fact that the situation is unusual produces uncertainty and the common response to uncertainty is fear. As you become more familiar with such situations, and as you become more accomplished in the skills described in this book, the uncertainty will diminish and much of the fear or anxiety will be eliminated.

The challenge presented by speaking situations is also an important factor in the physiological response. People give speeches about subjects that make a difference to them and they generally have a stake in the audience response to the presentation. The following examples show the kinds of stakes involved:

> A training officer is evaluated for his ability to present material in a clear and memorable fashion.
>
> A sales representative lives on the commissions from sales secured through formal presentations.
>
> An executive being evaluated for promotion may be asked to make a progress report to her supervisors.
>
> The chance of securing a major contract is determined by the quality of a briefing.
>
> A new employee is assigned to explain recent technical developments to his coworkers.

These examples represent common situations and they could be multiplied many times over. Faced with such situations, most people respond as an athlete responds to competition. More adrenalin is produced and the speaker becomes more alert to surrounding events and better able to respond to them—both physically and mentally. These physiological reactions actually work to the speaker's advantage, and it would be a mistake to try to repress or eliminate them. Instead, you can capitalize on them by directing the resulting energy into a dynamic presentation. Your efforts to cope with anxiety and to channel the resulting energy will be enhanced by the following guides.

Become Familiar with Various Speaking Situations

One source of anxiety is uncertainty about the speaking situation. This is especially common during the early years of a career and you can reduce the effects of this anxiety by paying attention to the expectations of audiences you are likely to face. Watch the way experienced speakers handle the situations you are likely to encounter and observe audience reactions to their presentations. You may even want to make brief notes about distinctive characteristics of the speakers you observe. When you have a chance, ask why they approached the situation as they did. In addition, discuss their speaking with other members of the audience. Try to learn what members of the audience expect from the speakers and then use these expectations to guide your presentational efforts. Such information can give you far more specific guidance than any textbook, but the object is the same: to learn a set of behaviors that are acceptable in the situations you are likely to encounter.

Canvass Your Speaking Assets

A second step in learning to control anxiety is canvassing your assets as a speaker. What things do you do particularly well? What abilities are important to the groups with which you work? Are you particularly adept at finding material, selecting visual representations, or organizing complex materials? Even if you have never given a speech before, you may be able to identify abilities that make you unique. What features of your personality are particularly attractive? Are you knowledgeable about particular subjects? Do others see you as trustworthy and honest? Do you display unusual amounts of energy or drive?

Your answers to these questions may help you identify abilities around which you can build your own speaking style. At the same time, you may want to identify personal characteristics or liabilities for which you must compensate. Some common liabilities are small stature, weak voice, unattractive mannerisms, and minor physical disabilities.

Identifying your own strengths and weaknesses as a speaker helps to control anxiety by pointing to characteristics you want to emphasize. Recognizing personal strengths and weaknesses gives you a set of very personal directions for managing your delivery.

Speak Often

While learning to control your reactions, practice by speaking as often as possible. The presentations need not be long, and many brief experiences are often better than a single long speech. You may need to seek out opportunities to give prepared speeches, and some that you may overlook can do a good deal to enhance your speaking abilities. Volunteer to assist in the presentation of routine reports at periodic meetings; help others who have prepared materials, but would like assistance in their presentation; search out and report materials requested by task groups; take an active role in periodic briefings; and prepare brief talks on subjects frequently discussed in staff meetings. In addition to these prepared activities, you can also gain speaking experience by participating in less formal settings. In the classroom, ask questions and volunteer information; in staff meetings, comment when asked to do so and make suggestions when they are appropriate; comment on and participate in the discussion of formal presentations of others; and volunteer to "fill in" when scheduled participants are unavailable. All of these activities can be overdone, but more people speak too little than too much. Be sure that your comments are appropriate, relevant, and in good taste; but by all means participate. At first, you may find it difficult to step forward, but this feeling will soon pass. In addition, as chairpeople and other speakers learn that they can depend on you, you will be called upon with greater frequency and both your speaking ability and your career are likely to benefit.

Tackle Manageable Tasks

If you wait until you are forced to speak, you may not have the leisure of picking your own opportunities. However, if you actively seek opportunities for practice, you will find that many are available. Start by picking those that make the fewest demands on your abilities. Initially, you will want to undertake presentations that are brief, simple, and on subjects popular with your audience. It is also wise to pick topics that do not vitally affect your interests until you have had an opportunity to develop more advanced skills. As your abilities grow, you will want to expand your speaking range by tackling longer, more complex, and more demanding subjects.

The rule of thumb is simple: *Tackle projects which tax but do not exceed your abilities.*

Prepare Thoroughly

The greatest single source of confidence is knowing that you are prepared for the presentation. Unfortunately, many speakers mistake knowledge of a subject for preparation to speak. No matter how familiar they are with the materials from which they are to speak, failure to prepare for the speaking situation is evident in poor organization, inappropriate selection of materials, inept use of visual materials, improper linguistic choices, and a faltering delivery. After a few experiences of this sort, these individuals learn to avoid speaking situations and the difficulties become progressively greater. Because speaking situations are uncomfortable for them, they avoid speeches and postpone preparation until the last minute. Since they fail to use adequate preparation time, each presentation seems worse than the one before and their ability to cope with speaking situations deteriorates rapidly.

This cycle can be avoided by taking time to prepare specifically for each presentation. Remember, knowledge of the subject is not an adequate substitute for speech preparation. Take time to compose your presentation systematically, and then take time to polish your delivery. The minimum amount of practice for a ten- to twenty-minute presentation is represented in the following schedule. The night before the presentation, read over the speech silently at least twice. Your objective is to learn the major ideas, the sequence in which they are to be presented, and the kinds of material associated with each. Avoid memorizing exact phrasing because some freedom should be retained, but try to set the major sequences in mind. After the silent practice, present the speech aloud two or three times. Some speakers find it helpful to have a small audience for these practice runs, and you may be able to call on friends, professional associates and subordinates, and family members. The audience isn't essential, but they help you control your rate of delivery and they can time your presentation. On the day of the presentation, try to set aside fifteen or twenty minutes before the gathering at which you are to speak. Although some schedules won't permit this luxury, it is a good time to run through the speech silently one or two more times. If additional time is available, it will also help to read the speech aloud once or twice. However, the silent runs are the most important.

More extensive practice sessions may be necessary for longer presentations, and your personal feelings of comfort with each speech should be the final guide. Some speakers can master their texts with very few trial runs, while others may require two or three times as many readings. Also, presentation of complex or difficult materials calls for additional practice time. With experience, you will be able to judge the number of practice sessions and the duration of each for yourself.

RUDIMENTS OF PLATFORM BEHAVIOR

Every speaking situation offers unique opportunities and makes specific demands on the speaker. Some audiences prefer a very casual approach, while others will be offended by anything less than a carefully polished oration. Some rooms require all of the speaker's vocal force, whereas others seem to echo with even the slightest whisper. Some auditoriums provide the speaker with a large stage from which to speak, but others offer only a small podium that greatly restricts physical movement, and some settings include no area designated for the speaker. Learning to capitalize on the opportunities provided by some settings, and to overcome the liabilities of others, is a lifelong task. Fortunately, adaptations to such settings can be thought of as variations on a generally accepted standard of delivery. Although it may not furnish optimum results in all situations, this standard will carry you through most presentations and it should be learned before you attempt to master variations. As you learn this standard, concentrate on maintaining eye contact, proper use of your body, normal use of your voice, and proper dress and appearance.

Eye Contact

Eye contact is as important in formal presentations as it is in conversation. Maintaining eye contact gives the audience a feeling that they are involved in an extended conversation and that you value their attention. Failure to maintain eye contact reduces your ability to direct the attention and reactions of your audience. In addition, maintaining eye contact provides you with an abundant source of information concerning audience reactions to your presentation.

To be effective, eye contact must be maintained throughout a presentation. The total amount of contact appears to be less important than the frequency with which it is made, and failure to look at your audience for a period as brief as a minute will have undesirable effects. Two hints may help you to avoid this difficulty. First, limit the amount of time spent looking at your text to roughly fifteen seconds of every minute. Of course, complex materials and manuscript reading may require some sacrifices, but adherence to the fifteen-second limit produces good results in most cases. Second, mentally divide the physical space occupied by your audience into three or four roughly equal areas and select a target person seated near the center of each. Think of yourself being engaged in a conversation with these three or four specific individuals and carefully observe their reactions to your major ideas. When the audience is large, this technique is particularly effective because people seated near the target individuals share the impression that you are looking directly at them and the entire audience will feel more involved in the presentation.

Use of Your Body

Many audiences view a speaker's physical behavior as an indicator of his or her composure—or lack of it. Any behavior that calls attention to itself distracts from your message and weakens your image as a speaker. The best stance, posture, degree of movement, and use of gesture is that which is unnoticed by the audience. To achieve a delivery that is unnoticed, you need to appear as natural as possible and avoid two extremes to which novice speakers often succumb. On the one hand, avoid rigidity and immobility, which indicate excessive restraints on natural patterns of behavior. On the other hand, avoid excessive informality indicated by a careless stance, frequent changes of stance and position, leaning on the rostrum, and gestures unrelated to the content of your message.

You can best avoid these extremes by establishing a habitual standard from which you make variations as necessary. Begin by finding a comfortable orientation to the rostrum or stand supporting your notes. Some speakers prefer a position directly behind the stand, while others prefer a spot slightly to the left or to the right. Once you have chosen a position, limit the distance you move from it to one or two paces. Avoid moving from one place to another frequently, but feel free to take a step or two every minute or so. Remember that being frozen in one position is as noticeable as moving about aimlessly.

Rest your weight evenly on both feet and bend your knees slightly. Audiences will seldom notice a bend of a few degrees and the flexed stance will insure good circulation and help to reduce tension. Stand erect and face the audience directly. Let your hands hang casually at your sides or rest them on the edge of the rostrum. Remember, the rostrum is there to support your materials and may not be able to carry the additional weight of a speaker leaning on it. Even if the stand will carry your weight, leaning on it will result in a stilted, unnatural position that calls attention to itself and limits your ability to move normally and to gesture appropriately. Above all, do not put your hands in your pockets and avoid holding objects while you are speaking.

Now that you have established a comfortable speaking position, avoid behaviors that would distract your audience. Foremost among the potential distractions are rocking on your feet, shifting your weight from side to side, shuffling one foot while resting weight on the other, and playing with objects in your hands.

Gestures are a natural complement to speech communication about subjects of concern to the speaker. However, planned gestures are difficult to execute successfully and they frequently become so artificial that they call attention to themselves. Learning to gesture naturally is largely a matter of observation and of paying attention to the ideas you want to express. Observe others involved in speaking and in conversation and you will notice that the gestures which are most effective are those which arise from the subject and which emphasize the ideas of the speaker. During a speech, attend to the ideas you wish to express; invariably you will feel a strong urge to gesture at certain points, while other points call for no activity. It is best to use gestures that seem appropriate at the points at which you feel a need to gesture. Avoid sweeping or dramatic gestures that are out of character in professional presentations. And, avoid gestures in the area of your face. Your hands and face are the two most noticeable parts of your body during a presentation and any gesture combining the two is almost certain to drown out your oral signals.

Use of Your Voice

The important characteristics of your voice are volume, rate, and pitch. Each of these is best managed in as natural a fashion as possible, but formal speaking calls for attention to a few factors that would not be encountered in other settings.

Volume should be adjusted to the size and acoustics of the room in which you are speaking. You should speak loudly enough that the furthest member of your audience has no difficulty hearing you, but not so loud that listening is uncomfortable for nearer members. Occasionally these concerns will force you to make compromises, but you can usually pick a level that will be comfortable to both you and your audience. Most modern meeting and conference rooms are designed with acoustics in mind and they are unlikely to cause problems. However, you may find yourself speaking in less than ideal conditions and some rooms tend to echo as sound waves bounce off reflective walls, ceilings, and other surfaces. In such situations, you should reduce volume and shorten the length of your presentation. This is an awkward compromise, but echoes are particularly annoying for an audience and most members will appreciate your sensitivity to the situation.

A normal speaking rate is approximately 145 words per minute, and you should attempt to maintain this rate in most presentations. Faster rates make it difficult for audiences to master the materials as presented and slower rates may give the impression that you are ''speaking down'' to the audience. However, formal speaking situations do require special attention to the use of pauses. In informal conversations, most people pause for nearly a second between sentences and use shorter pauses to mark less significant breaks. Unfortunately, beginning speakers often overlook the use of pauses and allow sentences to flow into one another without rest. This makes it difficult for audiences to understand the presentation and gives the impression that you are speaking "too fast" when your rate is actually within normal limits. In addition, failing to pause makes it difficult to find breathing points and results in gasping for breath at unnatural points. To avoid falling into this trap, consciously force yourself to breathe between sentences and employ graded pauses reflecting the content of your presentation. For example, each major idea should be preceded by a pause of as much as two seconds; pauses between sentences should be approximately one second; and pauses for breaks marked by commas should be approximately one-half second in duration. It may be necessary to build in slightly longer pauses when you address very large audiences. These longer pauses assist in securing audience comprehension and also provide the audience opportunities to react.

Pitch refers to the tone of your voice while speaking and is usually thought of as a point on a scale from low to high. Actually, it is more accurate to speak of "pitch range" because all voices vary through one or two octaves centered around a point. Your voice is strongest within its natural range, but some speakers try to disguise their natural range because low voices are thought of as masculine and high pitches as feminine. This is an inappropriate adaptation and should be avoided at all costs. Few people can maintain an altered pitch throughout a presentation, and those who can are expending effort that could be better used elsewhere. Moreover, there is a very real danger of overtaxing and damaging the vocal apparatus.

You should use a normal pitch range while speaking and make as few alterations as possible. However, tension requires special attention to vocal range. Tension constricts the vocal bands resulting in an abnormally narrow vocal range. This restricted range produces a sound pattern known as a "monotone," in which the speaker's voice does not respond to the varied materials presented. This pattern is unattractive and may give the impression that the speaker is uninterested. If you find yourself slipping into a monotone, concentrate on using normal vocal variations. Force your voice to rise with important parts of the speech and to fall with less important parts. As you become more comfortable in speaking situations, problems in pitch are likely to resolve themselves. However, your initial speeches may require the special attention just described.

Dress and Physical Appearance

Your physical appearance while speaking is extremely important, but the variety of settings in which you will speak makes it difficult to prescribe particular styles of clothing. Applied to your physical appearance, the principle that delivery should not generate conflicting centers of attention implies that your dress should not surprise or shock your audience. Anything unusual or unkempt in your appearance raises the prospect of distracting the audience. However, being uncommonly well dressed is equally dangerous and the common habit of "dressing up" for formal presentations needs to be tempered by the setting in which the presentation is to be made. A construction engineer or shop foreman wearing a three-piece suit on a job site is as conspicuous as an executive wearing coveralls. The best general advice is to pick a clothing style appropriate to the setting in which you will speak and which conforms to the expectations of your audience. If your audience expects you to wear a suit, wear the best you have. If your audience expects you to wear work clothes, wear what you normally would, but wear the best. While you are a student, dress as you normally would for class, but again wear your best.

DELIVERY FORMS

The third concern is choosing an appropriate delivery form. Full sentence outlines include sufficient material to ensure a careful plan while providing some flexibility during the presentation. Although the full sentence outline is ideal for preparing texts, it is less than ideal for some speaking situations. Personal preferences may influence your choice, and selecting a form with which you are comfortable is of paramount importance. To assist in making a choice, first consider the range of forms available and the characteristic uses of each.

The critical difference between the forms is the extent to which the speaker has prepared for the particular situation in which he will be speaking. Three variations are commonly recognized: *Impromptu, extemporaneous,* and *manuscript speaking.*

Impromptu Speaking

Impromptu speaking is used when the speaker has not prepared for the specific speech. It means that the presentation is based on the speaker's general knowledge of the subject and of public speaking skills. Although the speaker should have considerable knowledge of the subject, no time has been devoted to planning the presentation and neither an outline nor other notes are used.

The principal advantage of impromptu speaking is flexibility and it is commonly used in two situations. First, you may be called upon to speak without advance warning. Typical examples include responding to questions, presenting a project status report upon request, and press conferences. Second, impromptu speaking is also used when maximum flexibility in responding to audience interests is desirable. Any prepared speech may miss materials that the audience believes to be important. This danger is particularly evident when the speaker has little prior knowledge of his or her particular audience, or when audience interests are developing and changing rapidly. Impromptu speeches are ideal for these circumstances. Some common uses include conflict reduction sessions, in which each participant is asked to make a "what's-on-your-mind" speech; instructional presentations, in which the speaker wants to respond to very specific audience needs; and sales meetings, in which the speaker must quickly diagnose the demands of the audience and respond to them.

The principal disadvantages of impromptu speaking result from the limited preparation allowed for speaking. Novice speakers often feel particularly uncomfortable without a clear text before them. Similarly, situations in which either time or accuracy are important are not well suited for impromptu speaking. Since the text has not been prepared in advance, the duration of the presentation cannot be anticipated and the speaker may be forced to cut off ideas that are important. Accuracy may be a primary factor in presentations that have policy or legal implications. Instances in which impromptu speaking should be avoided because inadvertent slips may be damaging include reports to investors, introductory statements of new policies, public reports on labor negotiations, briefings outlining contract specifications, and all cases where your presentation may be recorded or quoted directly. In each of these cases, impromptu speaking ought to be avoided because misstatements may have serious consequences beyond the immediate speaking situation. There is simply too much at stake to rest your chances on an unprepared speech.

Extemporaneous Speaking

The most commonly used form is the extemporaneous speech. Extemporaneous presentations are partially prepared, but they leave the speaker some flexibility in responding to the situation. The portions that are planned in advance are the principal ideas, the sequence in which they are presented, the materials used to develop each, and some key phrases. Most of the particular phrasing is open for adaptation and the speaker may add or delete materials as he or she sees fit. Variations of this type also affect the total length of the speech and the relative amount of time allocated to each portion.

Two sorts of text may be used with extemporaneous speeches, and the difference between them reflects different levels of preparation. *Key word outlines* are very brief and remind the speaker of materials to be presented. Typically, they include a brief phrase for each major idea and one or two words—perhaps a title of some sort—for each item of developing material. For example, a key word outline of the speech reproduced as a full sentence outline on pages 18–19 might appear as follows:

    I.   Communication skills essential
         A.   list types
         B.   friend's experiences
         C.   Company X criteria
         D.   Pearse study
    II. Skills acquired
         A.   Syracuse University courses
         B.   Toastmasters
         C.   professional trainers
         D.   Smith says
    III. Corporate support
         A.   forms of support

B. Company Y
C. John Smith says
D. 80 percent figure

Full sentence outlines are the second form of text that may be used with extemporaneous speeches. They are illustrated in the chapter on developing materials and several other examples appear in this book. If you follow the recommended practice of composing speeches with full sentence outlines, you may find them to be your choice as a text because it eliminates the additional step of preparing a reading text.

The one difficulty in using full sentence outlines in an oral presentation is that the amount of material included sometimes makes it difficult to find your place quickly when glancing at your text; additional notes might reduce this difficulty. Marginal symbols in colored ink can help you find your place quickly, and colored arrows can be used to mark principal statements, while colored stars can be used to identify particularly important developing materials. You may use other symbols such as bars, rectangles, boxes, circles, or dots, but be sure to distinguish principal ideas from developing materials and follow a consistent pattern. It is also helpful to highlight particular phrases and key words, and two sorts of notation are helpful. With a typewriter, use all capitals for critical phrases and use a secondary color for key words when the typewriter is equipped with a multicolored ribbon. The second technique is to use a colored pen to underline key passages and to overline or highlight particularly important materials. A brief portion of an outline using these devices follows.

III. Corporations should **support** their employees' efforts to acquire communication skills.
   A. Companies can provide many forms of support: They can **pay** for all or part of the cost of training programs, they can provide **time off** during the day and furnish transportation to classes, and they can use bonuses and promotions to encourage employees who participate.
   B. Company Y found that **production increased by nearly 15 percent** after their supervisors were trained in communicating performance appraisals.
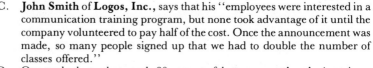
   C. **John Smith** of **Logos, Inc.,** says that his "employees were interested in a communication training program, but none took advantage of it until the company volunteered to pay half of the cost. Once the announcement was made, so many people signed up that we had to double the number of classes offered."
   D. One study shows that nearly 80 percent of the **top executives in** American companies believe corporations should take responsibility for developing their most promising employees.

Manuscript Speaking

Manuscripts are complete, word-for-word transcripts of a speech and they represent the most thoroughly prepared speech type. Using them effectively is difficult and makes special demands that most novice speakers should avoid. However, they are the best choice when extreme accuracy is required and when the speech is prepared by someone other than the speaker.

USING VISUAL AIDS

Visual aids should complement rather than conflict with your oral presentation. This means that the aids should be introduced with the ideas they develop and removed from view when you move on to the next idea. Visual materials have greater command of an audience's attention than your voice, and the worst thing you can do is force an audience to choose between looking at an aid and listening to what you say. Avoid this danger by organizing your speech and integrating the visual aids well in advance.

The following procedure is relatively easy for most speakers. Start by writing the entire speech as if you were not going to use visual materials. After the speech text is largely finished, look for points at which visual aids might be useful. Remember, visual aids are used to make ideas memorable and to explain complex relationships. You are likely to find more opportunities than you can conveniently use, so select the most important points and prepare appropriate charts. In the outline or text of your speech be sure to mark the points at which you will introduce the aids.

At the start of your presentation, place the charts face down on the table or desk from which you will speak. Each time you come to a point at which a visual aid is to be introduced, finish the sentence and stop talking before you hold up the chart. Allow the audience a few seconds to visually master the material before you resume speaking. Then talk about the material displayed and remove the chart from view before moving to the next topic. The general rule is that you should talk about nothing but the contents of the visual aid while it is in view.

There is only one exception to this rule. Sometimes it is convenient to have a single chart that summarizes the entire presentation. For example, a list might be used to outline an instructional briefing, a flow chart could be used to display an entire process, and a diagram may describe an entire factory. In these cases, leaving the visual aid in view while the speaker discusses constituent parts will help orient the audience. If you use an aid of this sort, place it where the audience can see it without straining and where you can easily refer to it. When you first introduce the chart, allow a little more time than usual for the audience to master it and explain that you will refer back to it at several points during your speech. During the presentation, refer to the chart every time you finish discussing one component and then move on to the next.

SUMMARY

Delivery is a general term that refers to all aspects of a speaker's behavior during a presentation. You should aim to deliver your message in a manner that does not call attention to itself, and you can avoid generating conflicting stimuli by controlling anxiety, mastering basic platform behavior, using an appropriate delivery form, and presenting visual aids properly. Anxiety can be controlled by becoming familiar with various speaking situations, canvassing your speaking assets, speaking often, tackling manageable tasks, and preparing thoroughly. The rudiments of platform behavior include eye contact, use of the body, use of the voice, and dress and appearance, and delivery forms consist of impromptu speaking, extemporaneous speaking, and manuscript speaking.

LEARNING ACTIVITIES

1. Find a spot where you can observe people engaged in conversation without their realizing that you are watching. Good spots include lunchrooms or cafeterias, lounges, airports, and social areas in public buildings. What gestures or nonverbal behaviors show that a person is highly involved in conversation? What shows that a person is uninvolved? Make a list of the involved behaviors that you could use in an oral presentation and a second list of the uninvolved behaviors to avoid in oral presentations.

2. Try to visualize a speaking situation in which you felt particularly uncomfortable. Divide a sheet of paper into two columns and in the first column list everything that made you uncomfortable. The items in this list are called anxiety triggers. In the second column, list things you could do to prevent the triggers from affecting you. For example, "lack of preparation" is a commom trigger and "more thorough research" and "select more familiar topics" are possible solutions. Keep the list and add to it as you gain presentational experience.

3. Meet with a professional who is now doing the kind of job that you would like to do. Ask him or her to describe a common presentational situation in detail. How many people were present? Who were they? What did they expect from the speaker? What techniques could the speaker use to satisfy their expectations? What did members of the audience say about the presentation? What were the results of the presentation?

4. Canvass your speaking assets by dividing a piece of paper into two columns. In the first column, list your personal assets—the things that make you a unique, valuable person. In the second column, describe behaviors that you could employ in a speaking situation to emphasize your assets. On a second sheet of paper, make a similar list of your speaking liabilities and the behaviors you could use to deemphasize them.

CHAPTER SEVEN
AUDIENCE ANALYSIS

Earlier chapters of this book have introduced you to most of the fundamental skills and concepts employed in presentational speaking; subsequent chapters discuss the application of these basic skills to specific speaking situations. The transition from basic skills to types of presentation is a critical juncture in your study of presentational speaking because neither systematic development of basic skills nor application to particular situations can take the place of sensitivity to the needs and interests of the audiences you face.

Analyzing the particular audience to whom you will speak is an essential step in preparing a presentation. To appreciate this generalization, imagine that you are a manager called upon to make a presentation. Assume that you know in advance that your speaking time will be limited to twenty minutes and the subject is limited to a proposal developed by your staff. These conditions reduce the complexity of your task because they reduce the number of choices you must make. However, a number of decisions remain. You must choose between five persuasive strategies, and you will use roughly thirty pieces of developing material and visual aids chosen from the twenty-five types surveyed in Chapters 2 and 3. You will probably employ a formal style, using either a consultative or frozen style on some occasions. In addition, you might use any one of three patterns of organization, and your delivery form may be impromptu, extemporaneous-key word, extemporaneous-full sentence, or manuscript. Although it is easy to list the

By permission of Johnny Hart and Field Enterprises, Inc.

choices as done here, few people realize the number of distinct possibilities available. Mathematically, the choices outlined above produce some 27,000 distinct presentations. More precise variations in language, organization, and delivery would substantially increase the number of presentations possible. Some of these presentations differ from one another in minor ways (for example, the substitution of one type of developing material for another), but some differ in critical ways (persuasive strategy, delivery forms, language style, and organizational pattern). Now, the point of the illustration is this: Any of the more than 27,000 presentations could be technically correct, but some will have a much better chance of achieving desired results than others. The only way to determine which of the potential presentations has the best chance of accomplishing what you want is to study the audience to whom you will speak.

The numbers in the preceding illustration may be difficult to visualize, while an example shows that attention to the needs and interests of the audience can make the difference between success and failure. In the following case, a manager is responsible for developing a proposal writing system and has made numerous presentations following the outline shown in Exhibit 7.1.

This manager realized, after many presentations, that he was not achieving

EXHIBIT 7.1

I. DEFINITION—what the proposal writing system is
II. HISTORY—when and how the proposal writing system was developed
III. IMPLEMENTATION—what must be done to make the proposal writing system operational
IV. TRAINING—what users need to learn to be able to use the system
V. APPLICATIONS—what the proposal writing system can be used for
VI. CURRENT PRACTICES and RESULTS—how members of the organization write proposals and what the results have been under current procedures
VII. ADVANTAGES—how the proposal writing system differs from current practices and what improvements could be expected
VIII. IMPORTANCE—showing that writing good proposals is essential to corporate survival and individual success

the results he had hoped for. He noticed that most audiences greeted him with polite attention, but the people seldom responded with enthusiasm or commitment. Understanding the concerns of his audiences then became instrumental in designing more effective presentations. Analysis made it possible to identify four typical audiences. One typical audience was composed of potential users who were unfamiliar with the system; the second was composed of managers who were unfamiliar with the system and who probably would not use it themselves, but who might require their subordinates to use it; the third group was composed of potential users who were familiar with the system, but had not begun to use it; and, the fourth type of audience consisted of managers who were familiar with the system, but had not committed themselves to its implementation. Each of these audiences had a different stake in the system and would be affected differently by a decision to implement it. Members of the first group needed to be introduced to the system in a manner that would not threaten them, but would allow them to learn about it. Members of the second group needed to be introduced to the system in a manner that would make them confident in recommending its use by their subordinates. The third group needed to be given a reason for using it and an effective strategy that would make it as easy as possible for them to begin. Finally, members of the

EXHIBIT   7.2

A presentation to potential users without prior knowledge of the system.

INTRODUCTION

ATTENTION MATERIAL   Examples and/or testimony showing that writing good proposals is fundamental to personal success

ORIENTATION MATERIAL   A brief review of current practices and results

PURPOSE   To explain an alternate approach to writing proposals

PREVIEW   First, I will define and describe a proposal writing system; second I will discuss its advantages; and third, I will discuss some potential applications.

BODY

 I.   Definition and description of the proposal writing system
 II.   Advantages of the proposal writing system
 III.   Potential applications of the proposal writing system

CONCLUSION

SUMMARY   The purpose of this presentation was to explain a new approach to writing proposals. I have defined and described a proposal writing system, presented the advantages of the proposal writing system, and discussed some of its potential applications.

FINAL APPEAL   Introduce training packages that are available to those who would like to try using the proposal writing system fourth group needed to be persuaded to actively support implementation of the system. The strategy chosen was to present reasons for adopting the system and establish a time table for its implementation. The presentations designed for these audiences are outlined in Exhibits 7.2, 7.3, 7.4, and 7.5. Notice that each one uses only a portion of the materials from the original presentation, while collectively they use all of the original material. As a result, each answers the questions most likely to be crucial in the minds of individual audiences and each emphasizes the concerns of a particular group.

It is doubtful that any speaker has ever made a presentation without devoting some attention to the audience. But, many speakers devote too little attention to the audience. In the end, they find that they did not achieve their intended purpose because the audience misinterpreted their message, lost interest in the presentation, or was unmoved by the arguments presented. You can avoid many of these difficulties by paying attention to the expectations of the audience. Audience analysis is defined as the systematic study of an audience for the purpose of identifying factors that will guide a presentation. Several methods have been

EXHIBIT   7.3

A presentation to managers (superiors) without prior knowledge of the system.

INTRODUCTION

ATTENTION MATERIAL   Examples and/or testimony showing that writing good proposals is necessary for corporate survival
ORIENTATION MATERIAL   Brief review of current practices and results
PURPOSE   To introduce an alternate procedure for writing proposals
PREVIEW   I will define and describe a proposal writing system; second, I will discuss its probable applications; and third, I will describe its advantages over our current approach.

BODY

   I.   Definition and description of the proposal writing system
  II.   Outline of its probable applications emphasizing current projects
 III.   Description of the advantages of the proposal writing system

CONCLUSION

SUMMARY   The purpose of this presentation was to introduce an alternate procedure for writing proposals. I have defined and described a proposal writing system, outlined its probable applications, and described its advantages over our current approach.
FINAL APPEAL   Mention the steps necessary to implement use of the proposal writing system; solicit questions to identify possible objections to use of the system

developed, and this chapter presents four that usually will yield profitable results: contextual analysis, demographic analysis, organizational goal analysis, and functional analysis.

CONTEXTUAL ANALYSIS

Analysis of the context or setting in which a presentation will be made is the first step in understanding the audience. This is called contextual analysis and its importance should be apparent from the discussion of the nature of communication in Chapter 1. Recall that each participant brings his or her own set of expectations to any communication event and that the setting is a relatively common feature that makes it possible to participate in meaningful interaction. Understanding the context or situation calls for attention to the physical environment and the purpose of the gathering.

EXHIBIT 7.4

A presentation to potential users who are familiar with the system, but have not used it.

INTRODUCTION

ATTENTION MATERIAL   Describe the planning and effort that have gone into developing the proposal writing system

ORIENTATION MATERIAL   Outline advantages of the proposal writing system emphasizing features that make life easier for those who must write or review proposals

PURPOSE   To encourage auditors to use the proposal writing system

PREVIEW   The entire body of the presentation should describe use of the proposal writing system on projects in which members of the audience are currently engaged. Each main head should refer to a specific application/project and the preview will reflect the applications/projects.

BODY

I.   Application/project 1
II.   Application/project 2
III.   Application/project 3

CONCLUSION

SUMMARY   The purpose of this presentation was to encourage you to use the proposal writing system. I have shown how it could be used for several of our current projects, including . . . .

FINAL APPEAL   Explain the procedure for initial use of the system, including the assistance available to those who would like to try the system

EXHIBIT   7.5

A presentation to superiors who are familiar with the system, but have not recommended its implementation.

INTRODUCTION

ATTENTION MATERIAL   Refer to difficulties caused by poorly prepared proposals submitted by subordinates

ORIENTATION MATERIAL   Briefly outline the history and development of the proposal writing system and explain how it can be implemented

PURPOSE   To show that the proposal writing system should be implemented

PREVIEW   The entire body should consist of reasons for implementing the proposal writing system.

BODY

   I.   Reason 1
  II.   Reason 2
 III.   Reason 3

CONCLUSION

SUMMARY   The purpose of this presentation was to show you why we should implement the proposal writing system. I have presented several reasons, including . . .

FINAL APPEAL   Emphasize the importance of rapid action and suggest a tentative date for implementation

---

Physical Environment

The physical environment affects the manner in which you make a presentation. The size and type of visual images, the form of your delivery, the amount to which you plan for interaction, the amount of movement permitted during delivery, and your ability to maintain eye contact with individual members of the audience are most directly affected by the physical environment. These concerns are determined by the size and shape of the room, the acoustics in the room, the presence of a stage or platform, the size and position of the audience, the availability of stands for notes or visual aids, and kinds of media available for amplifying your voice or enlarging visual images.

Nature And Purpose of the Gathering

The nature and purpose of the meeting specify the expectations of the audience and help you gauge the propriety of your response. The factors that should be considered are the time, place, and reason for holding the meeting; why individual members are present; why you were asked to speak; the relative formality of the meeting; the type of presentation expected; the presence of other speakers and opportunities for members of the audience to question or disagree with you; stated or unstated time limits for your presentation; whether the meeting is open to the public or closed to nonmembers; and whether or not your presentation will be reported to people not present. These concerns determine your subject, the materials you employ, and the extent to which you try to appeal to the immediate audience.

DEMOGRAPHIC ANALYSIS

The characteristics of any group of people can be described using statistics called demographics. These statistics constitute a profile summarizing the life histories of members of the audience by pointing to common features such as age, religion, and education. If preparing such a profile seems remote from the process of preparing a presentation, you should recall that receivers are active participants in the communication process. As explained in Chapter 1, each receiver determines which cues receive attention, organizes these cues into meaningful patterns, and determines how to react to the received message. Each of these activities is governed by expectations that receivers bring to the communication event. Theodore Clevenger, Jr., uses the term "images" to refer to these expectations and explains their importance:

> The significance of this point about images is not generally understood. Generally, it is thought to mean that, if the speaker is to achieve his desired effect upon an auditor, he must understand certain features of his auditor's image system. This is, of course, true; but even more important, it means that, if the speaker does not understand the auditor's image system, he cannot understand fully what he is saying to the auditor when he makes any statement, whether calculated to produce some particular effect or not. It is not just a question of whether the auditor develps some particular attitude toward the topic of the speech. It is a question of what "information" he will carry away from his encounter with the speaker.[1]

In other words, we can understand the way our messages are received only if we recognize the expectations receivers bring with them. This fact creates a paradox because we can never observe the images auditors bring to the situation. They are buried in their own minds and they may not even be aware of their existence. However, since the images are based on experience, tracing the experiences of individuals helps to identify the images that determine how they process information.

We can understand demographic analysis in less theoretical terms by saying that it will help you determine the level of knowledge that your audience possesses and their attitudes toward you and your subject. Public opinion polls repeatedly

---

[1] Theodore Clevenger, Jr., *Audience Analysis* (Indianapolis: Bobbs-Merrill, 1966), pp. 91–92.

show correlations between personal beliefs and experiences, and the following demographic variables:

1. Social and economic status
2. Occupation
3. Educational level
4. Geographical region
5. Place of residence: urban, suburban, or rural
6. Ethnic group
7. Age
8. Sex
9. Membership in special interest groups

Preparing a sketch of your audience using these variables and consulting frequently published opinion polls will help you make a pretty fair guess about the amount of information they bring to the speaking situation and their attitudes toward your subject. However, demographic analysis is, at best, an approximation, and it is unreliable when special circumstances create unrepresentative audiences or when audiences are so diverse that averages disguise the nature of the group.

ORGANIZATIONAL GOAL ANALYSIS

When an audience is composed of members of a single organization, your knowledge of the organization may give you insight into their interests and concerns. As you recall, organizations are defined as groups of people working together to achieve a common purpose within a defined structure. The common purpose is a goal and members of the organization can be expected to work to achieve this goal. This is important because you can make presentations interesting and attractive by showing that your subject is consistent with the organization's goals. To take advantage of goal analysis, you need to know the kind of organization represented by the audience and the level of the individuals within the organization.

Organization Type

All organizations may be classified by the *dominant goal* they attempt to fulfill. Focusing on goals at this level of analysis, Etzioni has classified organizations into three categories.

Organizations with *order* goals attempt to control actors who are deviants in the eyes of some social unit the organization is serving (frequently society) by segregating them from society and by blocking them from further deviant activities. This is a negative goal in the sense that such organizations attempt to prevent the occurrence of certain events rather than producing an object or a service. Order-centered organizations differ according to the techniques and means they use to attain their goals. Some merely segregate deviants; others segregate and punish; and still others eliminate deviants altogether. But all are predominantly order-oriented.

Organizations with *economic* goals produce commodities and services supplied to outsiders. These include not only the manufacturing industries but also various service organizations, from the post office and insurance companies to movie theatres, Chinese laundries, banks, and brokerage firms.

Organizations that have *culture* goals institutionalize conditions needed for the creation and preservation of symbolic objects, their application, and the creation or reinforcement of commitments to such objects.

Most culture-oriented organizations specialize in the service of one or two culture goals. Research organizations, for example, specialize in the *creation* of new culture (science is a subsystem of culture). Research-oriented universities emphasize creation of culture, although, like all educational organizations, they also contribute to the *preservation* of the cultural heritage by transferring it from generation to generation, mainly through teaching. Professional organizations specialize in the *application* of culture, mainly science and art. Churches strive to build in and to reinforce certain commitments to cultural objects. . . .

Organizations that have *social* goals are classified . . . as a subtype of those oriented to culture goals. Social goals are served by organizations that satisfy the gregarious needs of their members—for example, social clubs, fraternities, sororities, and the like.[2]

Position

Although all members of an organization are expected to contribute to its goals, many are directed by more specific concerns. The dominant, or official, goals can be thought of as providing the general direction for participants, while operative goals are more often involved in the behavior of members at levels below the top.

Official goals are the general purposes of the organization as put forth in the charter, annual reports, public statements by key executives and other authoritative pronouncements. For example, the goal of an employment agency may be to place job seekers in contact with firms seeking workers. . . . [But,] this level of analysis is inadequate in itself for a full understanding of organizational behavior. Official goals are purposely vague and general and do not indicate two major factors which influence organizational behavior: the host of decisions that must be made about alternative ways of achieving official goals and the priority of multiple goals, and the many unofficial goals pursued by groups within the organization. The concept of "operative goals" will be used to cover these aspects. Operative goals designate the ends sought through the actual operating policies of the organization; they tell us what the organization actually is trying to do, regardless of what the official goals say are the aims.[3]

Operative goals include maintenance goals and subsection goals. *Maintenance goals* are the conditions an organization needs to maintain its existence. Such goals often focus on personnel functions, resource management, market position,

[2] Amitai Etzioni, *Comparative Analysis of Complex Organizations* (Glencoe, Illinois: Free Press, 1961), pp. 104–105. Copyright © 1961 by the Free Press. Copyright © 1975 by Amitai Etzioni.

[3] Charles Perrow, "The Analysis of Goals in Complex Organizations," *American Sociological Review*, 29 (1961), 855.

and research projects. Each of these goals is subordinate to the dominant goal, but members in different parts of the organization are likely to rank them differently. In extreme cases, people become so involved with maintenance goals that they pursue them without regard to the purpose of the organization.

The final set of concerns are *subsection goals* or *missions*. Subsections or divisions within large organizations often have very specific goals that reflect their role in the organization as a whole. These subsection goals may be assigned by higher management or they may be developed internally, but they always reflect the desired contribution of the group to the total organizational effort. These missions are intended to contribute to the dominant or maintenance goals of the organization, but they are usually defined for the subsection without conscious attention to the organization as a whole. And, members of the division often internalize and respond to mission goals without considering their relationship to other goal categories.

An Application

All organizations have dominant, maintenance, and mission goals. In addition, these goals may be defined with varying levels of precision, and it is useful to describe "objectives" and "targets" as goals derived from dominant, maintenance, and mission goals. *Objectives* are relatively specific achievements that make it possible for the organization to fulfill its goals. *Targets* are more specific than objectives and they often include the time at which a project is to be completed. For example, some of the goals of one section of a manufacturing organization as understood by the participants are described in Table 7.1.

Preparing and reviewing the list of organizational goals shown in the table gives you insight into at least three factors relevant to most speeches. First, understanding the goals helps you identify topics of interest to the audience. From what is listed you learn that anything affecting profits, public image, staff qualifications, or technological leadership will interest the audience. You can use this insight when selecting subjects, choosing materials to secure and maintain attention, and adapting your vocabulary.

Second, the goals tell you what kinds of arguments will be persuasive. Anything that contributes to their goals will be an effective appeal, while anything not directly related to their goals will be ineffective. For example, with this audience you would accomplish little if you argued that the company should hire an industrial psychologist to improve morale. Morale isn't a major concern to them. However, you could make your case by arguing that the company should hire an industrial psychologist to improve recruiting procedures, improve salary and compensation programs, and to coordinate training programs.

Finally, the goals help you anticipate objections. In this case, anything that would interefere with the Market Analysis Program, the company park, the testing room, and so forth, is likely to be rejected. You should review your presentations before meeting the audience to make sure your remarks do not threaten

TABLE 7.1   Corporate Goals

GOAL	OBJECTIVE	TARGET
Dominant Profit	Reduce operating costs Increase market share Anticipate changing demands	Market Analysis Program (MAP)
Maintenance Good Public Image	Good neighbor policy Service existing products Develop better consumer products	Company park to be opened by July 4

Maintain a Qualified
    Staff
	Improve recruiting procedures
	
	Improve salary and compen-
	    sation
	
	Training programs to develop
	    current employees
		Internships for 6 students in Sep-
		    tember
		Train 20 recruiters by September
		"Pay for Performance" by January
		Revised appraisal procedure by
		    January
		Institute "Managerial Practices"
		    seminar
		Schedule another "Managerial Com-
		    munication" course for the fall
		Generate a list of instructional con-
		    sultants to assist participants
		Establish a permanent training budget
		    at 5 percent of gross revenues

Subsection
Establish Technological
    Leadership
	Increase influence within the
	    the company
	Upgrade facilities
	
	Encourage employee partici-
	    pation in professional
	    societies
	Encourage research and
	    publication
		
		New testing room to be operative
		    within 3 years
		5 people to attend the_____Society
		    Meeting

programs to which they are committed and to see that you have answers to probable objections.

FUNCTIONAL ANALYSIS

On some occasions, the forms of analysis described above will be insufficient to provide direction. Most people will have a similar understanding of the physical environment, but members may disagree on the nature and purpose of the meeting; members may have such scattered backgrounds that demographic analysis is meaningless; and, analysis of organizational goals may be inconclusive because members are drawn from different organizations or from different levels and divisions within the organization. Occasionally, these difficulties can be resolved through functional analysis.

Functional analysis takes advantage of the fact that most decision-making bodies in organizations are composed of people who have developed predictable ways of interacting with each other. These patterns of interaction create special roles or functions for members, and some of these roles are more important to a speaker than others. When you have sufficient information about a group, you should adapt your presentation to members performing the most important functions: *formal leaders, opinion leaders,* and *gatekeepers.*

Formal Leaders

The formal leader, the person "in charge," is often the most important member of the audience. This person may be in a position to make a decision or is so influential that other members will accept his or her decision without serious question. Identifying the formal leader is relatively easy and there are two common indicators. First, the formal leader is usually the highest ranking member of the hierarchy. A brief glance at the organization chart will tell you who this person is. When two members have the same rank, the one representing the more important functional area or the larger project is often assigned the leadership role. Second, a formal leader may be designated for a meeting or project. This person's authority is limited by the nature of the appointment, but he or she may have sufficient power for your purposes.

Whenever possible, you should plan your presentation to appeal to the formal leader of the group without alienating other members. However, there are some cases in which the formal leader lacks the authority or desire to make a decision. In these cases, you can plan your strategy to appeal to the opinion leaders.

Opinion Leaders

Opinion leaders are respected members of the audience who influence other members of the group. Opinion leaders may or may not have a formal position within the group, but their ability to influence other members stems primarily from their knowledge of the subject. In fact, the easiest way to describe opinion leaders is to say that they are members of the group who are usually asked for advice and whose advice is likely to be followed.

Identifying opinion leaders in corporate settings is relatively easy because they are often assistants or advisors to the formal leader. Decision-makers usually have personal staffs consisting of technical experts advising them on topics within their expertise. And, high level executives often remain "on call" as advisors after retirement.

In less clearly defined situations, opinion leaders may be spotted by their behavior. Erwin P. Bettinghaus has isolated a set of characteristics that are visible in most discussions.

1. Opinion leaders tend to be better informed than other members of the group in areas about which they are consulted.
2. Opinion leaders engage in more communication than others; they know more people, read more, listen more, view more, and have more than one circle of acquaintances.
3. Opinion leaders' impact varies with the topic under consideration; on some issues their word is final, but on other issues they have no more influence than other group members.
4. Opinion leaders' influence is usually limited to particular groups; within some groups they have substantial influence, but in other groups they are not seen to be authorities.[4]

Recognizing opinion leaders is important because you can appeal directly to them. This is useful whenever there is no formal leader or the formal leader is unlikely to act independently. Remember, however, that there may be several opinion leaders and you need to manage your presentation to appeal to those who are influential on areas affecting your topic while avoiding areas of concern to those who are less favorable.

Gatekeepers

If your analysis of an audience reveals neither formal leaders who are likely to act on your proposal nor opinion leaders who are influential on your particular topic, you should attempt to identify members of the audience who regulate the flow of communication from one group to another. To understand the role of these regulators, called gatekeepers, we need to look at the informal communication networks that exist in organizations.

Chapter 1 introduced formal hierarchies and pointed out that recognized channels of communication follow lines of authority and responsibility. However, communication is not limited to formal channels and a great deal of information passes through informal channels called *networks.* These informal channels are formed by groups of people who regularly communicate with one another regardless of their position in the formal channels. Social scientists have developed some very sophisticated procedures for identifying informal networks and it is common to diagram the networks using circles to represent individuals and lines showing the flow of communication. Figure 7.1 is typical and it shows the role of gatekeepers in a network.

The shaded areas in this diagram consist of groups of people who communicate with one another and who develop predictable patterns of interaction.

[4]Erwin P. Bettinghaus, *Persuasive Communication,* 2nd ed. (New York: Holt, Rinehart & Winston, 1973), pp. 109–110.

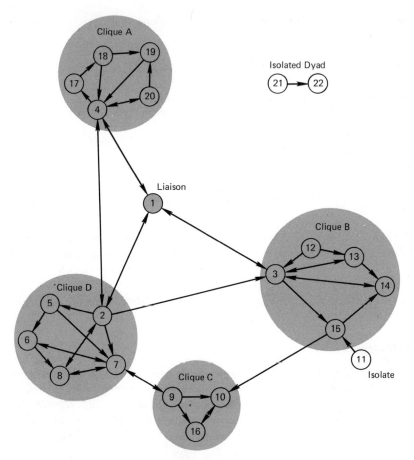

FIGURE 7.1. Sociogram of Four Communication Cliques in the ARC Company, Showing Liaison and Isolate Individuals

From Everett M. Rogers and Bekha Agarwala-Rogers, *Communication in Organizations* (New York: The Free Press, 1976), p. 129. Copyright © 1976 by The Free Press, a Division of Macmillan Publishing Co., Inc.

These groups called *cliques* and each would be isolated from the others if some members did not maintain contact with others outside of their group. These individuals, the gatekeepers, regulate the flow of information from one group to the others and are represented in the diagram by the numbers 2, 4, 7, 9, 10, 15, and 3. Individual 1 is a liaison whose role is similar to that of a gatekeeper. Liaisons regulate the flow of communication from one clique to one another, but belong to neither of the groups.

Whether or not your message is reported to decision-makers outside the immediate audience, and the accuracy with which it is repeated, depends on the extent to which it appealed to the gatekeepers in the audience. When several gatekeepers are present, you may attempt to appeal equally to all or you may adapt your message primarily to those participating in cliques that are of interest to you. The proper strategy depends on your topic, the organization, and the people present, but you can make a sound decision only after identifying the gatekeepers.

SUMMARY

Mastery of the basic skills introduced in the first six chapters will make it possible for you to compose a large number of presentations on any topic. Audience analysis is the process of studying the intended audience to determine which presentation has the greatest chance of accomplishing your purpose. There are several forms of audience analysis and each directs attention to a different aspect of the speaking situation. Contextual analysis focuses on the physical environment and on the nature and purpose of the gathering. Demographic analysis focuses on variables that help determine the audience's knowledge and attitudes. Organizational goal analysis helps identify persuasive premises by focusing on the nature of an organization and the position of audience members within it. And, functional analysis identifies particularly influential members including formal leaders, opinion leaders, and gatekeepers.

LEARNING ACTIVITIES

1. Any speaker makes assumptions about the interests and concerns of the audience. The assumptions may be carefully explored or unconsciously accepted, but they condition the presentation. Begin by looking at a speech presented by a public figure and identify assumptions about the audience addressed. What topics are thought to concern the audience? How does the speaker think that these topics will affect the audience? What appeals are thought to make the speaker's position attractive to the audience? Now, put yourself in the place of the speaker and ask how you would change the speech if you were presenting it to your classroom audience. Would you introduce different topics? Change the order of presentation? Change emphasis? Introduce different appeals to make the presentation attractive?

2. In the absence of more precise information, many speakers assume that the audience is similar to themselves. Determine how well this assumption fits your classroom audience by comparing your own demographic profile with that of other members of the audience. Employ the nine categories of demographic material introduced in this chapter and use three columns to record information. In the first column, record data about yourself; in the second column, record your observations about other members of the audience; in the third column, note differences that may affect the way your presentations are received.

3. Visit a public meeting of a decision-making group such as the board of education, city council, or state legislature. Before attending the

meeting, prepare a table like the one in Table 7.1 showing the dominant, maintenance, and mission goals and related objectives and targets of the organization. Use this table to analyze presentations made at the meeting. To what extent have the speakers identified topics of interest to members of the organization? Have they selected arguments that are likely to prove persuasive? Are they prepared to answer probable objections? And, do you need to reevaluate your understanding of the organization on the basis of its members' reactions to presentations? Has the table prepared you to analyze the speeches presented? Are there topics for which you were unprepared? Did unexpected arguments prove persuasive? Were there any objections you hadn't anticipated?

4. Analyze the functional relationships between members of an organization to which you belong. Who are the formal leaders? Who are the opinion leaders on topics frequently discussed? Who are the gatekeepers who control access to the group?

5. Assume that a close friend had been invited to speak to your class. You want to do everything you can to make the speech successful, but you have only a few minutes to talk to your friend before class. What five things would you tell your friend about the class?

PART TWO
TYPES AND APPLICATIONS

As your career develops, you are likely to face an almost endless variety of speaking situations. To visualize the variety, think about some of the factors that change from speech to speech.

AUDIENCE FACTORS	SPEAKER FACTORS	SITUATIONAL FACTORS
Size	Preparation Time	Subject[1]
Homogeneity	Knowledge	Time
Age	Skills	Date
Social Status	Comfort	Place
Economic Status	Interests	Room Size
Interests	Attitudes	Facilities
Attitudes	Values	
Beliefs	Beliefs	
Values	Health	

Some of these factors change in type and others change only in degree, but all change from speech to speech and all affect the total speaking situation. In fact, every situation presents the speaker with a unique combination of these variables. The speaking skills described in this text will work in the overwhelming majority of situations, but your ability to achieve the best possible results in each will be enhanced by more specific information.

It is not possible to describe or even to anticipate all of the situations you are likely to encounter. There are simply too many possible combinations of variables. But, because all situations share certain features, it is possible to group isolated speeches into recognizable classes. There is some variation in each class, but the variation within groups is small compared to the differences that distinguish each class from the others. This is important because it helps to solve the problem of diversity. If each speech were totally dissimilar from every other speech, it would be impossible to give meaningful directions that would apply to more than one. It would be impossible to learn from experience—from your own experience or from the experience of other speakers—because new situations would be unrelated to those encountered in the past. And, it would be impossible to build theories because past experience would be irrelevant to new and unique situations. There are several ways to classify speeches.[2] The method used here recognizes four general types: *informative, social, public interest,* and *persuasive* or *sales* presentations. These categories include all of the professional presentations you

---

[1] You may be surprised to see subject listed as a situational factor. Most people think of subject as something that the speaker is free to choose. However, recent theories have displayed the importance of the situation in deciding which subjects are appropriate for presentation in a given speech. For a strong statement of this position, see Lloyd Bitzer, "The Rhetorical Situation," *Philosophy and Rhetoric,* 1 (1968), 1–14.

[2] Various perspectives are discussed by Jackson Harrell and Wil A. Linkugel, "On Rhetorical Genre: An Organizing Perspective," *Philosophy and Rhetoric,* 11 (1978), 262–281.

are likely to encounter. Within each category there are many specific types, but the categories themselves are easily identified by the speaker's objective in making the presentation.[3]

Any speaker's objective may be identified by a simple statement indicating what he or she hopes the audience will do as a result of hearing the speech. At one extreme, there are some speaking situations that do not call for specific actions. This type of presentation is commonly called "informative," and it is defined by the fact that speakers are not attempting to produce action or alter behavior. People engaged in informative speaking are satisfied if the audience remembers portions of the message for a period of time. Greater amounts of information recalled and for longer periods of time indicate higher degrees of success, but facilitating recall alone is the object of the speaker's presentation.

At the other extreme, there are some situations in which speakers want the audience to undertake some very specific action. The action may be either immediate or potential, but the aim remains action. "Potential action" is not a difficult concept, but failure to recognize it may cause confusion. For example, some writers distinguish between speeches that aim at persuasion and those that aim at "conviction." In their schemes, speeches that aim at conviction try to change or reinforce beliefs or attitudes, while persuasive speeches try to get the audience to do something. However, the distinction disappears when you ask why a speaker would be concerned with beliefs and attitudes. The answer is that a speaker tries to alter beliefs and attitudes so that the audience will behave as the speaker wants when they encounter a particular situation. For example, a salesperson may give a speech on the advantages of a product, even though he or she knows that the audience will not be in a position to buy it for some time. The salesperson's pitch is, "Remember me when you need one." "When you need one," "when you get ready," and "when you run into it" are all references to future situations. The way the audience reacts when it encounters the situation is an action and may be the object of persuasion just like any other action. However, since it depends on future circumstances, it is only potential action. Speakers may be pleased if the audience remembers portions of the message for a period of time, but neither audience recall nor length of time are criteria by which success is measured. In persuasion, audience action is the only criterion by which success can be measured. Degrees of success may be defined according to the percentage of the audience acting, the frequency with which they act, the amount of energy the audience displays, and their resistance to counter-persuasion. But, the ultimate concern is their actual behavior.

[3] Until very recently, the speaker's objective has been the most widely used means of classifying speeches. Some writers have objected to this procedure because, they argue, it is impossible to look inside a speaker's head to find out just what his or her purpose is. As a result, they say, observers must infer the objective and reliable means for doing so have not been established. The objection is well taken if you are a social scientist interested primarily in describing different types of speeches and studying their effects. However, this problem doesn't reduce the value of the classification for practicing speakers. As a speaker, you should always be able to determine what your objective is. In fact, if you are not certain, there is a good chance that you should avoid speaking until you are able to clarify your purpose.

Social and public interest presentations occupy points intermediate between informative and persuasive speaking. Although the specific settings for social presentations are quite varied, they always attempt to facilitate interaction between participants. They accomplish this objective by calling attention to matters of common concern, identifying participants who are particularly knowledgeable on selected subjects, establishing ground rules for interaction between participants, and calming potentially disruptive emotions.

The term, "public interest presentation," will be used in a precise manner in this text in order to emphasize the unique feature of situations calling for public interest presentations. They are used when a group (that is, a public), which is not part of the formal decision-making structure, believes that its interests will be affected by the actions of an organization. One example that has been seen with regularity in recent years is the case of nuclear power plants which local residents believe present a danger to them. In such situations, public interest presentations should be used to avoid negative reactions that may produce destructive or counter-productive behavior. Thus, like persuasive speeches, public interest presentations are concerned with behavior; but unlike persuasive speeches, they do not direct behavior toward particular goals. Instead, they try to direct behavior away from a relatively limited number of destructive behaviors.

The four common types of presentation can be viewed on a continuum, with informative and persuasive presentations the extremes (see the illustration below). The intermediate points do not need to be defined precisely and numerous gradations are possible. However, as a speaker moves from left to right, progressively greater efforts are made to shape, direct, and control the behaviors of the audience. The informative speaker makes no effort to control the subsequent behavior of the audience; the social speaker attempts to create conditions favorable to interaction; the public interest speaker tries to prevent certain reactions, but leaves the audience with considerable behavioral freedom; and, the persuasive speaker tries to direct the audience to very specific behaviors that will satisfy his or her purposes. Thus, the informative speaker leaves an audience with the broadest range of acceptable behaviors, the social speaker makes only slight reduction in the options that would be acceptable, the public interest speaker rules out certain predetermined possibilities; and the persuasive speaker tries to leave only a very few possible lines of action.

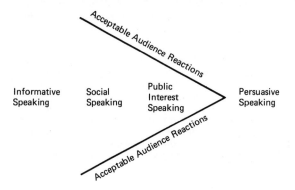

The four categories are highlighted in the following chapters, and the more common varieties of each are described in some detail. The descriptions are intended to help you prepare for specific speaking situations, and they will be most useful if you remember the context in which they are presented. The descriptions emphasize unique features of, special problems in, and preferred approaches to particular speeches. But, this information is to be used in conjunction with the basic skills presented in the first section of this book. The basic skills employed in developing ideas, providing visual representations, organizing materials, choosing appropriate language, and delivering the speech are essential to effective speaking. Descriptions of specific speeches are designed to help you to build on your knowledge of the basics, *not* substitute for it.

CHAPTER EIGHT
INFORMATIVE SPEAKING

The role of informative presentations can be understood by viewing them in a social context. Throughout most of human history, low levels of literacy and the scarcity of books made oral presentations the only effective means of recording and transferring information. In some periods, even teachers were only marginally literate and many learned their subject by attending lectures presented by a master. Few owned books or even consulted them, and most taught by repeating lectures they had recorded. Books remained scarce and valuable well into the seventeenth century, and in some libraries they were chained to walls to prevent theft.

The development of printing reduced demands for the oral presentation of information and the more recent introduction of other media has accelerated the decline. Think about the variety of ways in which you receive information every day. Books, newspapers, and magazines have been supplemented by specialized journals, monographs, and newsletters. And, commercial reprints and economical photocopying machines have made printed matter available in a much greater volume than ever before. Nonprint sources, including radio, television, and film, also provide substantial amounts of information, and the development of computerized storage and retrieval systems promises to make incredible amounts of information available on a moment's notice.

Although demand for informative presentations has been reduced, experience demonstrates that they remain necessary in three situations. First, oral presentations are necessary to "open up" a new subject to the audience. Used in this way, lectures provide the audience with concepts and other background information that enables them to employ other sources. Second, oral presentations are necessary when the situation requires all members of an audience to have relatively uniform exposure to the materials. A safety briefing required to insure that employees are aware of safety procedures is a typical case. Finally, oral presentations are necessary when the subject is changing so rapidly or the materials are intended for such limited distribution that use of other media is impractical. Project status reports and summaries of classified material that can be made available only to individuals who have obtained security clearances are common examples.

Presentations in all three of these situations are commonly called "briefings." However, differences in the situations require different approaches to the presentation, and a more refined vocabulary is available. To make clear the distinctions, we can call presentations introducing concepts or background material *lectures*; those providing uniform exposure to procedures *demonstrations*; and those summarizing current information for limited distribution *reports*.

LECTURES

Lectures are a form of oral presentation used to introduce fundamental concepts or background material. Their purpose is to introduce the audience to a subject and provide them with background so that they can take advantage of information available through other sources. Although they were once the only practical means of presenting information to students, many students, teachers, and administrators have protested their continued use. James R. Davis places these protests in an appropriate context.

> In recent years lecturing has been called into question. Traditional teachers lecture, it is said: while those who count themselves among the avant-garde, the innovative, and the experimental will avoid the formal lecture. This is a false and unfortunate dichotomy. Lecturing is neither inherently good nor bad. It has been and remains one of the chief strategies of the college teacher. What is wrong with lecturing is that it is so often done poorly. And it is done poorly because most college teachers don't understand the complexity involved in the transmission and reception of information.[1]

Understanding the relationship between the lecture and other sources of information is absolutely essential, and this author believes that more instructors fail here than at any other point in preparing lesson plans.

Within any instructional system, lecturing is only one means of transferring information. Alternate means include group discussions, directed study, and in-

[1] James R. Davis, *Teaching Strategies for the College Classroom* (Boulder, Colorado: Westview Press, Inc., 1976), p. 39.

dependent reading, and research indicates that all are superior to lecturing in some circumstances. Lectures are at their best when educational objectives are limited to recall and to the understanding of information. They are far inferior to other methods when objectives require application, analysis, synthesis, or evaluation of material. Moreover, lectures are a uniformly ineffective means of teaching physical movement and physiological control, and the value of oral presentation in developing patterns of emotional behavior is very low.[2] These findings are consistent with the specific application of lecturing described here.

These concerns point to the role of lectures in instructional systems. Lectures should not be the sole means of securing educational objectives and they are a cumbersome means of presenting highly detailed information. However, they are an ideal means of introducing new concepts because the lecturer can adapt the level and pace of a presentation to the abilities of the specific audience. This is something no other form of transmitting information can do because no other means gives the source such immediate feedback from the receivers. The teacher must make some initial assumptions about the audience while preparing a lecture, which is something that must be done when using any means of transferring. Only the lecturer, however, can constantly correct such assumptions on the basis of feedback from the audience.

As a result of their unique role in educational systems, lectures pose two distinct sets of problems. The first set results from the need to make novel ideas and concepts meaningful to the audience, and the second results from the amount of time customarily allocated to lectures. Making novel ideas and concepts meaningful to the audience requires selecting content with care because the lecturer must constantly balance the new and unfamiliar against the old and familiar. A lecture in which no novel material is introduced accomplishes nothing. Similarly, a lecture in which no ties are established between the new information and that with which the audience is already familiar is also a failure. To make the material intelligible, the lecture must develop from or extend what the audience already knows. This is a critical step and it usually takes place by using the orientation material. If the lecture is part of a continuing sequence, the orientation can simply explain how the current lecture fits into the sequence. However, if the lecture is the first one in a sequence or if it is an isolated presentation, other points of reference must be established. Determining what these reference points are requires knowledge of both the audience and the subject. But, as a general rule, you should not present a lecture that does not have some impact on the current activities of the audience, and these activities should be your reference points.

The amount of time normally provided for lectures causes a second set of problems. These problems involve maintaining audience attention and the need for elaborate organization. The following comparisons show the extent to which these factors distinguish lectures from other presentations. Most oral reports are

---

[2] For a convenient summary of research comparing lecturing to other instructional techniques, see the "Objective-Methods Matrix" developed by N. L. Gage and David C. Berliner, *Educational Psychology* (Chicago: Rand McNally 1975), p. 488.

less than twenty minutes long, social presentations may range from a few minutes for introductions to about twenty minutes for banquet presentations, and public interest and persuasive speeches are generally about fifteen to twenty-five minutes in length. In contrast, lectures in instructional contexts are generally fifty minutes and may be as long as ninety minutes. Of the other types of speech, only demonstrations approach this length, but the nature of a demonstration reduces difficulties caused by length. The problem in maintaining audience attention and receptivity was dramatically demonstrated in an experiment by Joseph M. Trenaman, who compared the ability of an audience to answer questions after presentations of various lengths. Audiences who heard presentations fifteen minutes long answered approximately 41 percent of the recall questions correctly; those who heard thirty-minute presentations answered 25 percent correctly; and those who heard forty-five-minute presentations answered less than 20 percent correctly. John McLeish explains these results in the following passage.

> With the increase in the duration of the talk the amount remembered thinned out. In the typical case, assimilation diminished severely after fifteen minutes. At thirty minutes, most listeners were approaching the point where the total taken in was zero. In some cases there was, in fact, a loss of material previously learned. This is, of course, the phenomenon known as retroactive inhibition.[3]

Overcoming attention effects due to the length of lectures requires special attention to verbal markers or transitions, techniques of emphasis, and variety.

Verbal markers and transitions are explicit statements about the relationship between particular items of information and the speech as a whole. The kinds of transitions commonly used are described in Chapter 4, and you should review the appropriate sections for detailed explanation.

In addition to using transitions to clarify the relationship between materials, it is desirable to use various techniques to call attention to particular statements. One technique that is particularly effective is repeating a statement at different times during a speech. The use of previews and summaries has the effect of building this technique into the format described above. Other techniques include the use of a verbal statement, indicating that an item is important ("Now get this" or "Be sure to remember this"), a slower than normal rate of delivery, a slightly longer than usual pause immediately before a statement, and a distinctive gesture to mark the idea. Curiously, some techniques suggested by common sense do not seem to be very helpful. Use of a soft voice or a loud voice and banging a fist on the table do not enhance retention.[4]

It is advisable to introduce as much variety into the lecture as possible. This

[3] John McLeish, "The Lecture Method," in N. L. Gage, ed., *The Psychology of Teaching Methods* (Chicago: The University of Chicago Press, 1976), pp. 269–270. Trenaman's research remains unpublished but is summarized by McLeish.

[4] This discussion of techniques of emphasis is adapted from Raymond Ehrensberger, "Experimental Study of the Relative Effectiveness of Certain Forms of Emphasis in Public Speaking," *Speech Monographs*, 12 (1945), 94–111.

may be done by using many kinds of developing material, using rhetorical questions periodically to force listeners to check their comprehension, employing modest amounts of physical movement and variation in vocal qualities, and pausing to invite questions and discussion.

The demand for particularly elaborate organization reflects the needs of both lecturer and audience. Relatively loose or casual structures may be satisfactory for brief messages, but as the length and complexity of a presentation increase, the demands for clear organization increase dramatically. For the lecturer, a precise structure makes it possible to integrate the large amounts of material required by a lengthy presentation. For the audience, a precise structure makes it easier to see how the various concepts or ideas presented relate to one another. Many different patterns will work, but the pattern you use should be substantially more elaborate and detailed than it would be in a shorter presentation. Precise guidelines are difficult to establish because speakers vary in organizational ability and memory. In an outline, however, the effects of greater precision should be evident in the number of levels of subordination employed. A relatively brief speech might employ just two levels: the major ideas and the materials used to develop each. A longer presentation should employ at least three levels: the major ideas, subordinate ideas derived from the major ideas, and materials used to develop the subordinate ideas.[5]

DEMONSTRATIONS

Demonstrations are presentations showing how something is done. By definition, the subject is always a process in which several distinct steps must be executed in order to achieve a predetermined end. The audience may be a single person such as a new employee learning a specific job, but it is more economical to address larger audiences.

Demonstrations are required whenever it is important to insure that all members have been exposed to a body of information. The requirements for uniform exposure may be legal, as in safety requirements, or they may be practical. A common example of a demonstration required by law is the initial safety meeting for new employees and periodic refreshers for continuing employees. Failure to demonstrate safety procedures in some industries is a criminal offense and it exposes the company to substantial damage suits if an employee is injured. Practical requirements for demonstrations commonly involve cases in which it is desirable for all members of the audience to do something in the same way. The demonstration may be part of a training session or it may be given to attract potential customers.

[5] Some studies have questioned the value of organization in facilitating audience comprehension, but most have used such brief treatment messages that the applicability of their findings to lectures is questionable. Whereas the typical lecture is nearly an hour long, experimental messages have ranged from a few minutes to twenty minutes in length. This problem is discussed in the instructor's manual and your teacher can probably provide a list of individual studies.

Demonstrations may be as long as lectures, and you may encounter attention lags when presenting them. When you do, you can employ the same techniques that you would in a lecture. Fortunately, you have two advantages in a demonstration. First, the activity resulting from the demonstration provides variety, which helps to maintain attention. Audience attention may well be captured by the constant changes in action, frequent introduction of new objects, and reworking of components introduced in earlier steps. Second, the basic organizational plan for a demonstration is determined by the process displayed. Although you may need to impose structure on the steps presented, the primary sequence of explanation and demonstration is established by the manner in which the process is actually conducted.

In spite of these advantages, demonstrations are among the most difficult presentations to make effectively. This is true because the nature of a demonstration presents some very specific challenges to your speaking abilities. These challenges arise from problems of orientation, complexity, pacing, and scale.

Orientation is a particular problem in demonstrations because you must constantly shift attention from the overall sequence of events to relatively detailed directions for particular steps, and then return to the general sequence. For example, in presenting a speech about performance appraisal systems, you would have to explain the major steps (establishing criteria, measuring employee performance, and communicating the appraisal), the relationship between the steps, and the procedures for each step. This constant shifting of focus makes use of visual aids essential. The preferred form is a flow chart displaying the major steps. The chart should be in view throughout your presentation and you should identify the point of your comments at each step by referring to the chart. Pointing at the step you are completing and tracing the line to the next step is an ideal means of marking the transition from one step to the next.

The complexity of the subject can be a challenge when a thorough exposition would require introducing more information than the audience can master in the time available. This may be a particular problem when the audience is expected to implement the procedure described. For example, safety briefings may require careful attention to complex processes to insure that employees conduct themselves appropriately under certain circumstances. However, if the procedures are explained in too much detail, the audience may conclude that the steps are too difficult to master and make no attempt to adopt the recommended procedure. Similarly, excessively detailed demonstrations may lead the audience to believe that use of a new product is too demanding, that adoption of a new procedure would be confusing, or that learning new skills is beyond their ability.

When you are faced with situations in which complexity is a problem, there is no fully satisfactory solution. The best you can do is to distinguish the minimum amount of information that will allow the audience to get started from refinements of the process. Once you have identified this information, you should plan a series of demonstrations. In the first, introduce the essential steps in an admittedly superficial presentation of the basic features of the procedure. Then, after the audience has had an opportunity to become acquainted with the fundamental steps, you can make a series of progressively more detailed demonstrations, focusing on particular elements of the system. For example, if you were introducing an audience to the use of a computerized text editing system, your initial demonstration might show how to use the standard features of the system. These might include creating files, simple editing procedures, and producing a finished copy. Subsequent demonstrations would include procedures for copying and storing files, more sophisticated editing procedures, transferring blocks of text, substituting extended strings, and producing multiple copies or copies with unusual formats.

For demonstrations to have the greatest possible impact, they should be paced so that oral comments accompany the physical act to which they refer. In most cases, this is relatively easy and you can usually add or delete oral amplification to correspond to the amount of time it takes to complete each step. However, pacing can cause problems when certain steps are easily explained, but demand long periods for execution. For example, some testing procedures require dehydration of samples while others need time for bacterial cultures to mature. Explaining that the sample must be dried or the culture developed will take a minute or two, at most, but the actual process may require an hour or more. Rather than asking the audience to wait while the process is executed, you should prepare another sample prior to the demonstration. When you come to the critical step, explain that it takes an extended period, set your first sample aside, and continue the demonstration using the previously prepared sample. If there are several steps that require such attention and time, you may need to prepare several samples, each at a different stage of development. Label each clearly to avoid confusion and store them out of sight to avoid distracting the audience. After the body of the demonstration has been presented, all of the samples may be displayed in sequential order to provide a physical summary of the process.

Finally, scale may present problems whenever objects employed in the process are either too big or too small to be used effectively in the presentation. For example, it may be physically impossible to manipulate large pieces of machinery, and there may be no convenient means of displaying microscopic components during a presentation. Challenges at both extremes can be overcome through the use of visual aids drawn to appropriate scales. Pictures, diagrams, and cutaways are often convenient, and physical models may be even better. A variety of techniques are described in Chapter 3, "Visual Developing Materials," and you should review the appropriate sections if you are unsure of yourself.

REPORTS

The word "report" is used casually by many people and may seem synonymous with "speech." In professional settings, however, a report is a very specialized kind of informative presentation governed by particular expectations. Characteristically, a report is understood to be an informative presentation in which the speaker describes a state of affairs. The state of affairs may be the status of a project, achievements of a research program, the financial condition of a company, or inventory levels for particular parts or supplies. Whatever the state of affairs, reports are essentially descriptive and the speaker's personal preferences or recommendations are seldom included. When recommendations are called for, they generally take the form of interpretations of the information presented, and the descriptive character of the report remains foremost.

Even understood in this restrictive manner, oral reports are the most pervasive kind of presentational activity encountered in modern organizations. Reports may be addressed to superiors, boards of directors, clients, customers, suppliers, shareholders, and so forth. The number of settings and the variety of audiences are almost endless. In all of these applications, two characteristics are evident.

First, reports are a response to a request for information. Reports answer questions raised by those who need specific information to fulfill their own responsibilities. In this sense, reporting is a "delegated function" assigned by people who lack the time, expertise, or position to secure the information on their own. Some examples illustrate this: At the conclusion of a research project you may be asked to report your findings to the funding agency; your immediate superior may request periodic progress reports on certain projects; customers may require status reports on contract items for which you are responsible; and, regulations require periodic reports to stockholders. The important feature of these situations—and of countless others—is that in making a report, you are presenting information for use by someone else.

The second characteristic of oral reports is that they are almost universally presented in conjunction with written reports. This characteristic results from the delegated nature of reporting because recipients often like to be able to study reports after they have been presented. Adapting to this situation is relatively easy if you understand the distinct functions of the oral and written reports; oral reports *develop interest,* written reports *document* material.

Because oral reports are such specialized forms of informative speaking, some special cautions must be observed in preparing them. The most important of these cautions is that you should prepare specifically for the oral report. Of course, preparation is essential for all kinds of speaking, but the characteristics of the oral report may deceive novices into thinking that preparation is unnecessary. The demand character of oral reports may suggest that all a speaker needs to do is show up to answer questions, and the presence of the written report may imply that the speaker already knows enough about the subject to "pull it off" without additional effort. However, effective oral reporting requires preparation to meet the demands of the audience and failure to prepare can have disastrous consequences. To illustrate the importance of preparation, Roger P. Wilcox of the General Motors Institute tells the story of a young engineer making his first project report.

> [The engineer] had been assigned an extensive study project, culminating when he finished in an oral report to top management. For months he carried on his investigation. Finally came the appointed day for his report. But he had been so preoccupied

with his investigation that he never thought to give any attention to preparing the report. He entered the room where the engineers and supervisors were assembled to hear his report. He heard himself being introduced and somewhat shakily approached the lectern. Only then, as he looked out over the collection of faces before him, did he begin to realize the situation he was in. His heart began pounding; he broke into a sweat. He became so unnerved that he had to be excused to an adjoining room, where he could gather his wits and make at least a few elementary notes while others preceded him on the program.[6]

This is an extreme example, but the point is clear: Knowledge of the subject alone is insufficient. Effective oral reporting requires specific preparation for the presentational situation.

The starting point in preparing an oral report—and probably the written one as well—is identification of the demands or needs of the person requesting the report. A complete understanding of the assignment should include the goal or purpose of the report; the materials to be consulted and the methods to be employed; the time(s) at which the report or its components are to be completed; and limits on the length or volume of the finished report. When these features are explicit in the original assignment, the task of preparing the report should not be difficult. However, more often than not, some or all of these components are unspecified, and the person making the assignment may be unable to state precise expectations. This happens because many reports are so routine that the demand character is all but forgotten.

When you encounter such a situation, keep in mind that the demands are just as real as if you were given a classroom assignment, but that you must do the added work of identifying critical features of your task. Initially, you know that the standard format for a technical report calls for attention to five topics: (1) a clear statement of the problem or topic explored; (2) an explanation of your research procedures; (3) specification of the "universe" or subject pool employed in generating data; (4) description of the procedures used in analyzing data; and (5) presentation of conclusions derived from the data. This format suggests the principal topics to be included in the report, and you may get additional direction from several other sources: Observe reports presented by others, examine file copies of similar reports from the past, and ask coworkers about expectations for such reports. In addition, you may be able to present a sample outline to your superior or the person requesting the report. If so, the final report should reflect any feedback that is received.

Once the expectations of the person assigning the report have been identified, make sure that the report is consistent with them. This recommendation sounds so obvious as to be unnecessary, but experience demonstrates that it is not. Many inexperienced reporters try to second guess the person requesting the report by making judgments about what he or she "really needs" or "ought to have." Even worse is the inclination to use the report as an opportunity to "make a per-

---

[6] Roger P. Wilcox, *Oral Reporting in Business and Industry* (Englewood Cliffs, New Jersey: Prentice-Hall, 1967), p. 7.

sonal statement'' or to ''call attention to more pressing matters.'' Of course there are times when it is necessary to display initiative by doing more than requested, and there are times when you should raise questions about company policy, but both are inconsistent with the delegated function of reporting.

Managing the content of an oral report can also be a problem when it is reduced from a much longer written report. A written report of fifty pages contains approximately 15,000 words and would require nearly two hours to read aloud. In contrast, oral reports seldom exceed twenty minutes—time for less than 3,000 words. Obviously, you cannot simply begin reading at page one and go until someone stops you. If you try, you will put the audience to sleep and may never get to the important components of your presentation. The problem you face is one of limiting the scope of your report without becoming superficial. Reducing the scope of the report can be difficult, but your knowledge of the character of the report and the interests of the audience can point to a solution. On one hand, oral reports are not well suited for presentation of highly detailed information. You may refer to characteristics of the data, but it is important to avoid extended analyses. On the other hand, the audience for an oral report is generally more specific than the one for whom a written report is prepared, so you can select topics of greatest interest to them. Capitalizing on the fact that the written report documents your work, you can use the oral report to focus attention on the novel, unique, or otherwise noteworthy and interesting features of the project. Make frequent references to the written report and be prepared to introduce some materials from it in response to questions. This does not mean that you can omit procedural features that are common or standard, but you can deemphasize them in order to highlight the distinctive contributions of your work. Generally, you will want to highlight your conclusions and any features of your work that are particularly noteworthy. In doing so, the speech format is valuable. The attention material should outline the problem and indicate its importance to the audience. The orientation material should outline the major topics in the written report and call particular attention to research procedures and subject population. The purpose of the oral presentation is to call attention to noteworthy features of your work, and the preview should list the topics discussed in the body. The body should concentrate on the distinctive features of the work, and it should explain their significance for the project as a whole. The conclusion should include a brief summary, and the final appeal should present the implications of the work and outline recommendations, if called for.

SUMMARY

Technological innovation has reduced demand for informative presentations, but three types remain important. Lectures are used to ''open up'' a subject, and they are best suited to introduce new concepts to an audience. To be effective, a lecturer must relate novel material to that which is familiar and control the effects of time by maintaining attention and employing a relatively elaborate structure. Demonstrations are designed to provide uniform exposure to a body of information and are used most commonly to show how something is done. Demonstrations pose special problems of orientation, complexity, pacing, and scale. Reports summarize information intended for limited distribution. They are presented commonly in response to a request for information and are almost universally accompanied by a written report.

LEARNING ACTIVITIES

1. Attend a presentation by a member of the faculty who has the reputation for being a particularly good lecturer. Take notes on the lecture and pay close attention to the manner in which the lecturer adapts to the oral setting. Have the materials been selected with an eye to the function of the lecture, or could some be presented more effectively through other media? What strategies did the lecturer use to relate novel material to concepts with which the audience was familiar? How did the lecturer compensate for the effects of time? What organizational patterns and devices did the lecturer use to maintain attention and focus?
2. Oral presentations in some fields are often more like demonstrations than lectures because the speaker is trying to show the audience how to do something. This is often the case in engineering, beginning mathematics, computer science, and public speaking courses. Attend a class conducted by a faculty member from one of these areas and observe how he or she adapts to the oral setting. Identify strategies used by the speaker to cope with the problems of orientation, complexity, pacing, and scale, which are described in this chapter.
3. Select an article from a professional journal in a particular field. For example, Speech majors may select an article from *Quarterly Journal of Speech, Communication Monographs,* or *Philosophy and Rhetoric.* Read the article carefully and consider the problems you would encounter in converting it to an oral report. Remember that the function of the oral report is to develop interest in the contents and only those features that contribute to this function should be developed. Using the format for oral presentations described in Chapter 4 and adapted at the close of this chapter, outline an oral report based on the article.

CHAPTER NINE
SOCIAL PRESENTATIONS

It is customary to call speeches that do not fit into other categories *ritual* or *ceremonial* speeches. Examples include speeches of welcome, introductions, award presentations, after-dinner speeches, and tributes. Lumping together such a variety of presentations fosters the impression that the category is a catchall for types that lack a common purpose. This impression is unfortunate because it obscures the function of social presentations. This function is *facilitating interaction* between the participants. All social presentations aim at enhancing interaction, and you can appreciate the importance of this function if you understand the factors that make it difficult for people to work together.

Groups working together can produce decisions superior to those of any single individual, but only when conditions permit effective discussion and interaction. Tension caused by unresolved issues may make it impossible for groups to work effectively, and social scientists have distinguished two types of tension. *Primary tension* results when people are placed in an ambiguous environment, and it reflects their natural tendency to withdraw until they know how they are expected to behave. *Secondary tension* is caused by competition between people trying to occupy the same role. The most common case occurs when two people struggle to become the leader and expend most of their energy contesting the position. Both types of tension reduce the effectiveness of a group, and the importance of social presentations in overcoming tension is evident in the four types discussed in this chapter.

Speeches of introduction are intended to facilitate interaction between the speaker and audience. They prepare the audience to receive the speaker's message by suggesting its importance and by establishing ground rules for subsequent discussion. Types of discussion that may be provided include questions and other remarks directed to the speaker after the formal presentation.

Chairing a panel discussion or symposium is the occasion for a second form of social presentation. The chairperson of a panel discussion serves a dual role in facilitating interaction between members of the panel and between the panel and the audience. To accomplish this dual function, the chairperson must make the audience receptive to the panel's message, explain the sequence of presentations by panel members, and establish ground rules for subsequent discussion.

Banquet speeches, often called after-dinner speeches, may appear to be intended for entertainment only, but they should always have a serious purpose as well. At elaborate banquets where several speeches are to be presented, the first may be used to mark the transition from purely social activities to more serious business. At less formal affairs, a single after-dinner presentation may both entertain and introduce concerns of lasting importance. In either case, the after-dinner speech should be calculated to make it possible for the audience to interact about topics of a semiserious nature.

Tributes memorialize the contributions of someone who is leaving the group, but the speaker's real contribution is to those who remain active. The emotions generated by the departure of an associate may make it difficult for members of a professional or social team to continue working together. Tributes facilitate continued interaction by quieting emotions and by channeling resulting energy in productive directions.

INTRODUCTIONS

Introductions facilitate interaction between speaker and audience by preparing the audience for the speech that follows. They prepare the audience by developing curiosity about the subject and by generating respect for the speaker. Neither of these tasks is difficult when the speaker is well known and introductions should always be very brief. The maximum length permitted is five minutes and most are much shorter. When the speaker is well known, introductions can be exceptionally brief and in the extreme case consist of nothing more than the conventional, "Ladies and Gentlemen, the President of the United States."

Because the presentation is so brief, elaborate organization is unnecessary and the speech format is normally compressed to four steps:

1. Welcome the audience.
2. Identify the subject of discussion.

3. Direct favorable attention to the speaker.
4. Introduce the speaker by name.

These steps take the place of the general format and should always be used in introducing a speaker. However, the specific materials used with each vary according to the situation, topic, and speaker. The welcome should include a greeting, a reference to the sponsoring organization, and something to identify the nature of the gathering. In addition, you may want to include your own name if there are people in the audience who may not recognize you.

The subject for discussion should be identified in a way calculated to develop audience curiosity. As you state the subject, you should also indicate why it is important or how it is likely to affect members of the audience. Your statement should be as precise as possible without causing difficulty for the speaker, and it is a good idea to check with this person prior to your remarks. You must avoid interpreting the topic in a manner inconsistent with the speaker's interpretation, and you should avoid stealing the show by disclosing too much of the speaker's thesis or purpose.

The third step, directing favorable attention to the speaker, should occupy the largest portion of your introduction. This step should generate respect for the speaker and two kinds of material are commonly used. The speaker's qualifications should be used to show that he or she is knowledgeable about the subject and warrants attention. Then, you may comment on characteristics or experiences of the speaker that demonstrate personal concern for the subject or audience. Finding materials for this step is easier than you may think. You can always check appropriate biographical dictionaries, and a reference librarian can help to identify several that are appropriate. Publication notices and news releases mentioning the speaker can be consulted as well. However, your primary source of information should be the speaker. Most people who speak frequently have developed a brief biography (often called a "bio") to assist people introducing them, and almost all professionals will furnish a copy of their résumé on request. In addition, a brief interview or phone conversation with the speaker should provide more than enough material. Gathering material is easy, but you should use it selectively. You must avoid embarrassing the speaker and boring the audience. A comprehensive list of accomplishments is unnecessary and your selection process can be guided by three considerations:

1. Avoid or deemphasize things with which the audience is already familiar.
2. Direct attention to the most distinctive qualifications and/or experiences.
3. Concentrate on qualifications and experiences most relevant to the particular subject and audience.

In addition, avoid references to your guest's speaking ability. Most audiences will want to judge for themselves, and your remarks may embarrass you, the speaker, or both.

Finally, introduce the speaker by name. Even if you have mentioned the person's name during the first three steps, say it clearly and correctly to mark the transition to the main speech.

An introduction employing these steps should sound something like the one given in the accompanying box.

Step I

Good evening. I'm John Smith, President of the Speaker's Board. I am pleased to welcome you to our fourteenth annual Campus Issues Forum.

Step II

In recent years the value of a college education has been questioned by many people. Several authors have emphasized the fact that time spent going to school could be spent earning an income, and a few studies have reported that the value of an education has declined to the point that lost income will never be made up. This is a particular problem for those of you considering graduate school because the income differential between college graduates and those with advanced degrees appears to be declining every year.

Step III

Our speaker this evening has spent the last fifteen years helping students select careers, and he is currently Associate Dean of the College of Education and Director of the Academic Placement Service. He has a doctorate in Education from Harvard University, and has published numerous articles and books. His most recent book, *Education at the Crossroads,* won the Smelling award and was nominated for a Pulitzer prize.

Step IV

Our speaker, Professor Joseph Daniels.

Your delivery should be extemporaneous and notes should be used sparingly or not at all. Your manner should match the setting, and some humor may be introduced in relatively informal settings.

CHAIRING PANEL PRESENTATIONS

As your career matures and you assume more responsible positions, you may be called upon to be the chairperson of a panel discussion or symposium. The difference between the two is that participants in a symposium present prepared speeches, while participants in a panel discussion respond to questions raised by the chairperson or audience. Conducting a symposium is more common in professional situations and will be discussed in more detail. Special responsibilities in chairing panel discussions are discussed at the end of this section.

Participation in a panel discussion or symposium requires few skills other than those necessary for any speech. Your presentation becomes part of a sequence defined by the remarks of the chairperson and other speakers. But, the chairperson assumes some particular responsibilities. These responsibilities include introducing the participants, managing interaction between participants and audience members, and supplying questions to keep the discussion alive. The directions for a speech of introduction govern your first responsibility, but discharging the others is easier if you understand why symposiums and panel discussions are used.

Symposiums are used when a presentation by a single speaker would be insufficient. These situations do not reflect on the abilities of the participants, but result from either the characteristics of the subject or from the demands of the audience. On the one hand, the subject may be so complex that no one speaker can do it justice in a single presentation. This is true when the subject is so broad that several areas of competence are necessary to comprehend it and when the subject is so complex that several points of view are necessary. When the subject is broad, it is common to bring together specialists who will comment on those aspects that fall within their areas of expertise; and, when the subject is complex, it is wise to assemble representatives of the relevant viewpoints. On the other hand, audience expectations may demand presentations by several people. Audience reasons for wanting to see several speakers vary with the situation, but there are some common cases. When a work group finishes a report or project, exposure through presentation of results may be regarded as a reward to be shared by all members of the team. Or, the panel presentation may serve as a substitute for personal contact when the audience is large and lacks other opportunities to meet noteworthy speakers. Finally, a panel presentation may be requested by a potential client who wants to observe several members of your organization before making a decision.

Both subject factors and audience expectations may require presentations by several speakers, and the outlines of the resulting panels are similar. However, when subject factors are of primary importance, you must do a good deal of work prior to the actual presentation to insure thorough coverage. By working with group members prior to the presentation, you should agree on a common definition of the purpose of the presentation, reach a mutual understanding of presentational roles, and determine the expected length of each presentation. To facilitate interaction between the participants, make sure that they all know what part of the subject they are to cover, when they will speak, how much time they can use, and when they are free to direct comments to one another.

When audience expectations are the primary factor calling for a group presentation, the participants should be given considerable freedom. Let each choose a subject and approach that allows for the display of the person's abilities and interests. But, coordination requires that the participants know the amount of time available per presentation and the order in which each will speak.

The preplanning mentioned in the last paragraph will make your job during the presentation much easier. You should begin the presentation by welcoming the audience and identifying the subject of discussion. These first two steps correspond exactly with the first two steps in a speech of introduction and the materials used are identical. The third step, introducing the speaker, is complicated by the fact that there are several speakers. As chairperson, you have two options. The older, more traditional approach is to introduce the first speaker, sit down while he or she speaks, introduce the second speaker, again sit down, and so forth. This approach has the advantage of identifying each speaker immediately before his or her presentation, but the amount of movement required can be awkward and frequent interruptions by the chairperson may prevent development of a coherent presentation. A less awkward procedure is to introduce all of the speakers in order before the first speaks and then let them speak in turn.

During the individual presentations, your primary responsibility is to monitor the time used by each speaker. Few people will deliberately exceed time limits, but many forget them while speaking. It is a good idea to seat yourself near the point from which the presentations are made so you can remind the speakers without distracting the audience.

The least conspicuous reminder is a written note, and you may wish to give speakers both "five minutes left" and "one minute left" reminders before giving them instructions to "STOP!" If someone exceeds his time, you should give him a few courtesy minutes to conclude, but you may have to actually interrupt him. Fortunately, few speakers are so unmanageable that actual interruptions are required. But, when one speaker takes too much time, it is the responsibility of the chairperson to take control and preserve opportunities for the others. Stand up, excuse yourself, comment on the time, and introduce the next speaker. It might go like this: "Excuse me, John, but our time is limited. The next speaker is. . . ."

After the presentations, you have two responsibilities. First, you should manage comments and questions from the floor. Do this by inviting comments or questions and recognizing members who would like to speak. When the audience is large, you also may repeat each question to insure that it is heard by everyone. The panelists usually can tell when a question is directed to them, but if several want to respond, you may recognize them in turn. Similarly, if no one on the panel responds, you may have to request answers from particular panelists.

After questions from the floor have been exhausted or the time allotted for discussion has been used up, you should conclude the presentation. If no further action is expected, you may simply say, "Thank you, our time is up. Good night." However, if further interaction is expected, you may call attention to future events. Your concluding remarks should indicate when you expect to meet again, what kinds of decisions are to be made, and/or what programs will take place in the immediate future.

One special caution should be noted: The fact that the chairperson is not responsible for presenting the content of a symposium should not mislead you into believing that an outline is unnecessary. In fact, an outline is as important as when you are speaking because you must plan both your own remarks and the structure of the whole presentation. A working outline for a panel presentation resembles the outline for a speech by a single speaker, but it goes one step further by identifying who is responsible for each topic. A convenient form of representation uses the left margin to identify participant roles. Time limits may be noted as well and many experienced chairpeople anticipate elapsed time for the entire presentation. For example, if the meeting is scheduled to start at 1:00, they plan to finish the introduction by 1:15, introduce the second speaker at 1:25, and so forth. Projected times may also be recorded in the left margin. Although it lacks some details, Exhibit 9-1 could be used by the chairperson for a symposium presentation on "academic dishonesty."

EXHIBIT 9-1

INTRODUCTION

[*1:00* P.M.]

Chairperson, Monica Smith

Attention Material: Welcome
Orientation Material: Our subject is cheating on campus. Academic dishonesty is defined as. . . . ; It affects everyone because. . . .
Purpose: To promote understanding of the issues.
Preview: Introduce the speakers and identify the topics for each presentation.

BODY

[*1:15* P.M.]

Professor David Smith

I. The extent of the problem.

[*1:25* P.M.]

Professor Stuart Alexander

II. Causes of the problem.

[*1:45* P.M.]

Professor Janet Davis

III. Possible solutions.

CONCLUSION

[*2:05* P.M.]

Monica Smith

Questions and comments from the audience.
Closing: Topic for next panel discussion.

[*2:30* P.M.]

The major difference in your responsibility when chairing a panel discussion is that you must be more active during the body of the presentation. Prior to the presentation, it is necessary to decide what topics should be explored by the panel and to frame questions that will allow the panel members to express their views. During the presentation, you should introduce all participants at once and then ask your first question. Allow each participant to answer in turn and then proceed to your second question. Each participant should be given an opportunity to respond to each question, and you should monitor the time to insure that no one individual monopolizes the discussion. To make sure that all members participate, you may need to address them in turn, and it is often desirable to change the order in which they respond to questions. For example, you may address the participants in the order A, B, C, D for the first question; B, C, D, A for the second question; C, D, A, B for the third question; and so forth. At the conclusion of the discussion, it may help the audience to frame questions if you summarize the position of each panelist. Do so only if you can do it with reasonable accuracy; misstatements will embarrass you and the participants.

BANQUET PRESENTATIONS

After-dinner or banquet presentations are an accepted part of most formal dinners, and many audiences will feel cheated if the program doesn't include at least one speech intended to entertain them. But, not any speech will do. The speech must be adapted to the condition of the audience and this is the major factor influencing the character of after-dinner speaking. To understand this factor, think about your own feelings after a large meal and, perhaps, a little too much to drink. Like most people, you are lethargic and want to avoid mental activity. Your attention span is likely to be relatively short and you may find yourself dozing off if activities do not hold your interest. Obviously, speaking to an audience in this condition requires careful planning to accommodate them. And, most after-dinner audiences resent a speaker who fails to adapt to their situation.

All of this means that your presentation must be consistent with the mood of the audience. Your speech should be brief—seldom more than twenty minutes— and its tone should be light and easy. The delivery should be relatively informal, jokes or other remarks may be addressed to particular members of the audience, and your style should be less formal than in other presentations. However, these adaptations do not mean that your presentation should lack a serious message or theme. A speech without a unifying theme is nothing more than a comedy monologue. Although the audience may find a monologue amusing at the time, it is soon forgotten and fails to facilitate serious interaction. Adapting to the audience means presenting a semiserious message in an enjoyable way.

> The after-dinner audience wants to be shown, not to be reasoned with; to watch, not to exert itself. Such concealed argument as there is must not be dry, heavy, or compact. It must be insinuated into the audience's minds, not loaded in or driven in. Hence the materials must be vivid; they must be capable of resting easily on a full stomach.[1]

[1] Donald C. Bryant and Karl R. Wallace, *Fundamentals of Public Speaking,* 4th ed. (New York: Appleton-Century-Crofts, 1969), p. 387.

Composing an after-dinner speech that makes a serious point in an appropriate manner requires special attention to choosing a subject, selecting materials, using humor, and organizing the content.

Selecting a subject may be particularly difficult. In some cases, you will be invited to speak, but you will be given no indication of what the subject is. Even if you know the audience relatively well, you may have to use a good deal of imagination to find a subject or thesis that is appropriate to the situation. In general, subjects for after-dinner speeches should be related to the common activities of the group and should offer pleasing prospects. Topics that fit these conditions can be found in accomplishments of the group and its members, current projects, and future prospects. One skilled speaker faced a unique problem in selecting topics when he was asked to be the main speaker at Christmas banquets for three interlocking companies. The dinners were less than a week apart and about half of the participants at the second had heard his speech at the first, and nearly all of those at the third had heard one of the first two. He solved this problem by using all three subject areas in turn. His thesis statement for the first speech was ''We've done some great things together''; for the second, ''We are involved in some really interesting projects''; and, for the third, ''The future looks good.''

The materials used in an after-dinner speech should be chosen with an eye to developing and maintaining audience interest and attention. Of course, extended quotations, detailed statistics, and summaries of empirical research are inappropriate. The materials should be examples, illustrations, and analogies that are interesting in-and-of themselves. Materials can hold interest when they involve familiar people, places, or events; when they present familiar items in a new or unusual context; and, when they are delivered in a lively and entertaining way.

Humor can be a great asset in after-dinner speaking, but few people have the wit necessary to compose an entire humorous speech on their own. Fortunately, the collections of anecdotal material mentioned in the chapter on developing materials include many humorous items. And there are many books of jokes and stories that may be used by a speaker. Find them in a library by consulting the librarian or the card catalogue. You should use care in selecting items and you may encounter a problem in creating the ''illusion of originality.'' Edward Rogge and James C. Ching explain this problem and its solution.

> Most anecdotes heard today as original humor are versions of originals told many times before and are the destined forerunners of original tales for future generations of hearers and readers. Moreover, even when a humorous idea seems new to a storyteller and his listeners, a knowledgeable critic could demonstrate probably that a particular story was told in other ways in the past. A wise speaker, understanding that narrative uniqueness is more in *characters* and *setting* than in *theme*, will not waste his time worrying over originality. Instead, he takes an old but good piece of humor and gives to it the illusion of originality by adding a new location, perhaps a new set of circumstances, or even a character or two.[2]

---

[2] Edward Rogge and James C. Ching, *Advanced Public Speaking* (New York: Holt, Rinehart & Winston, 1966), p. 257.

Finally, composing after-dinner presentations is facilitated by using an organizational plan called a "string of beads." This plan gets its name from the fact that materials are like attractive beads that hold attention, and the thesis is like a string holding them together. Using this plan, a speaker begins by acknowledging the audience and the introductory speaker, states the thesis, develops the thesis with an illustration or two, repeats the thesis, presents further material, repeats the thesis, and concludes by thanking the audience. The thesis may be restated as frequently as necessary to focus attention, and the amount of developing material can be adjusted to the time available.

TRIBUTES

Speeches of tribute are used whenever a valued member of an organization leaves the group. The most common forms are funeral orations[3] and presentations at retirement parties. Although the circumstances giving rise to these types of tribute are substantially different, the effects on a work group can be nearly identical. In both cases, a valued member of the organization has become unavailable. The person's talents and abilities may be replaced, but accomplishments of the individual are a constant reminder of his or her absence. This fact gives rise to powerful emotions that may make it difficult for members of the group to continue working together. Speeches of tribute facilitate continued interaction by helping members cope with their emotions, and by directing extra energy in productive directions.

Because of their potential impact and the frequency with which they are presented, tributes have become fairly stylized. Both the topics discussed and the order in which they are introduced have become standardized in the minds of audiences and you must fulfill their expectations in order to accomplish your purpose. The expected topics in a funeral oration are (1) memorializing the deceased, (2) consoling family and friends, and (3) providing direction for future activity. A speech celebrating retirement uses a parallel set of topics: (1) recognizing the accomplishments of the retiring worker, (2) celebrating the event, and (3) giving directions for the future. Because there is such a marked overlap between the two types of tribute, the following paragraphs will discuss the topics for both simultaneously, noting only major differences.

Memorializing the deceased or retiring person is the first step undertaken in a tribute. Themes employed for this purpose include the accomplishments, personal qualities, and concerns or interests of the person. Accomplishments include personal, professional, and economic or political achievements, and both physical and mental qualities may be mentioned. Concerns or interests may include hob-

---

[3]The word, "eulogy," may be more familiar to you and it is often used as if it were synonymous with "funeral oration." However, strictly speaking, funeral orations are presented at a funeral ceremony, while eulogies are presented some time afterward.

bies, avocations, and pastimes, as appropriate. Keep in mind that the tribute is not a biography and that you should not try to include everything that might be said. Focus on the best and most distinctive features of the individual. Be honest and sincere, but choose carefully to give an accurate impression of the individual. You can avoid the dry, stale taste of a biography by including large amounts of anecdotal material such as quotations, examples, and illustrations from the person. Humor may be introduced when it reflects favorably, but you need to be cautious to avoid offending the audience.

Most of the differences between funeral orations and retirement addresses are found in the second topic. In a funeral oration this step requires consoling family and friends. The themes that may be used depend largely on the audience and their interests, and you should make an effort to find out enough about them to adapt to their feelings. Highly religious audiences may be affected by references to divine purpose or design. When purpose and design are not consistent with the situation, it is conventional to refer to the "mystery" of God's plan. Less religious audiences may find consolation in the fact that life and death are part of a natural process. Death is as natural as life and the passing of one person is part of the progression from generation to generation. Finally, when the deceased has been critically ill for an extended period, audiences may find consolation in the fact that death is an end to pain and suffering.

At a retirement party, the second topic is celebration of the event. I have seen some speakers handle this as if they were conducting a mock funeral, but there is a considerable risk of offending the retiree. It is better to treat the retirement as a joyous event and focus attention on opportunities now available to the retiree. Some topics that may be mentioned include opportunities to develop hobbies or other interests, time for family and friends, a chance to travel, and anything else that the retiree might look forward to and enjoy.

The final step in both presentations is unifying the members of the group who remain active. Whenever members of the audience represent a cohesive group of mutually dependent people working towards common goals, the tribute should be an occasion for rededication to the common task. It helps to summarize what the departed coworker contributed to the effort, and contributions of a lasting character should be emphasized. Lasting contributions may include what participants learned from the person, projects he or she initiated, and policies or other guides to action that the individual prepared.

SUMMARY

Social presentations are intended to facilitate interaction between participants, and this chapter describes four common forms. Speeches of introduction facilitate interaction between a speaker and an audience by preparing the audience for the presentation and establishing ground rules for subsequent interaction. The chairperson of a panel or symposium has a dual role in facilitating interaction between members of the panel and between the panel and the audience. After-dinner speeches make it possible for the audience to consider semiserious topics, and speeches of tribute help members of a group to continue working together after a valued member departs.

LEARNING ACTIVITIES

1. Select a presentation by a major public figure and prepare the introduction you would use if the speaker were making the presentation in your class. Your instructor can help you identify a suitable speech or you may select one from *Vital Speeches.*

2. Planning a symposium will require you to work with several other students. You may assemble the group either by beginning with people from diverse backgrounds who would represent different functions in an organization or you may select people with very similar backgrounds and ask each to prepare a statement on a topic of common concern. Use either approach and plan a symposium presentation in which you are the chairperson and other members of the group are the principal speakers.

3. Imagine that your class is having a formal banquet at the close of the academic term. You have been asked to be the primary after-dinner speaker and you must begin planning the presentation on the basis of what you know about the class. What common activities or interests of the group could provide a theme for your presentation? What kinds of material would you use in developing the theme? What stories or anecdotes can you adapt for presentation to the banquet? In what order would you present the materials?

4. Prepare a speech of tribute for an historical figure of interest to you. Although the person's accomplishments may be known to you, selectively present those which are most likely to have affected the other students in your class.

5. Assume that your instructor is getting ready to retire at the end of the current school term. Prepare a speech of tribute celebrating the event.

CHAPTER TEN
PUBLIC INTEREST
PRESENTATIONS

Public interest speeches are among the most demanding professional presentations because the situations that call them forth offer both great rewards and great dangers. The need for effective communication with internal and external publics has become a fact of life in modern corporations. The case at Ford Motor Company is probably typical of most organizations.

> Last year, while putting together a streamlined, more coordinated corporate communications plan for senior- and middle-management, our Ford staffers found that 500 individual departments within 16 major company organizations were routinely carrying on corporate communications with employees and external audiences. Seventy-nine percent of those departments were providing information; and 35 percent were communicating in order to influence employee or public opinion.[1]

And, as greater emphasis is placed on public relations, demands for effective public interest presentations can be expected to increase.

As I use the term here, a public interest speech is a presentation to a group (that is, a "public") that is not part of the decision-making body, but that believes

---

[1] Stephen E. Madeline, "Eight Corporate Communication Challenges for the Eighties," *The Journal of Business Communication,* 17 (1980), 18. Mr. Madeline is the Manager, Chicago Regional Public Relations Office, Ford Motor Company.

its interests are affected by actions of the body. Some possible occàsions for difficulty and the potentially affected populations are listed below:

TABLE 10.1

SITUATIONS	PUBLICS
a utility reviews plans for a nuclear generating station	consumers, employees, area residents
a school board is faced with budget reductions	teachers, staff members, students, parents
a corporation's annual report is delayed	employees, creditors, stockholders
an organization's nominating committee fails to announce candidates when expected	current officers, regulatory bodies, members
a corporation considers a plant closing	employees, merchants, local workers, union officials, property owners in the area

The situations listed in Table 10.1 indicate the variety of cases in which public reaction may affect organizational planning. They also demonstrate the variety of publics that an organization may need to address.

The number and kinds of publics that may be affected by the actions of an organization depend on the type of organization, its role in the community, and the type of actions contemplated. However, most authorities recognize several common publics that may be affected by the actions of an organization. Common publics are stockholders, consumers, governmental and regulatory bodies, community members, dealers and distributors, suppliers, creditors, and employees. In addition, special publics may be defined by demographic features (as age defines "senior citizens"), race or religion, profession, or other features uniquely affected by actions of the group.

Most large organizations have regular programs designed to inform publics affected by their actions. These programs employ numerous vehicles to convey their messages, and the following list is a sampling of the techniques available:

1. News releases aimed at radio, television, and newspapers
2. Paid advertising in radio, television, newspapers, magazines, special interest journals, and billboards
3. Educational programs and films made available to public and private schools, and to community groups
4. Personal contacts with government officials, public figures, and interest group members
5. Direct mailing to government officials, public figures, and interest group members
6. Booklets and annual reports distributed to shareholders and other interested parties

7. Newsletters, bulletins, and announcements directed to employees
8. Plant tours, open houses, and exhibits
9. Speeches by members of the organization

As you can see, public interest presentations are only one part of a comprehensive public relations program. However, the personal contact provided through speaking makes oral presentations invaluable in some situations. Oral presentations are ideal public relations vehicles for developing contact with a public, maintaining interaction, and coping with potential crises. Speeches for each of these occasions are described in the following sections.

DEVELOPING CONTACT

Public interest presentations that develop contact with a group may be necessary whenever the organization with which you work decides to expand its public relations efforts. The factors prompting such a decision are largely beyond the scope of this text, but some typical cases are worth noting. Establishing contact with groups may be the first step in a public relations program for a new organization, and established organizations may seek to develop new contacts for several reasons: Management may recognize the importance of public relations and assign a higher priority to them; policy may call for expansion in previously unexplored areas, bringing the organization into contact with new publics; and, previously unrecognized groups may be called to your attention. Moreover, groups outside the organization may recognize that they have common interests, thereby forming new publics.

Developing contact with a public requires four distinct steps: finding an audience, securing an invitation to speak, planning the presentation, and making the appearance.

The first step is finding an audience, and a clear understanding of the public you want to engage will help considerably. What is the common interest that unites the group? Who is affected by this interest? Where do members of the group live, work, and socialize? Answers to these questions will help you determine who you need to talk to and where you are likely to find them. Of course, some research may be necessary and you should consult the following sources of information:

1. Local newspaper, radio, and television meeting announcements
2. Newspaper, radio, and television programs or talk shows featuring members of public interest groups
3. The local Chamber of Commerce, and other service groups
4. The editor or reporter responsible for the local news section of your community newspaper
5. The information desk at your public library—in some communities, libraries maintain a public events calendar listing meetings and officers of community groups

6. Individual members of the public
7. Professionals (doctors, lawyers, teachers, law enforcement officials) whose work may bring them into contact with the group

Your efforts to locate the public should identify officers or leaders of the group. This will make it possible for you to approach the group to secure an invitation. It is best to route your request to the program chairperson, but any officer of the group may be able to help. It is often easiest to initiate contact through a letter and then follow-up with a phone call after a few days. Another method is to start with a phone call, and either approach is acceptable. The initial contact should be relatively brief and it ought to include the following pieces of information: your name and title, the name of the organization you represent, your reason for wanting to address the group, an indication of the subject(s) about which you are prepared to speak, and any special conditions affecting your availability. If the contact is through the mail, you should also include arrangements for contacting the other person.

The response to your request will be affected by many factors. Remember that many organizations plan programs far in advance, making it difficult to secure an invitation on short notice. However, program chairpeople like to have speakers available to fill in when scheduled programs are cancelled. The more flexible you are, the better your chances of securing an invitation.

Planning the presentation is not difficult, but you should be sensitive to three factors. First, since you are a guest and other activities may be scheduled, find out how much time has been allowed for your presentation. Exceeding the time available will put the program chairperson in an awkward position and almost insure that you will not be invited back. Second, the fact that the presentation is your first formal contact with the group requires an informative presentation in which you introduce yourself and the organization you represent. Efforts to sell products or promote a proposal are inappropriate and should be avoided. Finally, subjects appropriate for presentation are defined by the manner in which your activities affect the interests of the group. Talk about activities of your organization that have an immediate impact on members of the audience.

Using the speech format described in the basic skills section of Chapter 4, you could organize this speech as follows. The attention material should acknowledge the introduction and thank appropriate individuals for inviting you. The orientation material should introduce the organization you represent, present a brief history of the organization, and explain your role in the organization. Your purpose should be to describe current activities, and the preview should list the main topics discussed in the body. The body should describe projects or activities of your organization. Each main head can refer to a different project or activity, and your explanation should include its purpose and size, and its projected effects on the public. The conclusion should include a brief summary, and the final appeal should emphasize common interests and open the floor for questions.

The primary concern in making the presentation is conducting yourself in a manner that reflects favorably on the organization being represented. Common sense is a good guide for most situations. Remember, most members of the public to which you are speaking make judgments about the organization you represent on the basis of their personal reactions to you. This fact has a number of implications for the manner in which you present yourself. First, and perhaps foremost, you can establish a competent, professional image by being in command of the material presented. This means that you should have a good knowledge of the subject matter *and* that you should be well prepared for the particular speech. Second, you should demonstrate respect for the interests and concerns of the audience. This is accomplished in part by selecting topics of interest to the audience, but the greatest impression is made by the tone of your presentation. Sincerity and respect should be evident in your tone of voice, facial expression, stance, and gesture. Finally, members of the public will observe you throughout your visit, not just while you are speaking. This implies that you should be friendly and approachable, even when you are not the center of attention. Be courteous to everyone present, engage in social interaction with members of the public, and pay careful attention to other group activities.

MAINTAINING INTERACTION

The second function of these oral presentations is maintaining interaction with the public. The frequency with which you need to make presentations to a group depends on several factors, including their importance to your organization, the nature of your relationship with them, and the speed at which programs affecting their interests change. If a group is relatively unimportant and other factors do not call for more frequent interaction, you may try to address them once a year. When more frequent contacts are called for, you may try to approach them twice a year, three or four times a year, or even on a monthly basis. Remember, however, that your decision to maintain interaction is subject to the group's approval and they may set their own schedule for contacts with you. Making yourself available to the program chairperson and indicating when you would like to speak again is the best way of securing an invitation.

Each presentation should be followed by a letter of acknowledgement addressed to the program chairperson and/or the official responsible for your invitation. The acknowledgement should include your thanks, any further information requested by the group, and an indication of when you can be available to speak again. Providing further information is particularly important and it suggests a useful attitude toward questions from the audience. In almost any situation, there may be questions you cannot answer. Novice speakers become flustered by such questions and either dismiss them or manufacture an answer. Neither strategy reflects well on the speaker and many experienced speakers have found another approach to be more consistent with the function of public interest presentations. These speakers treat questions they cannot answer as sincere requests for information that can be provided through subsequent interaction. When the information requested can be summarized quickly, you should include it in your letter of acknowledgement. Many organizations have prepared pamphlets or brochures to answer recurrent questions and they may be included with your letter. When the information requires special interpretation for the group or exceeds the space available in the letter of acknowledgement, furnishing it calls for another presentation. Your letter may mention the volume of information and indicate that you would like to make another presentation to answer the question. This approach capitalizes on unanswerable questions by treating them as invitations for future contact.

The content of speeches aimed at maintaining interaction is largely determined by the interests of the group. The introduction should acknowledge the welcome and, as you become familiar with the group, refer to members of the audience by name. If members may have missed your earlier presentations or if your current presentation extends topics from earlier speeches, the orientation material may summarize the earlier presentations. Your purpose should be to answer earlier questions, furnish new information, or present a progress report. As always, the preview lists the main topics from the body. The topics covered in the body should be determined by the interests of the audience, but three general themes may be employed: answers to questions asked at earlier presentations, descriptions of new projects affecting the group, and status reports on activities mentioned in earlier presentations. As always, the conclusion should include a summary, and the final appeal may open the floor for questions, suggest opportunities for future interaction, or invite the audience to an open house or other gathering.

Your conduct should be governed by the same factors governing initial contacts, but you can become more casual as you get better acquainted with the group. Your familiarity can be evident through more personal interaction with members, less formal manners during presentations, and greater use of humor. In the extreme, you may conduct yourself as if you were a member of the group itself.

COPING WITH CRISES

Presentations in potential crisis situations are the most challenging speeches of any type, and recognizing situations that may become crises is an important element. Any action by an organization that affects its relationship with the public or that affects the interests of the public can initiate a crisis. The following illustrates the manner in which a crisis may develop.

Recently, a particular company has been undergoing administrative reorganization. Initially, its primary structure was a typical hierarchical organization, but the demands of its current market required development of several project groups. As more and more project groups were formed, the administrative structure became so complex that top management decided to abandon the remaining hierarchical structures and implement a matrix structure. This decision resulted in the elimination of several work units defined by the traditional structure and word of the impending change circulated rapidly. The result was a high degree of anxiety and rapid circulation of rumors, which were injurious to the decision-making organization. The rumors were accelerated by a moderate recession and predicted wholesale layoffs. The atmosphere at the plant became increasingly uneasy, production declined, and many key employees began seeking alternate employment. In spite of the rumors, the company actually anticipated no layoffs and the displaced workers were to be reassigned to other units. Many were to be given more responsible positions because the restructuring highlighted areas in which the company was understaffed. Many current staff members were scheduled to assume managerial positions directing the activities of several hundred new technicians who were to be hired in the following months.[2] The object lesson is clear: In situations where people feel threatened and yet have relatively little information about the factors threatening them, rumors circulate rapidly. These rumors result from the need to make sense out of the environment and they usually cause needless damage because they tend to be more negative than the situation actually warrants.

In this example, crisis was precipitated by change in the work environment. In more general terms, a crisis may develop whenever an organization changes policies that affect a public, alters product or service lines, or responds to changes in its environment. The unique contribution of a public relations specialist in these situations is recognizing the potential for a crisis and presenting decisions to publics in the most favorable manner possible. Whenever possible, you should inform the publics before they get the news through other channels. This minimizes opportunities for damaging rumors and it reassures each public by demonstrating your concern for them. When prior notice is impossible, the presentation should follow implementation of the decision as quickly as possible.

When potential crises develop, you will probably need to arrange a special opportunity to address the public. If the public is an internal group, you can call a special meeting. When the public is an external group, you should approach the program chairperson or chief officer and ask for the opportunity to explain to the group changes made in your organization that will affect them. Occasionally, the group officer will say that there is little time available and he or she will volunteer to make the announcement for you. Although the offer may be well intended, you should avoid it because the extra link in the communication chain increases opportunities for distortion, and telling the officer makes it impossible for you to control the timing of disclosure.

Some people recommend a climax order of presentation for speeches of this

---

[2] Claude D. Beaver and Fred E. Jandt, "A Pilot Study on Alienation and Anxiety During a Rumored Plant Closing," *Journal Of Applied Communication Research*, 1 (1973), 105–114, report a similar incident. In their example, a plant manufacturing electrical appliances was compromised by the circulation of rumors. In the twenty-three years prior to the incident, the plant had grown rapidly and the parent company had transferred a number of production lines to the plant. Trouble was precipitated by the parent company's announcement that a new product line would be assigned to another plant and by local newspaper reports that the plant would be shut down for four weeks and production of a major product line would be reduced by 50 percent. The effect of these events was very predictable: high degrees of anxiety among the workers and rapid circulation of rumors predicting permanent closure.

type. Using a climax order, you begin by commenting on your relationship with the group, explain the factors responsible for your decision, and announce the decision near the end of the speech. The rationale for using a climax order is that it provides a favorable context for your announcement, but its value is often limited. In most situations, the fact that you have requested a special opportunity to address the group indicates that something special is happening and the group will want to hear it as quickly as possible. Moreover, if word of the impending change had "leaked out" and reached the group through other channels, the audience may be deaf to your explanations until you acknowledge the information they have already received.

An anticlimax order, in which you announce the decision early in the speech and explain it afterwards, is valuable in dealing with a potential crisis. Using an anticlimax order, you can begin with the attention material, thanking the group for inviting you on short notice. The orientation material summarizes the decision or action that may initiate crisis; your purpose is to explain why the decision was made or how it may affect members of the audience. The preview lists the main heads from the body. The body of the presentation should include reasons for the decision or action, the anticipated effects, and—when appropriate—measures you have taken to minimize hardships for the public. The conclusion should include a brief summary, and the final appeal should indicate whether or not you can answer questions and when additional information will be available.

Your manner in presenting the speech should be consistent with the situation. If the anticipated effects of change are favorable, you may appear pleased; if they are unfavorable, you should appear concerned and serious. Above all, you should demonstrate your concern for members of the audience by reflecting emotions appropriate for their situation.

SUMMARY

Public interest speeches are presentations to a group that believes its interests are affected by actions of the organization represented by the speaker. Major corporations have elaborate public relations strategies in which public interest presentations have specific roles in developing contact, maintaining interaction, and coping with potential crises.

LEARNING ACTIVITIES

1. Review the public relations activities of any group or organization to which you belong. Who are the publics affected by activities of the group? What media are used to inform these publics of the group's activities? Are there significant publics who are not regularly informed of the group's activities? What steps could you take to develop or maintain contact with

these publics? What procedures are available to inform the publics in event of a potential crisis?

2. With several other members of your class, form a hypothetical organization and begin planning a public relations strategy. With what publics should you develop and maintain contact? How will you locate them? How would the activities of your organization affect them? What public relations vehicles can you use to develop and maintain contact with them? Who will be the primary spokesperson for your organization? What personal qualities does your spokesperson have?

3. Major corporations usually manage public relations activities with considerable care. If there is such a corporation in your community, monitor their public relations activities for a period of time. Try to identify the rationale for these activities. With what publics are they concerned? How have they chosen their spokespeople? What procedures do they employ when faced with a potential crisis?

4. Assume that you have been asked to help an executive prepare a presentation for an organization's annual meeting with stockholders. You know that the presentation will be attended by representatives of the local news media and you know that the executive would like to create a favorable impression to encourage investors to purchase additional stock. Recent earnings have been substantial, reflecting a 25 percent increase in revenues over the previous year, but the company has been under attack from groups opposed to further corporate expansion. In addition, the company is engaged in hard negotiations with the union representing its employees, and you want to avoid discussion of profits because you don't want to encourage the union to make unrealistic demands. What topics would you recommend the executive discuss? How would you suggest they be organized? What kinds of developing material would you employ? What other factors would you want to consider?

CHAPTER ELEVEN
SPEECHES TO ACTUATE

Speeches intended to get an audience to take action are called speeches to actuate, and the most common forms are sales and persuasion presentations. Many authors distinguish between sales presentations and persuasive speeches, but commercial sales and persuasion are so closely linked that professional vocabularies seldom distinguish between them. It is common to call whatever the speaker wants an audience to do a *proposal,* and the term covers a myriad of activities. Proposals may call for the purchase of a particular product or service; for a change in company policy or for the establishment of new policies; for the development of new product or service lines; for the termination of commercial relationships; for the development of new sources of supply; and even for the initiation of legal action against suppliers, delinquent customers, or competitors. Thus all the activities that we normally associate with sales or persuasion in other contexts are included in the proposal concept. This usage causes some ambiguity, but confusion can be reduced by identifying what action any proposal calls for. For example, someone who ''makes a proposal'' is requesting the audience to take a specific action, a group ''accepting a proposal'' agrees to do what the speaker requested, and ''negotiating a proposal'' usually means requesting changes in some feature(s) of a product or action.

The use of the term, ''proposal,'' to describe the object of both sales and persuasive presentations is more than coincidental. From the receivers' point of view there is little reason to distinguish between these presentations. Buying a product requires action just as any other behavior requires action. Reliance upon the recommendations of another person—the speaker—involves the same requirements for trust in both cases. In other words, both sales presentations and persuasive speeches try to get the audience to act in the way the speaker wants. And, as you will see in a moment, the same strategies work in both cases.

Use of speech to affect the conduct of others is a significant part of our daily lives. Before we talk about approaches used to motivate an audience, it may be helpful to comment on some misconceptions surrounding the subject. People often identify persuasive speaking with a particular approach to delivery. A persuasive speech is thought of as one in which the speaker uses a loud and affected voice, displays considerable emotion, and employs dramatic gestures. And, effective salespeople are frequently thought of as aggressive or pushy people who "refuse to take 'no' for an answer." These images are misconceptions, not because the techniques described are ineffective—we know all too well that they work in some situations—but because they focus attention on secondary elements. The agitation displayed by some speakers is effective only when the speaker is well regarded by the audience, or when the audience believes its interests are similar to those of the speaker. Thus, the popular image of persuasive speaking is appropriate only in situations where the audience has already sided with the speaker. Capitalizing upon favorable reactions is an extremely effective technique, but even when the resources of personality are unavailable, effective speeches can still be composed through the proper management of content.

In a similar vein, the conduct of hyperaggressive salespeople is effective in some situations—such as bullying a timid person into signing a contract—but recent consumer legislation has reduced the effectiveness of such techniques. More significantly, the stereotypical behaviors of door-to-door salespeople are wholly inappropriate to professional sales situations in which prospective customers are generally well educated, intelligent, and accustomed to dismissing offensive individuals. Here again, proper management of speech content is a more certain route to success.

In most situations, the only approach to actuating an audience, which does not depend on audience reactions to the speaker or on personal aggression, is an approach that emphasizes the subject matter of the presentation. This approach is known as a *rational* approach to actuation. Its use requires identifying the demands of the audience with regard to the proposal and managing the subject matter of the presentation in a manner that answers those demands. The basic premise of this approach is that when you attempt to induce a group of people to take action, you must provide them with the kinds of information they demand as justification for action. Even though the members of an audience may be unable to articulate the specific materials necessary to move them, the questions, uncertainties, and objections that have prevented them from taking the desired action create a set of demands to which the speaker must respond in order to achieve his purpose.

These demands can be conceptualized as a call for materials that will overcome particular barriers to action. A review of these barriers may help you to visualize the rational approach. The first barrier encountered in attempting to produce action is *novelty* of the proposal. Novelty is a barrier to action because most people feel uncomfortable in situations where they do not know precisely what is expected from them, and this holds true whether the situation results from talking an action recommended by the speaker or from using a product with which they are unfamiliar. Audiences in this situation demand an extended description of the speaker's proposal.

Once novelty has been overcome, a speaker may encounter a second barrier: *Satisfaction*. Satisfaction is a barrier when an audience is so comfortable with existing conditions that it is unwilling to take the risk associated with change. A satisfied audience literally demands the speaker to show them a reason for change, a need to act. A speaker must answer this demand by demonstrating problems in the existing situation that could be rectified by adopting the proposal.

Once an audience is ready to act, *uncertainty* regarding the proper action is likely to pose a barrier. An audience in this condition demands that a speaker help them choose between alternative proposals. The choice is guided best by a careful comparison of the alternatives showing that the speaker's preference is also most desirable to the audience. Finally, an audience may understand the proposal, recognize the need to act, and accept the speaker's choice, but remain unwilling to act because of *objections*. These objections result from anticipation of negative consequences following action. A speaker faced with an audience at this point should try to identify as precisely as possible the objections and respond to each in turn. The audience demands the security of knowing that any potential difficulties have been anticipated and can be resolved.

It is extremely important to keep audience demands and appropriate answers to each in mind. An audience halted by novelty needs to have the proposal explained; an audience halted by satisfaction demands the speaker show them why the proposal should be accepted; an audience unable to choose between alternatives demands a careful comparison; and, an audience unable to act because of objections demands answers to its specific concerns.

It is easy to imagine an audience that makes all four demands upon the speaker. For example, a salesperson with a product unlike those used by potential customers in the past must first overcome the discomfort created by the novelty of the product. Then, the speaker must show that there is a need for the product, and that the particular product is superior to those offered by other manufacturers. Finally, he or she must answer any objections the audience may raise; typically, the speaker must show that the product is worth the expense and that appropriate financing is available. Thus, a speech might tackle all four steps in a single presentation. A speaker might start by explaining the proposal, show a need for it, demonstrate its superiority to other proposals and answer any objections the audience may raise. However, such a speech is most likely to be presented by a relatively inexperienced speaker. Most audiences lack the patience to sit through a speech long enough to deal adequately with all four topics. As a result, speakers who attempt all four steps in a single presentation usually find that they have accomplished little. They have said too little about too many distinct topics, and the audience remains unconvinced or becomes confused by the amount of new material presented. The alternative to such "one-shot" approaches is to plan a series of presentations. With an audience that knows nothing of the proposal, it may be necessary to arrange as many as four separate presentations, and in each cope with one of the specific demands made by the audience at the moment of presentation. Thus, while the overall purpose is moving the audience to action, the speaker must identify a series of intermediate purposes that enable him to achieve his final objective. These intermediate purposes consist of meeting the demands of the audience at each step in the progression noted. This approach gives rise to four distinct streategies of actuation displayed in Table 11.1.

TABLE 11.1

BARRIER	AUDIENCE DEMAND	IMMEDIATE PURPOSE/ SPEAKER STRATEGY
Novelty	Explanation	Describe product or action
Satisfaction	Reasons for action	Create need
Uncertainty	Comparison of alternatives	Demonstrate superiority of product or action
Objections	Response to objections	Answer objections

Bear in mind that you might attempt to answer all four demands in a single presentation, but your chances of doing so successfully are quite small. Chances of success are increased markedly by tackling each barrier in turn through a series of presentations. The notion of series or sequence in answering the demands of an audience underlies the specific strategies outlined in this section. Choice of strategy should result from understanding the specific audience to which a speech is addressed. Prior knowledge of the audience is an invaluable guide in making the selection, and chatting informally with members of the audience prior to a presentation will provide considerable assistance. When there is no opportunity to evaluate an audience in advance of the presentation, you may prepare all four speeches and choose between them on the basis of initial audience reactions.

STRATEGY I: OVERCOMING NOVELTY

Speeches to actuate through explanation are used in situations where the audience is unfamiliar with the proposal. In these cases, novelty is the primary barrier to action and your immediate purpose is to overcome this barrier by explaining the action or product. You will probably find this strategy relatively easy to employ because finished speeches are most similar to informative speeches you have mastered already. In fact, employing this strategy requires no concepts that you don't know already and few specialized adaptations are necessary. The only real "trick" is recognizing that a speech of explanation is required to overcome audience resistance. However, you should pay particular attention to the topics introduced, your use of language, and the introduction.

A special topic pattern of organization in the body gives great flexibility and the topics explored should reflect the probable concerns of the audience. Generally, an audience of potential customers will want answers to the following questions:

1. What is it?
2. How does it work?
3. What must I do to use it?

An audience asked to take an action will usually ask a similar series of questions:

1. What do you want me to do?
2. How do I do it?
3. What will happen to me as I do it?

Answering each of these questions in turn, you should aim to make the audience feel as comfortable as possible, and the bulk of developing materials should be types that explain or clarify. Definitions, restatements, and real or hypothetical examples and illustrations are all ideal forms of developing material in such speeches. However, comparisons and contrasts are particularly useful because they enhance audience comfort by identifying the novel with the familiar.

Use of language is a special concern in employing this strategy. Since novelty is likely to make the audience uncomfortable, use of words, terms, or phrases that are unfamiliar will cause severe problems because they make the audience feel even less at ease with the materials. Avoid this difficulty by using terms from the active vocabulary of your audience, defining unfamiliar terms that you must employ, and use frequent comparisons and contrasts to relate items to things with which the audience is familiar.

The introduction to the speech should be structured as any other, but composing the attention material may be more difficult than usual because direct references to the product or action may prove disquieting to the audience. Humor may be particularly effective if it emphasizes interests and experiences you share with the audience. Moreover, it may establish a relaxed tone for the presentation. Direct references to the product or action may be incorporated in the orientation material, and a brief historical sketch of the product or proposed action may be included. The purpose statement should indicate the speaker's intention to explain the product or action, and the preview will list the topics explored. Finally, the conclusion will include a summary, as always, and the final appeal may begin by suggesting the need for the product or action.

STRATEGY II: CREATING A NEED

A second type of situation is created when the audience already understands the proposal. These situations may be generated when you have already given a speech explaining the product or action, or when your audience has received information from another source. Novelty is no longer a barrier to action, but the fact that the audience has not done what you want them to do indicates that there is some other barrier. The barrier you now face may be *satisfaction*. An audience that is satisfied with the existing situation will be reluctant to act because the existing situation is "good enough" for them. The product or action you have explained may be interesting, but they feel no need to adopt it. This barrier exists because people feel secure in using accepted products and following accepted patterns of action. Any change involves some risk, and few audiences are willing to accept a risk when there is no reason to make a change.

Satisfaction and the security of accepted patterns are powerful barriers to action. Throughout history they have represented a major barrier to technological innovation. The maxim, "Build a better mouse trap and the world will flock to your door," is true only when the world feels a need for a better mouse trap. In most situations, changes and innovations are matters of curiosity until someone shows that they are needed—that is, until someone finds something wrong in existing situations that can be rectified by using the innovation.

When you face an audience that is satisfied with the existing situation, your task is to create a need for the product or action. Unfortunately, the simplicity of the foregoing statement belies the actual difficulties you are likely to face in attempting to create a need. Overcoming these difficulties requires that you have an understanding of the kinds of things that motivate people to act and of the way these things may be employed by a speaker.

Abraham Maslow has developed a theory of motivation that throws considerable light on human behavior. According to Maslow, people are motivated to behave in ways that satisfy five types or groups of needs. These needs are physiological needs, safety needs, membership needs, esteem needs, and self-actualization needs. *Physiological needs* consist of everything that affects the physical functions of our bodies. This category includes nourishment, shelter, clothing, and sexual activity. These physiological needs are immediate concerns only in primitive societies, but they are affected by many features of organized societies. For example, in modern societies, the primitive needs are satisfied through employment and income, which makes it possible to purchase food, drink, housing, clothing, and so forth. *Security* needs center on the desirability of a stable, predictable environment. In primitive terms, they involve protection from physical attacks and measures to insure the continuity of food supplies. In complex societies, they include the provision of police and fire protection, insurance coverage, and preservation or accumulation of financial resources. *Membership* needs are concerned with an individual's desire to be part of an organization or social group. In primitive areas, developing and maintaining stable relationships with a family, clan, or tribe are membership needs. In complex societies, the need focuses on opportunities for participation in social activities and professional associations. *Esteem* needs relate to an individual's need for both self-respect and the need to be respected by members of groups with whom he or she associates. Primitive societies recognized these needs by presenting the choicest cuts of meat to the best hunters and other rewards to especially capable warriors. Modern organizations do the same with trophies, awards, and bonuses. Finally, *self-actualization* needs are displayed in an individual's desire to do the best job possible in selected activities. They always involve the development of personal attributes and abilities for the pure pleasure of doing so. Rituals in primitive societies may recognize these needs, but the demands for survival are so great that self-actualization plays a limited role in daily activity. However, self-actualization is quite apparent in modern society. Many hobbies—especially solitary ones—result from the search for self-actualization, and people who work to develop abilities unrelated to their professional and personal responsibilities do so in response to these needs.

The order of categories in Maslow's theory reflects the sequence in which people experience the particular needs. According to Maslow, people experience the needs in a predictable order, beginning with physiological needs and progressing in steps or levels to self-actualization needs. Thus, physiological needs are the most basic needs and are experienced before any of the others. Someone who is hungry probably does not recognize any other need until he or she has been fed. Similarly, someone who has had physiological needs satisfied will begin to experience security needs, once a sufficient food supply has been established, for example, the person will take steps to preserve food for the days when hunting is poor. It is easy to observe life patterns consistent with Maslow's predictions. Physiological needs are the primary motivators of the urban poor. Urban residents who have satisfied their physiological needs find security to be their greatest concern. They often attempt to move to more desirable (that is, safer) neighborhoods. Suburban residents are likely to join neighborhood or community organizations to fulfill membership needs, and they may enroll in self-improvement courses to enhance their esteem. Finally, hobbies are likely to occupy significant amounts of time only for those who have fulfilled other needs.

This sequential ordering is important for you as a speaker because it may help you determine which need or motive is most likely to influence your audience at a particular time. Whenever an audience has fulfilled a given need, the next level is most likely to be pursued. That is, the next level is most likely to provide a compelling motive for action. Thus, you may plan a persuasive presentation to appeal to the particular unfilled need.

Alternately, you may generate a need by showing that the existing situation somehow threatens to undermine the existing levels of need satisfaction. For example, continued dependence on a currently-used product may threaten security because the manufacturer is unstable; reliance upon a particular executive may be unwise because he does not feel a personal attachment to the firm; and continued production of a particular model may threaten physiological need satisfaction because it is becoming less popular and will become a drain on resources. Developing a need this way has been studied under the headings "threat appeals" and "fear appeals," and the two terms are used more or less interchangeably to "refer to those contents of a persuasive communication which allude to or describe *unfavorable consequences* that are alleged to result from failure to adopt and adhere to the communicator's conclusions."[1]

Although generating a need by showing that existing situations threaten current levels of satisfaction is an effective strategy, special caution must be used. This caution is necessary because showing that current levels of satisfaction are threatened may generate levels of fear that could immobilize the audience or lead them to reject the speaker. Research to date is not conclusive in defining situations in which high levels of fear or threat work to a speaker's advantage, but it appears that high fear appeals are useful only when the speaker is a highly credible source, the topic is important to receivers, and the receivers believe they can do something to alter the situation. Erwin P. Bettinghaus' discussion is a handy summary.

> Obviously, additional work needs to be done on this topic. But the research suggests that if the communicator knows little about his audience, he is better advised to cast his message into a form which does *not* use high levels of fear appeal. On the other hand, if the communicator knows something about the importance of the topic to the receiver, or knows something about the credibility of any sources to be used in the message, or knows the personality of the audience, much higher levels of fear appeal might prove to be effective.[2]

In composing a speech to develop a need, you should be sure to take advantage of materials the audience has already accepted. It is especially important that you remind them of the special features of the product or action, and that you remind them of materials used to overcome novelty. This is best done in the introduction and a fairly long orientation section may be the result.

STRATEGY III: COMPARISON OF ALTERNATIVES

A third type of persuasive problem may arise when the audience understands your proposal and accepts the need for adopting it. This situation usually results when there are several competing products on the market or when several actions might satisfy the needs developed in the second step. An audience at this point is literally unable to select between the alternatives available to them. This situation calls for decisive action by the speaker because the time and effort you have already invested may be lost. The need the audience feels may lapse, or the audience may

[1] Carl I. Hovland, Irving L. Janis, and Harold H. Kelly, *Communication and Persuasion* (New Haven: Yale University Press, 1953), p. 60.

[2] Erwin P. Bettinghaus, *Persuasive Communication,* 2nd ed. (New York: Holt, Rinehart & Winston, 1973), p. 159.

buy another product—in effect, your efforts have been turned to a competitor's advantage.

An audience that is unable to choose between the alternatives understands the product or action and recognizes a need for it. Your job as a speaker is to help them make an intelligent choice by comparing the available alternatives. Your knowledge of the product or action should enable you to identify a number of comparisons that can work to your advantage. But, not all comparisons are of interest to an audience and some comparisons that work to your disadvantage may be prominent in the audience's mind. Choosing comparisons requires attention to the interests of the audience you encounter. When the audience is composed of members of a single organization, the organization's goals tell you which comparisons are interesting. When audience members do not represent a single organization, you can employ critical dimensions that should interest members of any audience.

These dimensions are determined by very general conceptions of good and bad, right and wrong. Such general conceptions are called "values" and they become "social values" when shared by members of a society. A precise definition is difficult because the concepts have been used in many different contexts. However, most applications display common properties that are convenient means of characterizing values.

> What are experienced by individuals as values have these qualities. (1) They have a conceptual element—they are more than pure sensations, emotions, reflexes, or so-called needs. Values are abstractions drawn from the flux of the individual's immediate experience. (2) They are affectively charged: they represent actual or potential emotional mobilization. (3) Values are not the concrete goals of action, but rather the *criteria* by which goals are chosen. (4) Values are important, not "trivial" or of slight concern.[3]

From our point of view, it is important to emphasize that values are not merely individual or personal phenomena. They reflect the nature of society and general value orientations characterize all members of a society. This is important because you can be pretty sure that any member of the society will be interested in comparisons that involve the values of the society.

The dominant values that characterize American society are presented here:

Achievement and Success	Progress	Science and Secular
Activity and Work	Material Comfort	Rationality
Moral Orientation	Equality	Nationalism-Patriotism
Humanitarian Mores	Freedom	Democracy
Efficiency and Practicality	External Conformity	Individual Personality

This list should not be used as a substitute for an understanding of the particular audience you face because there is considerable variation from group to

---

[3] Robin M. Williams, Jr., *American Society: A Sociological Interpretation,* 2nd ed. (New York: Knopf, 1966), p. 400. © Alfred A. Knopf, Inc.

group within a society. Major variations include the way in which the values are interpreted, the relative importance of each, and accepted means of fulfilling each. However, when you have no surer guide, these general values are all items that may suggest important comparisons.

As you develop comparisons between products or actions, you are bound to discover some areas in which your proposal is inferior to others. This is inevitable because there are very, very few perfect solutions. This fact may force you to make some very difficult choices. Should you mention comparisons that work to your disadvantage? How much attention should you give to negative comparisons? How should you build negative comparisons into your speech? Unfortunately, there are no easy answers to these questions because both ethical and pragmatic concerns must be considered. The ethical factors are most difficult to discuss. My personal preference is to include the negative information in sufficient detail to give the audience a reasonable understanding of the situation they face. This ethical position includes some latitude because ''reasonable understanding'' is an imprecise notion.

Pragmatic concerns in deciding whether or not to include negative information involve four factors: audience sophistication, audience knowledge, audience exposure to other information, and continuity of your relationship with the audience.

Less sophisticated audiences usually expect easy answers and may be confused or unsettled by the inclusion of negative information. Sophisticated audiences realize that few choices are clear-cut and expect you to present both sides of an issue. Failure to present negative information to a sophisticated audience reduces your credibility and increases the probability that they will search for additional information.

Audiences lacking prior knowledge about the alternatives are more likely to rely solely on your recommendations and may have difficulty mastering complex comparisons. Audiences already familiar with the alternatives will expect you to answer their questions and to acknowledge the superiority of other products in areas they have already mentioned. Failure to recognize the advantages of other alternatives will make you appear less knowledgeable and trustworthy, and increase the chances that your audience will try to find a more reliable source of information.

The extent to which your audience will be exposed to presentations favoring other alternatives also requires attention. If the audience is unlikely to hear opposing viewpoints before the final decision, you may not need to include negative information. However, if they hear opposing presentations, negative information you have not anticipated will have enormous impact. You should introduce negative information if only to reduce its effects when someone else discusses the subject.

Finally, you should consider the continuity of your relationship with the audience. If you are unlikely to encounter the audience or its members in the future, you can feel relatively free to omit negative information. However, if you are likely to work with them in the future, you should build a trusting relationship by presenting all of the relevant information—even if it costs you a sale this time. Failure to present negative information that your audience discovers on their own can be a substantial embarrassment. The more negative the information, the greater the chance it will cause your audience difficulty in the future and the greater the demand for its presentation.

When any of the preceding considerations indicate that you should include negative information, you need to choose where in the speech to present it. This is a relatively easy decision. Research on the order of presentation shows that an audience is most likely to remember and to act upon information presented in either the first third or the final third of a presentation. This means that you should introduce materials favoring your position during the first and final thirds of a presentation, and block the negative information into the center third. This also provides a convenient limit to the amount of negative material you include: It should consist of no more than one-third of the body of your presentation.

There is one exception to the practice of presenting negative information in the center third of the speech. This exception covers cases in which the audience is so impressed by negative information that they are unwilling, or unable,[4] to listen to your presentation until their concerns have been addressed. These are very difficult situations, and your only chance is to review negative information very early in the speech, perhaps even in the introduction, in order to make the audience responsive to your presentation. This does not mean that you must agree with the audience, but it does mean that you must show that you understand their concerns. You may even go so far as paraphrasing what you understand their concerns to be before launching into the material favoring your position. The effect of this step is similar to the effect of active listening discussed in Part III, and it works because it allows you to deal with the audience's emotions before working through the subject matter.

In comparing alternatives in the persuasive speech, you should retrace the earlier steps in the persuasive process. Your orientation explains the product or action, and recalls the need for it. The preview will list the topics explored. Finally, the conclusion will include a summary, as always, and the final appeal may begin by suggesting the need for timely commitment.

STRATEGY IV: ANSWERING OBJECTIONS

The final type of persuasive strategy is answering objections. This is a very specialized type of presentation and it is used less often than the other three because it is designed for an audience at a stage in the decision process that is

---

[4] Research on perception shows that an audience may be literally unable to receive information that is inconsistent with their expectations. Related studies of persuasion demonstrate that an audience not only fails to hear opposing points of view, but actively develops arguments to defend their own point of view.

relatively rare. Specifically, this speech should be used only when the audience (1) feels comfortable with the proposal, (2) recognizes a need for action, and (3) agrees that your proposal is the best option available. This particular strategy is used less often than the others because most audiences that meet these conditions are ready to act without further effort by the speaker. However, some audiences still hesitate because specific objections have been raised. These objections may be shared by many members of the audience or they may be of concern only to a few, respected members. However, the opposition of even a few members can cause action when the group as a whole is unwilling to offend them and is unable to answer them.

Dealing with this situation is particularly difficult because you must respond to objections without offending the audience. By the time an audience reaches this stage, you are likely to have developed sources of information that can help you identify the objections. If you are a member of the group, you should have been present when the objections were voiced. If you are an "outsider," members who favor your alternative are probably more than willing to share information with you. Finally, you may call upon officers or influential members of the group to explain the continued inaction.

Whatever source you use—and you may want to use several—you should start planning your presentation by compiling a list of objections. The list should be as thorough and accurate as you can make it, and you should state each objection in a fair and neutral manner. You want to look at the objections objectively and you may be forced to agree with some of them. Once you have listed objections, cluster them into units sharing common themes. You must reduce them to a small enough number so that you can handle them meaningfully in the time available. Then, develop responses to each. Common responses include providing further information, making concessions, identifying misconceptions underlying the objections, and agreeing with the objection in principle, while pointing out that it is less important in practice.

Composing the speech by responding to objections is ticklish business because you must deal with the substance of the disagreement without creating hard feelings. This calls for careful planning of the speech and particular care in stating your responses. Above all, you must avoid attacking—or seeming to attack—individual members of the audience. You may secure good will by acknowledging the importance of their concerns, and it is best to begin by emphasizing common interests and points on which everyone agrees. The points of aggreement should include an understanding of your proposal, the need for action, and a preference for your alternative. In fact, if agreement on these points has not been reached, a speech of response is inappropriate.

The summary of common concerns and points of agreement should occupy most of the introduction. Your purpose is to "respond to some objections that have been raised," and the preview should list the objections in the order you will discuss them. Each main head in the body of the presentation should be an objection, or a closely-related group of objections, and the material you use in responding to it. In each, state the objection(s) fully and accurately, taking care to show that you understand it and the reasons supporting it. You may also wish to acknowledge the good faith and sincerity of people who introduced the objection. Then, answer the objection to the best of your ability without attacking the people who introduced it. Avoid personal attack because you must avoid alienating members of the audience.

SUMMARY

Speeches to actuate include all efforts to get an audience to accept a proposal and common forms include persuasion and sales. This chapter introduces a rational approach to persuasion in which the speaker first recognizes the barrier(s) preventing an audience from acting and then presents material designed to overcome the barrier(s) encountered. Common barriers are novelty, satisfaction, uncertainty, and objections, and specific strategies are used to overcome each.

LEARNING ACTIVITIES

1. Some door-to-door salespeople are very skilled at identifying barriers to action and introducing appropriate material. When a salesperson calls on you, your parents, or a friend, observe the way he or she deals with the potential customer. Less-skilled salespeople will launch into a predetermined pitch regardless of audience reactions, but more skilled salespeople will begin by asking questions to determine what they must do with the audience. Is the salesperson you are observing working through a predetermined pitch or adapting to the audience? How did he or she identify demands of the audience? What barrier is this person attempting to overcome? What kinds of material are being used? Is the salesperson's approach consistent with your knowledge of the audience and of persuasive strategies?

2. Select a product and prepare to sell it to your classroom audience. To what extent is the audience familiar with the product? Do they feel a need for a product of this type? Do they have sufficient information to choose between this and competing products? Are there objections to be answered before they are willing to buy? If you can't answer these questions with certainty, prepare several potential speeches: one to overcome novelty, one to generate a need, one to compare alternatives, and one to answer objections. In addition, prepare a general introduction that you could use with any of these presentations and that solicits audience reactions (feedback) to the product. If you have a chance to make the presentation, begin with the general introduction, but present only the body that seems most appropriate to the audience reactions.

3. Assume that you are an extremely persuasive speaker and that you can talk your classroom audience into doing anything you want. There are no

limitations on what you can accomplish except those you impose. Which of the following speeches would you be willing to make under those circumstances? Which would you be unwilling to make? Why?

    a. A speech to convince members of the audience to contribute to a scholarship fund from which all students would benefit.

    b. A speech to convince members of the audience to contribute to a scholarship fund from which minority students would benefit.

    c. A speech to convince members of the audience to contribute to a scholarship fund from which only members of your family would benefit.

    d. A speech to convince members of the audience to contribute to a scholarship fund from which only you would benefit.

PART THREE
PRESENTATIONS IN DYADS AND MEETINGS

Earlier chapters of this text have introduced communication skills by explaining their use in formal speaking situations. These situations are defined by the fact that a single speaker presents a body of information to a relatively passive audience composed of people who are unlikely to interrupt. Because these situations limit opportunities for interaction, speakers must rely on largely predetermined message units to achieve their purposes, and the demand for thorough preparation is at a premium. Of course, in even the most restrictive settings speakers need to monitor audience reactions and adapt to particular interests and concerns evidenced by feedback. And the audience usually has an opportunity to ask questions following the presentation.

Even when speakers and audiences take full advantage of the variations possible, the formal character of most presentational settings restricts the amount of interaction between speaker and audience, and it imposes a number of other limitations on each. Faced with the mechanics of gathering an audience, speakers may lose the chance to: (1) determine when a report is to be made, (2) select the specific topics discussed, (3) choose the social context and location, and (4) tailor content and structure to the unique abilities and interests of each recipient. Audiences are unable to ask questions and secure clarification, make suggestions or openly share ideas and reactions, react to or extend the comments of the speaker, or solicit immediate responses from the speaker on related concerns.

The limitations imposed on speakers and audiences during formal presentations distinguish formal presentations from other forms of oral communication. Public speaking courses are taught throughout the country largely because learning to cope with these limitations is a demanding task. However, oral communication often occurs in contexts other than formal presentations. These other contexts include dyadic (two person) encounters and small group meetings. These other situations are encountered far more often than formal presentations. Many of the skills used in formal presentations are equally serviceable elsewhere, but their application to dyadic and small group settings requires sensitivity to the characteristics of each. The following chapters are intended to offer guides for applying presentational skills to dyadic and small group settings.

CHAPTER TWELVE
PRESENTATIONAL ACTIVITIES IN DYADS

Dyadic communication is any communication that takes place between two people. It is far less formal than presentational speaking and it usually occurs in situations that allow both participants to assume active roles. Textbooks often refer to it as interpersonal communication, and studies have shown it to be a nearly constant activity in most professions. The occasions for interpersonal communication are almost endless, and you are likely to experience dyadic communication in many forms: giving instructions to a subordinate, receiving directions from your superior, soliciting information from coworkers, building relationships with customers, and sharing ideas with professional colleagues. You may also discuss programs with potential customers, interview prospective employees, conduct appraisal interviews, receive and make informal progress reports, and learn to appreciate the problems of coworkers and subordinates.

In the last few years, a number of excellent books on interpersonal communication have become available, and many books on organizational communication include lengthy sections on dyadic communication. This chapter and the next discuss five of the most important dyadic communication activities you are likely to encounter: building relationships through communication, receiving information, being interviewed for a position, reporting to your boss, and performance appraisal and feedback.

COMMUNICATION AND INTERPERSONAL RELATIONSHIPS

Interpersonal relationships in all fields are extremely complex and those on the job are no exception. In fact, they are more complicated than most because work may place people with few things in common together and may make them dependent upon one another. A project manager with nearly twenty-five years of experience describes relationships between superiors and subordinates as the "most complex interpersonal relationship anyone ever encounters." This is certainly true, because all of the factors affecting any interpersonal relationship are operative at the same time that both people must perform the roles dictated by their formal positions. Moreover, the professional and interpersonal roles may conflict with one another and both participants may suffer as a consequence. Effective communication is essential to establishing a relationship that will allow two people to work closely with one another.

Interpersonal Relationships Are Complex

Interpersonal relationships are complex because we think of and react to other people according to a number of different concerns. These concerns are often called "dimensions," and they have been organized in different ways by several scholars. The central factors seem to be liking, trust, shared meanings, and role definitions.

Of these four dimensions, most people are aware of the first two, and the terms, "liking" and "trust," are used in ordinary conversation. Liking is nearly synonymous with "affection," and the degree to which people in a relationship like each other determines the amount of time they are willing to spend together. Trust reflects the extent to which one person is willing to rely on or put faith in another. Daily activities require us to trust those we encounter to a limited degree, and growing relationships are usually associated with increasing amounts of trust. For example, when driving a car we must trust other drivers to keep right, and riding in a car driven by another person implies that we trust them to exercise a certain amount of caution and good judgment.

We speak the same language as so many other people that we seldom think of shared meanings as a dimension of interpersonal relationships. However, as was pointed out in the chapter on language, the meaning we attach to words depends on our experiences with them. We share certain experiences with large numbers of people—for example, reading the morning newspaper—and we share meanings that are broad enough for the task. When two people live, work, and play together, they share a broader range of experiences and the language they use reflects that fact. The pet names members of some families have for one another are good examples of this phenomenon. These names embody experiences shared by the family members, and much of the meaning is lost to outsiders, even though they may understand the literal meaning of the words used.

The final dimension is the extent to which the participants in a relationship share common role definitions. This does not mean that both participants do the same thing in every situation, but it does mean that both can anticipate what the other will do. For example, most of us experience some discomfort when we meet another person for the first time because we are not sure how we are expected to react and how our behavior will be interpreted. As our relationships grow, we become more comfortable as we learn what the other person expects and how he or she behaves. Both parties in mature relationships react in predictable ways and the strength of the relationship results from the value of predictability in coping with frequently encountered situations.

Dimensions in Professional Relationships

All four of the dimensions mentioned above are important in professional relationships. Liking is the dimension most frequently questioned by many professionals. Occasionally, people still make statements such as, ''I don't care if my men like me as long as they do what they are told.'' There would be few problems if things were as simple as the statement implies. However, employees are unlikely to perform well for someone they dislike, and they may even deliberately sabotage an unpopular superior. There are numerous stories of subordinates who seriously damaged the career of a superior through malicious obedience—doing exactly what they were told even though they knew it would produce disastrous results.

The importance of the other three dimensions is seldom questioned. An employee's willingness to support a superior on policy questions, to accept his or her recommendations, and to perform services with little personal benefit is determined by the extent to which the employee trusts the superior. More importantly, the level of trust determines a subordinate's ability to discuss problems with a superior and to report problems to the superior. The critical feature of interpersonal roles is the extent to which participants share a common definition of their relationship. To the extent that they share a common understanding of the rights and responsibilities, the relationship will function smoothly and the job will proceed unhindered. To the extent that they disagree—even through a misunderstanding—there is likely to be conflict and the job may suffer. Traditional superior roles include giving instructions and receiving reports while subordinates take orders and make reports. These traditional roles have been clouded by the development of new patterns of management, giving subordinates opportunities for active participation in decision making. In addition, the introduction of matrix structures has obscured the patterns of command and report. However, in these uncertain environments, it has become necessary for participants to define their own roles and to reach some sort of mutual agreement concerning the appropriate conduct of each. Moreover, many people maintain both professional and social roles with regard to one another. Both must understand when one set of roles is in effect and when the other may be applied. For example, John Jones is called Dr. Jones by his colleagues in professional settings, and he addresses them as Doctor or Professor according to their preferences. Socially, however, he is John, and his colleagues are referred to by their first names. The changes in title alone are trivial, but they serve as convenient notices that different sets of expectations are in force and that violations of the norms associated with the social or professional roles are inappropriate.

The existence of a large range of shared meanings makes it possible for two people to communicate accurately with minimal effort. Professional vocabularies—jargon to the outsider—result from the need of people working together on specialized projects to convey quantities of information quickly and with minimal chances of error. In many cases, the words used in professional vocabularies are also used by nonspecialists in a much less precise way. For example, the nonspecialist uses the word ''motivate'' in a vague way as something to do with getting someone else to do something. In contrast, for the personnel specialist, the word has a relatively precise meaning as part of a systematic theory of behavior. When the specialist and nonspecialist talk to one another much meaning is lost; in contrast, two personnel specialists can communicate readily because they share a broader range of meaning associated with the word.

Communication and Relationship-Building

Communication is influenced by and has an effect on all four elements of interpersonal relationships. Accuracy in communication is facilitated by a strong, positive relationship on all dimensions. High degrees of liking promote openness and make it possible to discuss topics that otherwise would be difficult to approach; high levels of trust make possible frequent feedback; a common understanding of roles establishes common expectations, reducing the chance of conflict and disagreement; and shared meanings reduce opportunities for misunderstanding and error.

In addition, communication patterns determine the extent to which relationships develop. Frequent communications that produce positive feelings are bound to liking; consistently open and honest communications increase the level of trust; candid discussions of roles produce common sets of expectations; and clear directions and reports increase the range of shared meanings. Unfortunately, poor communication habits weaken interpersonal relationships. Frequent communications with negative effects decrease liking; closed communications reduce trust; deceptive communications confuse the roles of participants; and unchecked ambiguity reduces the extent of shared meanings. The interaction between communication and interpersonal relationships is illustrated in Figure 12.1.

This interaction between communication, interpersonal relationships, and performance should be recognized because it points to an important attitude toward interpersonal communication on the job. Every time you communicate with a coworker, you have the opportunity to improve interpersonal relationships, which will facilitate further communication and improved performance. Conversely, every instance of communication is a potential threat to interpersonal relationships. Poor communication damages interpersonal relationships, reduces

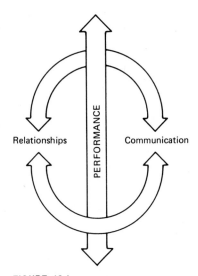

FIGURE 12.1

the quality of subsequent communication, and threatens the level of performance. Of course, a few isolated instances of communication that differ from the normal pattern are unlikely to have a marked impact on your relationships. Those with whom you have good relationships will excuse a few blunders, and those with whom you have poor relationships will think a few good experiences result from chance. However, in the long run, the quality of your communication with coworkers will have a marked impact on your relationships and levels of performance.

RECEIVING INFORMATION

For most people, receiving information in oral settings (that is, listening) is at least as important as transmitting messages. Consider some of the common situations in which you may need to listen to others: You are given a new assignment and your immediate supervisor explains the responsibilities it entails; at a meeting, the corporate research director summarizes what is known about the problem to be resolved; a subordinate hands you a report he has just completed and wants to discuss the assignment; the productivity of your work group has declined and you must learn why; the personnel officer describes a new corporate hiring policy and you need to determine how it will affect your division; and, you must learn what changes your clients and customers want made.

Each of these situations offers potentially great rewards, and each poses substantial danger. Your success in each case depends on your ability to listen effectively and to secure the information of greatest value to you from the person making the presentation. The importance of such situations is generally recognized by those who experience them. In fact, one study asked recent graduates who had majored in business administration to list the communication skills "most important to one's job success." Listening was the skill regarded as most important by the overwhelming majority of the respondents.[1] Curiously, a number of studies show that most people are not effective receivers. Ralph G. Nichols conducted several tests of his students' listening abilities and the results are startling. Immediately after a lecture, the students remembered less than half of what they had heard; after two months, they could recall less than one quarter of the information presented.[2] Still fewer people are able to accurately summarize and repeat information received orally. One study found that only one out of every four listeners is able to summarize a message with reasonable accuracy.[3] These research findings are consistent with the impressions of personnel managers and training directors who find listening ability to be the most common deficiency of their entering trainees.[4]

A major cause of ineffective listening is a widespread misconception. Many people assume that listening is a wholly *passive* activity in which they need merely sit back and "soak in" the message. The passive approach to listening allows distractions to interfere with the message because the human mind is able to process information at a rate much faster than most people speak. A normal speaking rate is approximately 145 words per minute, and the human brain processes information at a rate in excess of 400 words per minute. When listeners are not actively involved in the communication process, the "free" time provided by the rapid rate of mental information processing creates distractions that eventually command more attention than the message. The solution to this problem is to find means whereby listening can become an active part of the communication process. Fortunately, the relatively informal character of dyadic communication provides several ways of being involved, and we shall look at three of the most useful: creating a favorable emotional environment, paraphrasing for accuracy, and soliciting clarification of emotionally charged messages.

Emotional Environment

In ancient times, some rulers were in the habit of executing messengers who brought bad news. History does not record the effects of this practice on the speed with which information was brought to monarchs, but it could hardly have been advantageous. Modern professionals are not free to dispatch the bearers of bad tidings quite as quickly, but many managers engage in practices that have equally

[1] Vincent DiSalvo, David Larsen, and William Seiler, "Communication Skills," paper presented to the International Communication Association, 1974.

[2] Ralph G. Nichols and Leonard A. Stevens, "Listening to People," *Harvard Business Review*, 35 (September-October, 1957), 85–92.

[3] Martin Maloney, "Semantics, The Foundation of All Business Communication," *Advanced Management*, 19 (July, 1954), 26–29.

[4] Jan E. Meister and N. L. Reinsch, Jr., "Communication Training in Manufacturing Firms," *Communication Education*, 27 (1978), 235–244.

disastrous consequences. Sherman K. Okun, Vice President of Folger & Co., Inc., managerial consultants, records the following example:

> A recently appointed vice president of operations of a machine tool manufacturer found that unanticipated problems—such as materials shortages, cost overruns, machine downtime, and lost orders—kept cropping up. Evidently, he assumed, the company's reporting system was not providing him with adequate timely information.
>
> He called in the corporation information system's staff and asked them to review his reporting systems. The staff then developed a new set of reports—but he found the same unforeseen problems kept recurring.
>
> The vice president then felt sure that a basic organizational problem was leading to these difficulties. He called in a management consultant, and the consultant soon spotted the trouble. The information the vice president needed was readily available. But it was not being presented to him. The fault lay with the executive, not with the organization. Whenever potential problems were being discussed, the consultant discovered, the vice president quickly began to assess blame instead of calmly seeking solutions.
>
> As a result, no one dared to bring potential problems to his attention.[5]

Reprinted by permission of Tribune Company Syndicate, Inc.

The executive in this example was penalizing those who brought him the information sought, and the effects of his behavior were very predictable. At-

[5]Sherman K. Okun, "How to Be a Better Listener," *Nation's Business* (August, 1975), 59.

tributing blame is the most obvious penalty, but two other sets of behavior create environments in which employees are unlikely to report fully and accurately.

Giving less than full attention to the person reporting also penalizes the reporter and reduces the likelihood of future reports. Failing to give your full attention implies that you place little value on the person or the report. And failing to give your subordinates visible credit or to report back to them when their comments, suggestions, and/or complaints have resulted in subsequent action creates a sense of futility. The futility resulting from these behaviors reduces employees' willingness to report to you because they see no reward for their efforts, and because "nothing ever seems to get done."

Being an active participant means creating an emotional environment that is conducive to full and open reporting by actively working to eliminate penalties for reporting. Three concrete steps are necessary to eliminate these penalties. First, make it clear to your subordinates that "news is news," and be receptive to both the good and the bad. No one enjoys receiving bad news, but the ability to cope with awkward situations before they become crises is essential. To solve problems, you must know they exist, and the best sources of information are subordinates who see difficulties affecting their daily activities before the problems are recorded in job logs and "discovered" when they become major problems.

Second, when you are listening, give the other person your full attention. Look directly at the person, set aside papers or other materials with which you are working, and let your hands rest comfortably and unobtrusively. They should be in a comfortable position and they should be empty of pens, calculators, papers, and other objects that might be distracting. Your posture should become slightly more erect as you listen to the person with whom you are speaking and you should use nonverbal signs of acceptance to promote further reporting. These signs include encouraging expressions, nodding "yes" in response to statements, and nearly continuous eye contact. If you are in a position to do so, ask your secretary to hold calls, close your office door, face the reporter, and make it clear that you are giving your undivided attention. Of course, you may be operating under pressure as deadlines for other work draw near. But, one minute of total attention is time much better spent than five minutes of partial attention. When time is a critical factor, make the limitations clear at the outset. By establishing a limit (for example, one minute, five minutes, or one hour) at the start of the conversation, you condition the reporter to "get to the point," and you reduce the chance of creating hard feelings by dismissing someone before his or her report is completed. If the limited report for which you have time indicates that you need further information, you can either extend your time limit or schedule another appointment. Some employees may resent the imposition of time limits, but most find your total and undivided attention to be more than sufficient compensation. And, your decision to give them extra time when justified is high praise for the value of their report. One word of warning: If you are forced to cut a report short and promise to set aside time for the discussion later, be sure to follow through. Failure to meet with the person later will damage your relationship and may weaken your credibility with the entire team.

"Look at me, Carruthers, when I'm speaking to you."
Reprinted by permission of Tribune Company Syndicate, Inc.

The final step is to reward your subordinates by giving them credit and by letting them know what has been done as a consequence of their report. Giving them credit by directing your superior's attention to their good work will increase their exposure and also their faith in you.

> The most convincing demonstration of your interest in your people's best interest, is your eager dedication to pushing them as far as possible: thrusting them into the limelight, giving them all possible credit and exposure, promoting them—even if it means spinning them off to other groups.[6]

And, while you are giving them credit for recognizing potential problems and calling them to your attention, be sure that they know what action was taken as a consequence. Even if their suggestions cannot be implemented at the present time, be sure they know what you have tried to do and the reasons that nothing could be done.

Paraphrasing for Accuracy

A second way in which you can become actively involved in the listening process is by paraphrasing messages as you receive them. The relative informality

---

[6] Robert J. Schoenberg, *The Art of Being a Boss* (Philadelphia: Lippincott, 1978), pp. 72–73. Copyright © 1978 by Robert J. Schoenberg. By permission of Harper & Row, Publishers, Inc.

of dyadic communication provides frequent opportunities to interrupt the speaker, and you should make the most of these opportunities by repeating portions of the speaker's message in your own terms. Paraphrasing is simply the process of repeating portions of another person's message in your own terms. Its primary use is to ensure that you have interpreted the message as it was intended. Some common errors in interpretation are described in the chapter on language, and Saul W. Gellerman uses the following example to show how paraphrasing can be used to avoid confusion:

> The word *average* is used quite differently in practice (especially by managers) than its dictionary meanings. The word has a rigid mathematical definition and another perfectly respectable meaning as the central tendency of a distribution or as the most typically expected instance in a group. But it has come to be a way of damning with faint praise, especially when evaluating people or their performance. Thus we hear of someone who has done a "merely" average job. (How can the most commonly expected level of performance be "mere"?) And when managers are asked to evaluate their subordinates for salary increases, the great majority are nearly always "above average," which is, of course, a mathematical absurdity. (If pressed, managers may rationalize their ratings by suggesting that the "below average" people who counterbalance their own "above average" subordinates will all be found in some other manager's department.) Clearly one is never quite sure what *average*—or many other words that have accretions of acquired meanings—really means.
>
> The most practical way to cope with the problem of private meanings and nonstandard vocabularies is through paraphrasing. All participants in a dialogue can restate the others' messages in their own words or in terms of their own experience, and the others can either approve that interpretation or point out that it was not exactly what they had in mind.[7]

As important as they are, misunderstandings concerning the meaning of words are only one type of problem that paraphrasing can help to avoid. Confusions about a speaker's purpose in making a statement and about the relative importance of various parts of a message may also be reduced through effective paraphrasing.

Most statements are made with a specific purpose in mind, and speakers may avoid explicit statements of purpose as a means of making unpleasant news more palatable. Although their intentions are laudable, the danger of confusion looms large in these attempts, and it is up to you to secure the full meaning. For example, consider the range of meanings present when your immediate supervisor comments that the last person to hold your job was fired because he failed on a particular assignment. Of course, she may be simply sharing information, but because the risks are great, it would be beneficial to explore every possibility. She may be warning you that you face termination because your work has been unsatisfactory, encouraging you to put in extra time on the project, or even promising advancement for successful completion of the assignment. The best way to sort

[7] From THE MANAGEMENT OF HUMAN RESOURCES by Saul W. Gellerman. Copyright © 1976 by the Dryden Press, a division of Holt, Rinehart and Winston. Reprinted by permission of Holt, Rinehart and Winston, CBS College Publishing.

out these possibilities is to paraphrase the message and allow your supervisor to correct any misunderstandings. In this case, you might use any of the following:

> If I read you correctly, you are warning me that my work has been unsatisfactory.
> I think you are telling me to give this project a higher priority.
> You think this is an important project and I can help myself by doing it well.

Active Listening for Emotional Content

Finally, your receiving skills are incomplete until you develop the habit of actively listening for emotional cues that accompany explicit messages. Emotional content is present to some degree in all messages, and the following example shows how important the feelings can be:

> John was assigned a particularly important report and allowed to set his own deadline. Unfortunately, the report required much more time than expected because certain pieces of information were not available locally. To insure accurate presentation of the material, John spent two weekends traveling to remote locations to examine documents stored there. In addition, he worked overtime several evenings compiling data and drafting his recommendations. In spite of his extraordinary efforts, the typist made several errors and the whole report had to be retyped. As a result, John was three days late in submitting the final copy to his boss. When he handed the copy to his superior, all John said was, "Well, it's finished."

John's remark sounds like a simple statement of fact, but it is unlikely that his nonverbal message was neutral. However, even if his nonverbal communication failed to portray his feelings about completing the report, it is probable that strong emotional reactions are just below the surface and you risk serious consequences if you fail to explore the possibilities. Think for a moment about your own reactions if you were in John's situation. The emotions that might be prominent at this moment include relief at having finished, pride in the report, regret for being late, anger at having been given such a demanding assignment, frustration as a result of the typist's errors, fear that the delay will have a negative effect on your performance rating, and concern that you will not be given credit for the extraordinary effort put forth. The important thing to remember is that John's supervisor will not know which emotion predominates unless he takes time to initiate discussion. The emotional reactions have important implications for the supervisor's response to John's statement. The very least John probably expects is acknowledgement that the report is complete, and he may also need help in coping with his feelings. Moreover, knowledge of John's feelings may help to revise report and data gathering procedures, work assignment schedules, and secretarial responsibilities.

The skills that will allow the supervisor to solicit additional remarks from John are collectively known as "active listening." Four active listening techniques are particularly effective in dealing with situations like the one described. First, show interest in the person and his or her feelings. We have already mentioned some nonverbal means of showing interest, and you may also use verbal signs of attention. These signs should be used whenever the other person pauses as if seeking encouragement, and they should always be short and to the point. Their purpose is to indicate your interest in and attention to the other person's statements. Typical examples include "I see" and the streetwise "got cha." Others are "Yes," "OK," "Uhm-hum," "Yep," "Sure," "Right on," and "I hear you." Select phrases that are appropriate to you, your respondent, and your relationship.

Second, suppress personal reactions that might cause the other person to feel defensive. Statements that imply evaluation are particularly dangerous and even advice should be avoided because it suggests the other person erred by not doing things correctly in the first place. Jack Gibb explains the danger of implicit evaluations in the following manner.

> If by expression, manner of speech, tone of voice, or verbal content the sender seems to be evaluating or judging the listener, then the receiver goes on guard. . . . Because our attitudes toward other persons are frequently, and often necessarily, evaluative, expressions which the defensive person will regard as nonjudgmental are hard to frame. Even the simplest question usually conveys the answer that the sender wishes or implies the response that would fit into his value system.[8]

Of course, there will be a time for advice and evaluation, but initially it is most important to hear the other person out.

Third, use mirror statements to reflect the emotions you believe the other person feels. Good mirror statements are always brief, convey neither approval nor disapproval, and represent your best guess about the other person's feelings. For example, John's supervisor could use any of the following to help John to express his own feelings:

I guess you are pleased to be done with it.
It seems like you found this a frustrating assignment.
It sounds like you are proud of the report.
Sounds like you are pretty tired.
I bet you're anxious to see how it is received.

John's nonverbal behavior may indicate that some of these responses are inappropriate. But any one of them opens the door for him to express his feelings, and they might even help him clarify his own mixed emotions concerning the report.

Finally, once your respondent is talking freely, you may ask questions to secure clarification. Because some questions may imply evaluation, avoid using them until the other person is talking freely, and use them sparingly. When used,

---

[8] Jack Gibb, "Defensive Communication," *Journal of Communication,* 11 (1961), 142–143.

questions should be brief, targeted to secure clarification from the other person, and free of evaluative implications. Their proper use is to find out what the other person means by particular remarks. They should not be used to "remind" the other person of items they may have overlooked or to suggest ways of avoiding the problem. For example, none of the following questions would be appropriate in talking with John because they all imply that he made an error:

> Why didn't you tell me you were having problems?
> Couldn't you get someone else to gather information?
> Shouldn't you use a different secretary for matters like this?

However, you could ask for clarification on some of the following points:

> How many tables needed to be retyped?
> How many extra hours did you work?
> How many trips did you make to each remote site?

SUMMARY

Five types of interpersonal communication will have immediate impact on your career, and this chapter discusses the first two; building professional relationships through communication and receiving information. Interpersonal relationships are complex because they involve four dimensions: liking, trust, shared meanings, and role definitions. All four dimensions are involved in professional relationships and both affect and are affected by communication. Few people are effective listeners, and you can enhance your abilities by creating a favorable emotional environment, paraphrasing for accuracy, and using active listening techniques to clarify emotionally charged messages.

LEARNING ACTIVITIES

1. Think about your relationship with someone you know well and with whom you interact on a regular basis. Characterize your relationship with him or her in terms of the dimensions described in this chapter. How well do you like the other person? How much do you trust the other person? Have you developed specialized or shared meanings for terms you use in talking with the other person? Have you developed specific role expectations in dealing with the other person? Now, try to answer each of these questions as you think the other person would.

2. Try to identify ways in which your relationship with another person affects communication between you. Is the amount of time you spend communicating limited by the nature of your relationship? How is the accuracy of communication affected by your relationship? Are there ways in

which improved communication would improve the relationship between you?

3. Go to a location where you can observe a person who has to interact with a large number of other people. For example, observe your instructor dealing with students, a receptionist greeting people, or a bus driver involved with people boarding the bus. Does the person appear to encourage or discourage conversation? What behaviors encourage people to talk? What behaviors discourage people from talking?

CHAPTER THIRTEEN
PRESENTATIONAL
SKILLS
IN INTERVIEWS

Relatively formal types of dyadic communication are called *interviews*. Interviews differ from less formal kinds of communication in that at least one of the participants has predetermined objectives, and the interaction is structured to facilitate the objectives. In this chapter, you will see three of the most common professional interviews: selection interviews, in which you can use presentational skills to secure a position; informational interviews, in which you can use presentational skills in reporting to your boss; and appraisal interviews, in which you can use presentational skills to give employees feedback.

SELECTION INTERVIEWS

Selection interviews probably will have greater impact than any other kind of communication on your early career. The way you present yourself during selection interviews will determine where you are employed, at what level and salary you start, and your prospects for advancement. This fact should concern you because a growing body of literature indicates that interviews are an unreliable means of assessing the abilities of job applicants.

The face-to-face interview is . . . the most expensive, least reliable way to select people for a job. No two interviewers ever seem to agree on an individual; in the
research, interviewing comes off second best to almost every other selection approach
save handwriting analysis.[1]

Even though their limitations are recognized, interviews are the primary
means of selecting employees and are likely to remain so. The unreliability of interviewing forces you to come to terms with an undeniable consequence of most
personnel systems: Your qualifications alone are not enough to win the job you
want because interviewers are influenced by far more. Moreover, most attractive
positions will have several applicants, many of whom are as well qualified as, or
even more qualified than, you are. What this means is that you need to present
your qualifications most favorably and distinguish yourself from other applicants.
Presentational skills can help you to prepare for and participate in selection interviews.

Preparing for Interviews

Failing to prepare for an interview is as great an error as failing to prepare
for a formal presentation. Just as knowledge of a subject is inadequate to carry you
through a formal presentation, knowledge of your experiences and qualifications
is inadequate to carry you through an interview. In both cases, your knowledge of
the subject is not sufficient because it is not adapted to the situation and audience.
Analysis of the audience—the potential employer—is essential if you hope to present yourself in the best possible light. Fortunately, there are several sources of
information available, and you should start preparing by developing a mental pic
ture of the organization and position for which you are being interviewed. Particularly helpful sources of information include annual reports to stockholders,
current articles in the *Wall Street Journal* and the financial pages of other papers,
product and other reports in appropriate trade journals, and files maintained by
placement offices. The information you gain through analysis of the audience will
help you prepare a résumé highlighting your special qualifications and develop
answers to probable questions.

Preparing your résumé   Your résumé should be a reasonably concise
document listing experiences and abilities *relevant* to the positions for which you
apply. The word "relevant" is emphasized because many students make the
mistake of producing a life history instead of a résumé. A résumé should focus attention on experiences and abilities that uniquely qualify you for positions you are
seeking. Remember, interviewers try to determine whether or not you are

---

[1] Ron Zemke, "Legally Speaking, Don't Take Interviews for Granted." Reprinted with permission from the December, 1980 issue of *Training,* The Magazine of Human Resources Development. Copyright 1980, Lakewood Publications, Minneapolis, Minnesota (612) 333–0471. All rights
reserved.

qualified for a position and where you rank compared to other applicants. A résumé should be a persuasive document showing your qualifications for a position *and* your unique abilities that distinguish you from other applicants.

The first step in preparing a résumé is selecting information about yourself. It is conventional to include a statement of your career objective and this statement may be the most persuasive part of your resume. You should devote considerable attention to phrasing it: It should be relatively specific, reasonably brief, and designed to show that you fill the needs of prospective employers. Most students err here by stating an objective that shows their needs and many make a poor initial impression as a result. The following examples show the difference between statements emphasizing the applicant's needs and those emphasizing the employer's needs:

> An entry-level personnel position that provides security and a chance for advancement.
> An entry-level personnel position requiring a mature and responsible professional.

The first statement tells prospective employers what the applicant wants, while the second tells them what the applicant has to offer.

Beyond stating your career objective, there are few hard and fast rules about what should be included in a résumé. A recent survey revealed a consistent pattern of preferences among the chief personnel officers of *Fortune* 500 companies, and you should include the information they would like to see.

1. personal information such as date of birth, address, marital status, dependents, etc.,
2. general as well as specific educational qualifications such as majors, minors, and degrees,
3. scholarships, awards, and honors earned,
4. previous work experience including jobs held, dates of employment, company addresses, and reason for leaving,
5. special aptitudes and abilities,
6. the names and addresses of three references,
7. military service,
8. willingness to relocate, and
9. the major source of your financing while in college.[2]

Citing reference names is a noteworthy departure from usual practice. The common procedure is to exclude names of references and substitute a note saying "references will be furnished on request." Including references, however, saves time, and the names can be a persuasive force on your behalf.

[2] Barron Wells, Nelda Spinks, and Janice Hargrave, "A Survey of the Chief Personnel Officers in the 500 Largest Corporations in the United States to Determine Their Preferences in Job Application Letters and Personal Resumes," *The ABCA Bulletin,* 44 (June, 1981), 3–7. Published by the American Business Communication Association.

The second step in preparing a resume is choosing the form in which you present the information. The majority of personnel officers surveyed (67 percent) prefer a one-page resume, but two-page resumes are also acceptable. Questions about the order of presentation produced inconsistent findings because respondents agreed to a pair of potentially contradictory statements. Seventy-one percent agreed to the statement, "The traditional order in which information is presented in a resume is desirable (personal information, education, experience, references)." But, 49 percent agreed to the statement, "The applicant's strongest points (education, work experience, etc.) should be listed first in the resume, without regard to any rule for presentation." It appears that you have some latitude in choosing an order of presentation, but you will be safest if you use a traditional order, and most distinctive if you use a novel order emphasizing your strong points.

The final step in preparing a resume is creating a master and having copies printed. It is well worth the cost to have your resume set and printed by a professional. Most placement services can handle the job for you. Exhibit 13.1 shows what finished copies should look like. Pay particular attention to the use of open spaces and headings to make the finished product attractive and to make it easy to find particular items of information.

Preparing answers   After you have prepared a resume, you should plan answers for the questions you expect to be asked. This is an area in which your presentational skills can be particularly valuable, and you should understand what constitutes a "good" answer. A good answer is *responsive* to the question asked; an *accurate* and *honest* statement about yourself; sufficiently *detailed* to distinguish you from other applicants with similar qualifications; and stated to make you appear as *interesting* and *attractive* as possible. Making yourself an attractive job candidate does not require falsification, but you should be careful to develop answers that emphasize positive attributes. The impact of even very negative information can be softened through phrasing that is free of negative connotations. For example, interviewers often test candidates' self-awareness by asking about their greatest weaknesses. Comparing the following pairs of answers shows the value of careful phrasing:

I am intolerant toward people who are always complaining.
I am not always as sympathetic as I could be to other people's problems.

I cut corners when under pressure.
I like to get things done and sometimes work too quickly.

I am disorganized and usually make a mess when working on a project.
I get so involved in projects that I become disorganized and my work area gets cluttered.

Each statement could be accurate and honest, but the second one in each pair presents a far more positive image.

EXHIBIT 13.1

MARGARET L. WASHINGTON

211 Swanson Hall   Syracuse, New York 13210   (315) 423–2308

OBJECTIVE

An entry-level personnel position requiring a mature and responsible professional who enjoys working with people and developing problem-solving teams.

EDUCATIONAL BACKGROUND

Bachelor of Science, *cum laude,* in **PERSONNEL AND INDUSTRIAL RELATIONS** from Syracuse University, June 1982. Named the "Outstanding Personnel Major" by the departmental faculty, 3.87 G.P.A., Dean's list 6 semesters while working an average of 15 hours per week to finance 50% of education.

PROFESSIONAL EXPERIENCE

For the past four summers worked for Paul Stromer Construction, Inc. Starting as a laborer, I was assigned greater responsibility every summer and advanced to **BENEFITS COORDINATOR** during my final summer. Mr. Stromer has asked me to become an **OFFICE MANAGER** if I decide to remain in construction.

During school years, I have supported myself as a waitress at several local clubs including the Marshall County Club, University Club of Greater Syracuse, and the Morgan County Country Club. All of my employers have asked me to return and all have volunteered to provide references.

RELATED EXPERIENCE

I have polished my managerial ability by serving as **SECRETARY** and **TREASURER** Alpha Omega Lamda Sorority, and as **CAMPUS COORDINATOR** for the 1981 March of Dimes campaign.

PERSONAL DATA

I was born on February 7, 1956 and am in **EXCELLENT HEALTH.** I am an active person and my activities include intramural athletics, swimming, and dancing. I enjoy travel and am **WILLING TO RELOCATE.**

REFERENCES INCLUDE

Eric Skopec,
Associate Professor
Speech Communication
Syracuse University
(315) 423–5555

Paul Stromer,
Owner and General
  Manager
Paul Stromer Construction
Bethel, New York
(315) 555–1212

Arleen Smith,
General Manager
Marshall Yacht Club
Marshall, New York
(315) 445–1937

Marshall Johnson,
Club Manager
Morgan County Yacht Club
Morgansville, New York
(315) 555–1037

By preparing answers in advance, you can avoid being caught off guard and you should be able to make a more effective presentation on your own behalf. The specific questions you are asked in an interview depend on the position for which you are applying, the material you have included in your resume and correspondence with the interviewer, the skills and interests of the interviewer, and a number of other factors. This variability complicates the task of preparing answers, but you can expect to be asked about your education, personal interests, work experience, qualifications, and professional expectations. Common questions that attempt to explore each of these topics are listed below.

EDUCATION

Why did you choose your particular field of study?
How did you choose your major?
What courses did you like best? Why?
What courses did you like least? Why?
Do you feel you have done the best scholastic work of which you are capable?
If you could start over in school, what would you do differently?
Do you plan to continue your education? When? In what areas?

PERSONAL INTERESTS

Tell me about yourself.
What are your three biggest accomplishments?
Do you generally speak to people before they speak to you?
How have your goals or objectives changed in the last five years?
How would you describe the essence of success?
What was the last book you read?
What was the last movie you saw?
What was the last sporting event you attended?
List your extracurricular activities.
What offices have you held?

WORK EXPERIENCE

What jobs have you held? How were they obtained?
Why did you leave your last position?
What portion of your college expenses did you earn?
What features of your previous jobs have you disliked?
Would you describe a few situations in which your work was criticized?

QUALIFICATIONS

What qualifications do you possess for success in your field?
What are your major strengths?
What are your major weaknesses?
What can you do for us that someone else cannot do?
Why should we hire you?

Can you work under pressure, deadlines, etc.?
Are you creative? Give an example.
Are you analytical? Give an example.
Are you a good manager? Give an example.
Are you a leader or a follower? Explain!

PROFESSIONAL EXPECTATIONS

What are your long-range goals?
Specifically, what position are you interested in?
Why are you interested in our company?
What do you know about our company?
What are your short-range objectives?
What do you look for in a job?
What is your philosophy of management?
What kind of salary are you worth?
Why do you want to work for us?
How long do you plan to stay with our company?

You may find it helpful to prepare your answers in three stages. First, answer each question as accurately and honestly as you can. Second, rewrite your answers to include as much detail as possible, using the kinds of developing material discussed in Chapter 2. Finally, check the wording in your answers and rewrite any that have negative loadings or connotations. Make sure that they present you in the most favorable light possible.

Participating in Interviews

Hiring practices have been the subject of increasing legal scrutiny and many companies have developed sophisticated screening systems to protect themselves. In spite of efforts to eliminate bias and error, the impression you make while participating in an interview can determine whether or not you are hired, and, if you are hired, your salary level, location, and future prospects.

Many interviewees are nervous, and skilled interviewers will try to set you at ease. Unfortunately, anxiety will reduce the quality of your answers and your ability to cope with the situation. You should work to control your tension, and many of the techniques of controlling anxiety in formal presentations that were presented in Chapter 6 will work in interviews as well.

Beyond controlling anxiety, making a favorable impression requires avoiding negative factors and adapting to the style of the interviewer.

Avoid negative factors   The accidental cues generated by job applicants often carry greater weight than intended messages. This is so because interviewers assume that the unguarded reactions of interviewees are more indicative of personality and ability than carefully prepared answers. You cannot always tell what will create a favorable impression, but you can avoid some behaviors that will count against you. Frank S. Endicott, Director of Placement at Northwestern University, has isolated fifty negative factors evaluated during interviews that frequently lead to rejection of applicants.

1. Poor personal appearance
2. Overbearing—overaggressive—superiority complex—know it all
3. Inability to express oneself clearly—poor voice, diction, grammar
4. Lack of planning for career—no purpose or goals
5. Lack of interest and enthusiasm—passive or indifferent
6. Lack of confidence and poise—nervous, ill at ease
7. Failure to participate in activities
8. Overemphasis on money, interest only in the best dollar offer
9. Poor scholastic record—just got by
10. Unwilling to start at the bottom—expects too much too soon
11. Makes excuses, evasiveness, hedges on unfavorable factors on record
12. Lack of tact
13. Lack of maturity
14. Lack of courtesy—ill-mannered
15. Condemnation of past employers
16. Lack of social understanding
17. Marked dislike for school work
18. Lack of vitality
19. Fails to look interviewer in the eye
20. Limp, fishy handshake
21. Indecision
22. Loafs during vacations—lakeside pleasures
23. Unhappy married life
24. Friction with parents
25. Sloppy application blank
26. Merely shopping around
27. Wants job only for short time
28. Little sense of humor
29. Lack of knowledge of field of specialization
30. Parents make decisions for him
31. No interest in company or industry
32. Emphasis on whom he knows
33. Unwillingness to go where we send him
34. Cynical
35. Low moral standards
36. Lazy
37. Intolerant—strong prejudices
38. Narrow interests
39. Spends much time in movies
40. Poor handling of personal finances

41.   No interest in community activities
42.   Inability to take criticism
43.   Lack of appreciation of value of experience
44.   Radical ideas
45.   Late to interview without good reason
46.   Never heard of company
47.   Failure to express appreciation for interviewer's time
48.   Asks no questions about the job
49.   High pressure type
50.   Indefinite response to questions[3]

Adapting to interviewers   Many interviewers will make judgments about you on the basis of their comfort in interacting with you. Some interviewers want to do all the talking while you listen, others want to relax and listen while you talk, and most prefer an interaction pattern somewhere between these two extremes. If you do not adapt to the interviewer's pattern, or if the interviewer does not adapt to yours, both of you will be uncomfortable and both may form negative opinions of the other. Skilled interviewers will avoid these difficulties by explaining what kind of answers they would like, but many lack the necessary sophistication. Most of the time, you will have to recognize the interaction pattern of the interviewer and respond accordingly. Although the division is somewhat arbitrary, you can expect interviewers to use one or more of the following four styles.

Nondirective interviewers exercise little control over the content of interaction and will give you considerable freedom in selecting topics for discussion. They ask questions infrequently and prefer long answers (5 or more minutes) in which you present your qualifications without much prompting. Your role in the interview can be thought of as presenting a series of short speeches showing that you are the best candidate for the position. When this style is used it is possible that important topics will not be introduced and you may lose the position simply because you didn't mention relevant qualifications. To avoid this danger, use the sample questions above as a checklist to insure that you have discussed each of the major topics outlined.

Somewhat more directive interviewers use a style that can be characterized as *question-probe*. Few questions are asked, but these interviewers constantly probe for additional details. They usually have a set of topics they want to explore, but they may get sidetracked by following up on incidental features of the answers. You should give moderately long answers (about two minutes each), but you should pause frequently to give the interviewer an opportunity to probe. Interviewers using both the nondirective and question-probe styles relinquish control of the interview, and it becomes your responsibility to focus attention on job-related topics that present you in a favorable light.

Highly directive interviewers control interviews using two styles. Inter-

---

[3] Adapted from the Syracuse University *Placement Manual* (Spring, 1980).

viewers using the *question-question* style approach the interview as if their responsibility were limited to filling out a form. They ask large numbers of questions, cut off long answers, and take brief notes about the answers. They may even use your phrasing to fill in an employment form. Your best strategy is to give brief answers (about thirty seconds) using key words that summarize your qualifications and can be recorded easily. Phrase your answers so that it is easy to record expressions that will make a favorable impression on people reading the interviewer's notes. In many cases the person using this style lacks authority to hire you, but his or her report may determine whether or not you are called for a second interview.

Finally, some interviewers use a *talk and observe* style. These interviewers do most of the talking and approach the interview as an opportunity to talk about topics that interest them. You become a captive audience, but you should not believe that the interviewer is learning nothing about you. Skillful interviewers using this style form judgments about you on the basis of your nonverbal reactions to them. They watch to see what interests you, how you respond to statements about the company and position, and how you react to the slightly strained social setting. When you encounter an interviewer using this style, you can make good use of your listening skills by maintaining a posture of involvement, focusing your attention on the interviewer, avoiding distractions, and occasionally paraphrasing or echoing the interviewer's comments. If the interviewer appears to run out of things to talk about, you can show interest by asking questions that prompt further remarks, but your primary role is as an attentive observer.

Figure 13.1 summarizes these interview styles and the appropriate reactions to each. If the interviewer does not tell you how the interview will be conducted, you can use a trial-and-error system to judge the style. Begin with answers of intermediate length and see how the interviewer responds. If you finish an answer and the interviewer is not ready to ask another question or probe for additional details, you should lengthen the answers. If the interviewer appears anxious to cut you off, begin reducing the length of your answers. You should be able to strike a comfortable balance within ten or fifteen minutes, but adaptation can be a continuous process because the interviewer may change style or ask questions calling for different types of answers.[4]

[4] Interviewing textbooks distinguish several types of questions, and differences between them may help in planning your answers. Free association questions invite you to talk without restricting your range of answers; for example, "Tell me about yourself." Open questions ask you to talk about a more specific topic; for example, "Tell me about your education." Closed questions ask you to pick one of a stated or assumed set of answers; for example, "Roughly what percentage of your college expenses did you earn: less than 25 percent, 25 percent to 50 percent, 50 percent to 75 percent, or more than 75 percent?" Bipolar questions ask you to choose between two answers; for example, "Did you earn more than 50 percent of your college expenses?"

It would be easy to gauge your answers if all interviewers used questions systematically. If this were the case, you could give long answers to free association and open questions, and short answers to closed and bipolar questions. Unfortunately, many interviewers are not skilled at phrasing questions and may ask bipolar questions, expecting you to expand on the answer, while some ask open or free association questions when they want a brief answer. Therefore, judging interaction style is the best guide you have in pacing your answers.

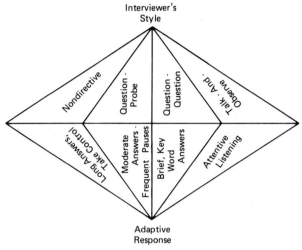

FIGURE 13.1

INFORMATIONAL INTERVIEWS: KEEPING THE BOSS INFORMED

No matter what position you occupy in an organization, you will always have a boss. Even at the highest levels in modern corporations, executives have little difficulty identifying the person(s) to whom they are expected to report and from whom they receive instructions. Of course, the amount of direction your boss will attempt to exercise varies widely with the type of organization, your role in the organization, and the particulars of your relationship with the boss. However, the basic pattern of receiving instructions and reporting results is universal in modern organizations.

Formal reports concluding assignments will usually be in writing accompanied with an oral briefing of the type described in Chapter 8. However, few supervisors are satisfied with a single report at the conclusion of a project and most will want to receive some information while the project is being conducted. The boss's "need to know" while assignments are being conducted arises from a number of factors: he or she may be called upon to report to a superior at any time in the course of the project; other programs may need to be adjusted or decisions made on the basis of your progress; and the boss should be able to anticipate and correct problems arising from difficulties you encounter while working. In addition, many managers are anxious to serve as instructors and develop the abilities of their subordinates. From your point of view, keeping the boss informed is an ideal way of calling attention to your abilities; building a reputation for honesty, even when obstacles are encountered; and ensuring that your final results are consistent with the needs of the organization. In addition, maintaining contact with

5-24

"You'll get along here, Wilmerton, if you just remember that
internal progress reports are our most important product."

Reprinted by permission of Tribune Company Syndicate, Inc.

your superior gives you access to this person's knowledge and experience, both of
which are important resources. These factors should promote frequent contact
between you and your boss, and call forth a large number of informal reports.
However, several factors reduce the amount of time your supervisor is able to
spend with you and the frequency with which reports are to be made. Depending
on the structure of your organization and your position in it, your immediate
supervisor may give instructions to and receive periodic reports from fifteen or
more subordinates. The time required for the supervisor to fulfill responsibilities
that cannot be delegated to subordinates further reduces the amount of time he or
she can spend with you. These limitations exist regardless of the perspective from
which the supervisor-subordinate relationship is viewed. When viewed from the
perspective of communication theory, one further limitation becomes apparent.
All systems have limited capacity to process information and managers often face
situations in which there is too much incoming data to be processed efficiently.
This fact gives rise to "information overloads" and some sort of breakdown in the
system. Mechanical systems can be redesigned to eliminate overloads, but
humans must resort to other techniques. E. E. Jennings describes this situation in
graphic terms.

The corporation is a vast communication medium in which information competes with information in an endless array of variety and with varying degrees of intensity. In this medium, everybody fights against being bowled over by excessive information. Managers at all levels have screening devices based upon priorities that identify relevant information and filter out the mass of irrelevant information.[5]

Many managers cope with this problem by refusing to pay attention to sources of information that have proven to be of relatively little value. For example, some executives routinely discard third-class mail unopened. In other cases, reports from some subordinates are routinely filed or referred to a secretary for disposal.

Clearly, you need to manage your informal reports to your supervisor in a manner that insures that necessary information is transmitted while not making excessive demands on this person's time or attention. Unfortunately, establishing procedures for such interactions is an area in which supervisors have chronic difficulty. Few are able to spell out precisely what kinds of information they want to receive or to identify the frequency with which they want to receive progress reports. More often than not, colleagues become accustomed to working with one another through a process of trial and error. Subordinates make reports as they think appropriate and then judge their supervisors' reactions. If reports are made too infrequently, the boss will begin asking questions and searching for information; if reports are made too frequently or contain too little information of value to the supervisor, progressively less attention will be paid to the subordinate. Trial-and-error methods may eventually produce a smoothly functioning relationship, but the process is time-consuming. Moreover, subordinates who find the "magic" pattern that pleases their boss most quickly are often seen to be particularly promising, while those who are slow on the uptake may find their relationships deteriorating.

Research to date is inconclusive, but it appears probable that every individual's expectations are unique and that the relationships that evolve between superiors and their subordinates may be highly characteristic of them. However, three general concerns emerge so frequently that they demand specific attention. These factors seem to be the principal areas in which agreement produces smooth superior-subordinate functions. They are earning your superior's trust, determining what information is to be reported, and timing your reports.

Earning Your Superior's Trust

One of the most common errors young employees make is in assuming that the only factor affecting their superior's faith in them is their task performance. Although task performance is important, it is only one of several factors affecting a superior's reaction to a subordinate, and even task performance must be communicated to ensure that you are given full credit for your accomplishments. In

---

[5] From E. E. Jennings, *The Mobile Manager*, p. 41. Copyright © 1967 by McGraw-Hill Book Company. Used with the permission of McGraw-Hill Book Company.

his book, *The Mobile Manager,*[6] E. E. Jennings isolated four conditions necessary to earn a superior's trust. The first of these conditions is accessibility. Jennings thinks of accessibility as openness to the thoughtful exchange of ideas, and the illustrations he uses all point to cases in which the subordinate assists a superior in exploring and developing ideas. Related research conducted from a communication theory perspective has described a similar phenomenon under the terms self-disclosure, openness, and respect. Although the vocabulary used in these studies and the theoretical implications differ from Jennings's interpretations, the specific behaviors to which they point are remarkably similar. The object lesson from all of them is that in order for your boss to trust you, you must act as if you trust your boss. That means you must share your ideas and openly accept his or her reactions and feedback. Of course, this can be difficult when the reactions are negative, but in the long run, encouraging an atmosphere in which your boss freely shares ideas with you will go far to aid your career. Being receptive and open to the boss's ideas doesn't mean that you always agree. In fact, the "yes man" is of little value when your boss wants to try ideas because simple agreement does not provide the critical testing he may want. Only by raising objections, identifying potential difficulties, and suggesting alternative approaches can you provide your superior with the kinds of input needed in order to make a thoughtful decision. Robert J. Schoenberg interviewed nearly one hundred business leaders and found remarkable consensus on this question. The subordinate has a responsibility to disagree with the boss!

> Part of the process is seeing the drawbacks in ideas that originate with the boss. You must be, on occasion, the loyal opposition. "You run a risk, as a manager, of coming off the wall, of making a decision too soon," says Thomas Plaskett [Senior Vice President for Finance, American Airlines]. "You have to have somebody who will say, 'Now, goddammit, that's not right! You can't do that! And here's why.' You have an obligation to keep him from making what you think is a wrong decision." It is especially important to question decisions if you essentially agree on most issues. The most dangerous yes-men are those who genuinely mean it, precluding closer examination, or reexamination, of policies and positions.[7]

Although disagreement is essential to the process of testing ideas, it should not be carried past the point at which it is useful. Once the decision has been made, continued disagreement only weakens the cohesiveness of your working group. Disagree while a decision is being made, but lend your full support after the conclusion has been reached.

Once you have demonstrated your accessibility by openly sharing ideas and disagreeing as necessary, you must preserve the relationship by respecting your superior's need for confidentiality. Ill-timed or misdirected disclosure of ideas that your superior shared with you may have a serious adverse effect on his or her plans

---

[6] Ibid., pp. 47–50.

[7] Robert J. Schoenberg, *The Art of Being a Boss* (Philadelphia and New York: Lippincott 1978), pp. 79–80.

and may otherwise prove embarrassing to the supervisor. To avoid this, it is wise to avoid sharing your boss's ideas with others. If some advantage will result from disclosure, try to persuade your boss to disseminate the information. It is critical that the supervisor always decide what is to be made available and with whom it is to be discussed.

The second condition Jennings identifies is *availability*. In the most immediate sense, this means that the subordinate is physically present when expected to be there. As a student, you have probably experienced the frustration of trying to find an instructor who failed to be available during office hours. A few absences can be excused, but repeated disappointments cannot be tolerated. You know how you would evaluate an instructor who consistently failed to be available, and you can readily imagine the reactions of a supervisor who had difficulty in locating employees. Physical presence is especially important when corporate activity is in peak periods because your superior may need you at a moment's notice.

As important as it is, physical availability is only the steppingstone for psychological availability. This means that your boss needs to feel that you are interested in his or her work and that your talents are available to help out when necessary. To achieve this condition, you should practice the receiving skills described above by creating a favorable environment, paraphrasing messages to ensure accuracy, and actively listening for emotional content.

In addition, you should give your supervisor's needs a higher priority than your own. Norman C. Hill and Paul H. Thompson use the following example to explain the availability of resources:

> Recently, one of the authors was under pressure to complete several projects with very tight deadlines. One of his subordinates became upset because he was not receiving the help he needed on a project the author felt was of less importance. Another subordinate took a different approach. In one of their meetings he said: "I know you're under pressure right now trying to complete high-priority projects. This article we're working on is less important, so I'm quite willing to let it wait for a while. In addition, if I can be of help on any of your projects, just let me know. I've got a little extra time, and I'm willing to pitch in and help any way I can."
>
> The second subordinate was invited to work on two of the projects and not only helped his boss but helped himself as well. It is not difficult to guess which individual received the most favorable letters of recommendation.[8]

The third condition Jennings describes is *predictability*. Of the four, it is most specifically related to task performance. Predictability means that the subordinate can be expected to perform in a consistent manner, regardless of the specific task. Simply stated, "Managers don't like surprises," especially ones that "embarrass them or make them look bad."[9] A major source of information for a superior

---

[8] Norman C. Hill and Paul H. Thompson, "Managing Your Manager: The Effective Subordinate," *Exchange* (Fall/Winter 1978), 10.

[9] Ibid., p. 11.

about your performance is your communication with this person. This fact poses an especially difficult problem because there is always the danger of appearing immodest, of being labelled a "horn blower." Schoenberg found this to be one of the most important problems for young executives to solve and his advice is worthy of attention.

> The issue of self-advertisement is critical, particularly at lower levels in large corporations where there may be considerable insulation between you and the boss whose recognition of your merits means most. There are four exceptionally effective techniques.
>
> First, *selectively* send the right people copies of conclusive memos and correspondence. Restraint is everything. A blizzard of paper will soon be ignored, so you must save your shots, sending only those that signal particular triumph: superb test results, commendation from the outside, breakthroughs on a project of first importance. The test is whether intermediate bosses may want to brag about it to *their* bosses. If so, send the original with a simple, handwritten notation like, "Thought you'd want to know about this," in red ink.
>
> Second—and more informally—keep the right people abreast of any project you know interests them by mentioning it in passing. "You catch them in the hallway," says Litton Microwave's Rick Shriner. "You know some people are pushing a project you're on, so you say, 'Hey! we made some good progress today!' And that afternoon they come down to actually *see* what you've done." That gives you immediate exposure at the best possible time, in the throes of success.
>
> Third, increase your exposure and identification with good results by being circumspect about when, where, and with whom you share the fruits of your labors. Gary Tessitore, manager of operations cost and profit analysis in Louis Ross's group at Ford, knew there was going to be a presentation to executive VP Donald Petersen of some vital figures Tessitore's group had generated in conjunction with the finance staff. There was no argument about the figures or their implication. "This was a case where we all agreed," Tessitore says. "One of the finance staff was going to present it, or I was going to present it. And I wanted visibility with Petersen." So he arranged for it—by the simple expedient of not releasing the final figures to the finance staff ahead of time. The moral is to save your crowing for when it counts.
>
> The fourth way of letting the boss know how well your group is doing, without seeming immodest, is something you should be doing anyway: lavishly praising the accomplishments of your subordinates. From your boss's viewpoint, "My guy, Joe, did a great job," means your group is producing good results, and since your group is your boss's group, it is welcome news. It also might be called socially acceptable personal hornblowing, since your people's record is eventually your record. Your boss, in turn, can blow your horn a couple of levels up, thus (by the same indirection) blowing his own. Why deprive your boss of such generous pleasure? Praise your people for all that you—and they—are worth.[10]

The final condition Jennings mentions is *loyalty*. The loyalty Jennings has in mind is personal loyalty of the subordinate to his immediate superior, and its importance is evident in several situations. An effective working relationship may require sharing sensitive information with the boss, and the boss needs to be sure that the subordinate will not use this information to the superior's disadvantage.

---

[10] Schoenberg, *The Art of Being a Boss,* pp. 77–79.

Similarly, discussion of projects and proposals in their preliminary stages may include comments that should not be repeated, and your superior must be able to trust you. Finally, from time to time, your boss is likely to make an error and he or she must feel free to call on you for help in correcting things while knowing that you will not broadcast the mistake.

Each of the foregoing is a more or less positive instance of personal loyalty. Unfortunately, there are also cases in which personal loyalty may conflict with other loyalties and values—cases in which actions by your immediate superior are in conflict with your values, threaten the security of your friends and coworkers, reduce the effectiveness of the organization as a whole, or even violate laws or social policies. These conflicts are extremely difficult to resolve and there seem to be no clear guides for dealing with them. The approach you use is ultimately your own decision, but caution is especially important. Approaches that aggravate the conflict seem to be particularly fruitless. Either sacrificing other principles to personal loyalty or finding a boss with whom you are comfortable are preferable to keeping your job while doing battle with your superior.

What to Report

Deciding what to report to your superior is complicated by two factors. First, most work environments make demands upon the participants, and your supervisor's expectations have been shaped by unique experiences in these environments. Since you have not shared many of these experiences, there is a broad area of discretion in which you may have few guides. The situation in which subordinates find themselves in this regard is not unusual, and many studies have revealed broad areas of disagreement or misunderstanding between supervisors and their subordinates. For example, B. B. Boyd and J. M. Jensen found that superiors and subordinates did not agree on who had the responsibility to purchase materials in 44 percent of the cases studied and on who was responsible for equipment maintenance in 59 percent of the cases studied.[11]

The second problem in deciding what to report results from the broad range of information directly available to the subordinate, but not to the superior. In addition to technical feedback about goal accomplishments, David Katz and Robert Kahn list eight classes of information that the subordinate *might* pass on to a superior. These classes are:

1. What the person has done
2. What those under him have done
3. What his peers have done
4. What his problems are
5. What the problems of his department are
6. What he thinks needs to be done

[11] B. B. Boyd and J. M. Jensen, "Perceptions of First-line Supervisor's Authority: A Study in Superior-Subordinate Communication," *Academy of Management Journal*, 15 (1972), 331–342.

7.   What his perception of his job performance is

8.   What organizational policy and practices need adjusting.[12]

The reason I say that these classes of information *might* be reported is that not all superiors want to receive this much information and certain categories may be regarded as inappropriate. For example, some supervisors prefer not to hear about problems (classes 4 and 5), especially when they are not in a position to solve them, and recommendations for changes (classes 6 and 8) may be taken as challenges to the supervisor's authority. As an individual you are unlikely to be in a position to change corporate policy or the preferences of your immediate supervisor. You will learn what the supervisor wants to know as your working relationship matures, but three generally accepted guides may make the adjustment easier. These are a prohibition against reports that transfer responsibility, predetermined levels of initiative for certain tasks, and the principle of exception.

Do not transfer responsibility   One of the most common problems managers encounter is called "upward delegation." Upward delegation occurs whenever a subordinate uses a report to transfer responsibility for a project or decision from him or herself to an immediate supervisor. William Oncken, Jr., and Donald L. Wass use an illustration to explain how this happens:

> Let us imagine that a manager is walking down the hall and that he notices one of his subordinates, Mr. A, coming up the hallway. When they are abreast of one another, Mr. A greets the manager with, "Good morning. By the way, we've got a problem. You see. . . ." As Mr. A continues, the manager recognizes in this problem the same two characteristics common to all the problems his subordinates gratuitously bring to his attention. Namely, the manager knows (a) enough to get involved, but (b) not enough to make the on-the-spot decision expected of him. Eventually, the manager says, "So glad you brought this up. I'm in a rush right now. Meanwhile, let me think about it and I'll let you know." Then he and Mr. A part company.[13]

Once the manager said, "I'll let you know," the problem became his, and his subordinate was relieved of responsibility for further action. In fact, the manager had voluntarily assumed a subordinate role by accepting responsibility *and* promising to make a progress report.

Oncken and Wass describe several techniques that the manager might use to escape upward delegation. Even escaping the situation places additional demands upon the manager that few will appreciate. As a subordinate, you should communicate in a manner that avoids transferring responsibility to your boss.

Of course, there are many occasions when you will want to solicit your

[12] David Katz and Robert Kahn, *The Social Psychology of Organizations* (New York: John Wiley, 1966), p. 245.

[13] William Oncken, Jr., and Donald L. Wass, "Management Time: Who's Got The Monkey?" *Harvard Business Review* (November-December 1974), 76. Copyright © 1974 by the President and Fellows of Harvard College; all rights reserved. Reprinted by permission of the *Harvard Business Review*.

supervisor's recommendations and you may also need assistance in making policy decisions. In these cases, you will want to check with your supervisor before taking action, but you can avoid transferring responsibility by the simple method of suggesting a course of action. Plan the action in advance and be prepared to give a brief report, which should include a statement of the problem and an explanation of what you intend to do. This allows your supervisor to become involved, and gives the person a chance to see if any dangers lie ahead. But by reporting both the problem and your proposed solution, you retain responsibility and give your supervisor an option.

Predetermined levels of initiative   A second factor determining what you should report is the amount of initiative the boss expects you to exercise. Although the level of initiative is seldom specified in job descriptions, finding a level that matches your supervisor's expectations is an important part of developing an harmonious working relationship. In some cases, your supervisor may have difficulty voicing expectations, but it is a good bet that they fall somewhere within the following range. Whenever a problem comes to your attention, you can

1. Do nothing until told—this is the lowest level of initiative
2. Ask your supervisor what to do
3. Recommend some action and do what your supervisor directs
4. Act on your own, but report to your boss immediately
5. Act on your own and report routinely—this is the highest level of initiative[14]

As you can see, acting at level 1 requires no initiative and is generally improper in professional contexts. Acting at level 2 is a form of upward delegation and should be avoided. Thus, the real choice is between levels 3, 4, and 5. Unfortunately, the choice is complicated by the fact that your supervisor may have different expectations for different parts of your job. For example, a training director for a large firm occasionally is responsible for purchasing instructional packages subject to the following budget limitations. If the price is under $2,500, she may purchase it and account for the money in her monthly report (level 5); if the cost is between $2,500 and $4,000, she is expected to act on her own, but make a special report to the accounting department (level 4); and, if the cost is over $4,000, she may recommend purchasing it, but do nothing until she receives authorization (level 3).

The expectations in this example are spelled out fairly precisely, but other supervisors may have difficulty in voicing their expectations. You are always free to ask your supervisor how much initiative you should exercise; some people find it helpful to schedule a conference with their immediate supervisors to discuss the question. It works best if both parties compile a list of duties and try to set levels of

[14] The characterization of initiative is developed by Oncken and Wass, "Management Time: Who's Got The Monkey?", *Harvard Business Review* (November-December 1974), p. 79. Copyright © 1974 by the President and Fellows of Harvard College; all rights reserved. Reprinted by permission of the *Harvard Business Review*.

initiative for each. When an open discussion is not possible, and when your supervisor cannot give you meaningful directions, you may use a trial-and-error approach. The safest point to start at is level 3: Recommend a course of action and do what you are told. At the same time, you can learn from the experience by asking your boss, "How would you like me to handle this in the future?" After several tasks, you should be able to form a clear idea of your supervisor's expectations while avoiding conflict that could be generated by misunderstanding.

The principle of exception   The principle of exception is the final guide in deciding what to report. This principle is the outgrowth of scientific theories of management in which many managers have been trained, and it has remained popular in some applications. According to this principle, managers make the most efficient use of their time and talent by delegating routine matters to subordinates. The proper use of the manager's time and ability is in coping with exceptional, unusual, or unexpected items.

From the subordinates' point of view, the principle of exception means that anything that departs significantly from the normal course of events should be called to the supervisor's attention. The problem, or course, is in determining what constitutes a significant departure from the normal course of events. In some cases, it is easy to set standards. For example, on some projects the normal overhead is 15 percent of the budget, but any figure between 12 percent and 18 percent is acceptable. In this case, then, figures that fall outside of the range should be reported immediately.

Few applications are as uncomplicated as the example, but after a short time you should be able to determine what your superior considers to be a normal course of events. Anything that you have not encountered before should be called to the attention of your boss, and you should treat each surprise as an opportunity to learn. After notifying your supervisor, find out if you should report future occurrences or if your supervisor would rather have you take care of them. The question, "Would you like me to report similar instances in the future?" should be sufficient and will help both of you to clarify your expectations. After you have established a good working relationship, identifying exceptions will be almost second nature and you will be pleased to see how easy it is to identify events that the boss will regard as exceptional.

Timing Your Report

Many executives set aside time for regular reports from their subordinates. The time may resemble the formal office hours used by college and university faculty, or they may take the form of lunch meetings held with individual subordinates. Some will set aside portions of staff meetings for "concerns of the group" during which participants are invited to discuss potential problems. Unfortunately, many executives do not provide regular opportunities for informal reports, and some who claim to have an "open-door" policy act in a manner that discourages frequent interaction. In addition, matters that require immediate attention or that are excluded from regular schedules may require you to secure special opportunities for informal reports. When you must secure special time for an informal report, the phrasing of your request may determine your chances and will almost certainly affect the amount of attention you receive.

The most common error subordinates make is catching their boss off guard and launching into a lengthy report without first securing attention. Most executives will resent the unexpected demand on their time and few will listen attentively. The proper approach is to begin by requesting an opportunity and allowing your superior to decide whether or not it is a good time for the report.

However, merely requesting time doesn't give the other person sufficient information on which to make a judgment. The phrase, "Got a minute?" is one of the most feared expressions in management because it seldom means that the person making the request only wants one minute. And again, it doesn't give the person sufficient information on which to base an answer.

An adequate request for time should always include four elements: a greeting, an indication of the subject to be addressed, an estimate of the time required to make the report, and an expression of the urgency of the situation. The following is a good example:

> Steve, I need two minutes of your time to discuss a problem on machine number 6. It's urgent, and we may have to stop production if we can't get it solved.

A request phrased in this manner does two things most supervisors will appreciate: It gives them the information they need to establish a priority for your report, and it gives them the option of deciding when they will talk to you. Of the four components, the greeting is the least important. However, if the contact is by telephone, the greeting should be expanded to fully identify you to the other person. For example,

> Steve, this is John Smith in Shipping. I need you for five minutes to discuss a problem with our primary carrier. It's not urgent, but I'd like to clear it up by the end of the week.

The subject to be discussed should be identified quickly, but in sufficient detail to indicate the kind of decision to be made. Your estimate of the time required should be as accurate as possible, and the more experience you have with your supervisor, the more accurate you can make it. If you don't know how long it will take to solve the problem, say so and indicate how long it will take you to explain the situation. You might phrase your request as follows:

> Marsha, this is Eric in Maintenance. I've got a problem with the new floor in the production area, and I'd like to correct it before we begin the new run next week. I can show you the problem in less than ten minutes, but I don't know how long it will take us to solve it.

Finally, your expression of the urgency of the situation should be an honest one. Although there are many qualifiers available, the following sequence represents the most commonly used gradients:

1. Not critical, not urgent
2. Moderately important
3. Important
4. Very important
5. Critical, urgent

Many beginners find that overstating the degree of the problem gets their boss's attention more rapidly. However, the tactic soon loses its effectiveness and the subordinate using it soon may lose credibility. The subordinate for whom everything is a crisis is either untrustworthy or unreliable, while the subordinate who gives accurate appraisals of the situation soon earns respect. Using the key words, "critical" and "urgent," only when they are appropriate helps to ensure that your boss will be available when needed.

APPRAISAL INTERVIEWS

If your career develops well, you should someday find yourself managing the work of other people. This is an important step and it is an added responsibility: Once you have taken this step, you assume responsibility for the work of your subordinates as well as for your own. It has been said that the most important attribute of a skilled manager is the ability to get the most from subordinates. One of the primary tools available is the systematic appraisal of the people who work for you, and most companies have developed elaborate appraisal procedures for this. Properly employed, such systems have a number of desirable effects.

1. Motivating employees by establishing merit foundations for raises and promotions
2. Providing employees with a sense of accomplishment when their work is reviewed
3. Giving employees directions for development of their careers
4. Providing management with feedback about changes in the work environment
5. Identifying areas in which corporate training and hiring policies need revision
6. Selecting promising employees for advancement and reassignment
7. Allowing employees to build records of success on which to base their expectations

In spite of these praiseworthy goals, no managerial practice has been the object of more criticism. One critic observes that "in government, performance appraisal is largely a joke, and in both private and public enterprise, merit ratings are hollow."[15] The problems that prompt his criticism include use of arbitrary or subjective judgments of performance, systems that collect insufficient or irrelevant information, different rating patterns used by different supervisors, reliance on inappropriate survey instruments or measures of performance, evaluation on

---

[15] Harry Levinson, "Appraisal of *What* Performance?" *Harvard Business Review* (July-August, 1976), 31. Copyright © 1976 by the President and Fellows of Harvard College; all rights reserved. Reprinted by permission of the *Harvard Business Review*.

criteria other than those specified in job descriptions, and the inability of many managers to communicate necessary information to subordinates. Awareness of these difficulties has prompted the development of more sophisticated systems of appraisal. However, even the most comprehensive and well-intentioned system of appraisal is liable to break down when managers are unable to effectively communicate the results to employees. Such difficulty is likely to surface in two ways. First, a supervisor may communicate negative information in a way that causes the employee to become defensive. These supervisors like to "lay it on the line," but they fail to realize that once the employee is made to feel like the object of a personal attack, very little real communication will take place. The second difficulty stems from the discomfort most managers feel when they are asked to evaluate their employees. Many report that they do not like "playing God," and they often find ways of avoiding performance appraisal interviews. Some delay and postpone unfavorable reviews, leaving the employee in a state of uncertainty. Others withhold negative feedback until formal reviews so that the appraisal sessions become annual (or semiannual) explosions. Some managers are dishonest with the employee by failing to acknowledge negative reports, and they either refuse to deal with them or report them without discussion with the employee. All of these responses are manifestations of the managers' discomfort with the evaluative element of performance appraisal. Since most people have difficulty coping with such situations, it is not difficult to see why even the most elaborate appraisal systems may fail to produce desired results. Saul W. Gellerman has described the feelings of many professionals in the following paragraph:

> Few, if any, aspects of management reveal as disappointing a gap between potential and actuality as does performance appraisal. Under certain conditions, performance appraisal can contribute to . . . laudable goals . . . [But] those 'certain conditions' are seldom created. To make matters worse, many organizations act as if they were unaware of them.[16]

Recognizing that the ability of individual appraisers is critical to the entire appraisal system is less important than training them to use systems effectively.[17] Much of the necessary training is outside the realm of communication and centers on criteria for evaluation, objectivity of judgment, and statutory requirements for evidence of nondiscrimination. However, the means whereby information can be presented to the appraised employee is first and foremost a communication problem. The information presented to an employee concerning his or her performance is known as *feedback* and the communication skills involved in presenting feedback have many applications. This section describes the characteristics of ef-

---

[16] From THE MANAGEMENT OF HUMAN RESOURCES by Saul W. Gellerman, pg. 165. Copyright © 1976 by the Dryden Press, a division of Holt, Rinehart and Winston. Reprinted by permission of Holt, Rinehart and Winston, CBS College Publishing.

[17] Alan H. Locher and Kenneth S. Teel, "Performance Appraisal—A Survey of Current Practices," *Personnel Journal* (1977), 245–247, 254.

fective feedback, discusses the characteristics of defensive communication, and presents an approach to conducting appraisal interviews.

Characteristics of Effective Feedback

To be effective, feedback should be marked by five characteristics. First, effective feedback is prompt. To be prompt, feedback should follow the behavior recognized as quickly after it occurs as possible. Failure to acknowledge good work promptly reduces employee motivation, and allowing inferior performance to continue sets a bad example for other workers. Thus, someone who submits a report should get a response as quickly as possible, a salesperson who exceeds the specified quota should be rewarded as soon as practical, and an employee who fails to meet a deadline should be questioned about the failure soon after the deadline passes. The one thing that can justify postponing feedback is anger. You should never try to conduct an appraisal or disciplinary interview while you are angry. Always give yourself time to "cool off" before approaching an employee, and make sure that your subordinate also has time to get in control before discussing a situation that has angered either one of you.

Second, effective feedback is ongoing. This notion is closely related to the first because prompt feedback will usually be constant as long as two people work together. However, ongoing feedback is especially important as a means of developing a trusting relationship between coworkers. By establishing a norm of openness through constant feedback, a supervisor can establish a relationship that allows for discussion of even negative aspects of an employee's behavior with much less danger of unpleasant or defensive reactions.

Third, effective feedback focuses on specific behaviors. Focusing on specific behaviors both reduces the possibility of defensive reactions and gives the person receiving the feedback a clear impression of what was done and how it was viewed. Contrast the following statements:

1. You are lazy.
2. You are not working up to par.
3. You are not producing enough widgets per hour.
4. Yesterday, you stopped for seven water breaks between 2:30 and 4:00 P.M.

Only the final statement identifies a specific behavior that an employee could change in order to improve performance. In addition, it opens the way for further discussion, as the employee might explain, for example, that the doctor advised drinking more water to cure an illness.

Fourth, effective feedback fits the context of the relationship between participants. That is, effective feedback is relevant to the situation that brings the participants into professional contact with one another. This means that the feedback is based upon performance monitored by the person giving the feedback. Discussion of matters that are not directly related to work may be seen as unwarranted invasions of the employee's privacy unless the supervisor and employee have developed a personal relationship in addition to their professional one. However, even in that case, personal discussions should be kept distinct from professional ones.

Finally, effective feedback is structured to avoid defensive reactions. These reactions inhibit communication and may produce behavior opposite of that desired. Jack Gibb coined the term "defensive communication," and he describes its consequences as follows:

> Defensive behavior is defined as the behavior which occurs when an individual perceives threat or anticipates threat. . . . The person who behaves defensively, even though he also gives some attention to the common task, devotes an appreciable portion of his energy to defending himself. . . . Defensive recipients distort what they receive. As a person becomes more and more defensive, he becomes less and less able to perceive accurately the motives, the values, and the emotions of the sender.[18]

Avoiding defensive reactions does not mean that only positive aspects are discussed, but feedback must be presented in a way that minimizes the chances of a defensive reaction. Avoiding defensive communication is so important that we will further explore its characteristics.

Characteristics of Defensive Communication

Gibb based his description of defensive communication on the study of small groups, but the characteristics of communication likely to produce defensive reactions also apply to interpersonal communication and feedback. Gibb identified six qualities that produce defensive climates and six opposed qualities that produce supportive climates. These qualities are listed in Table 13.1.

TABLE 13.1   Communication Qualities

DEFENSIVE CLIMATES	SUPPORTIVE CLIMATES
Evaluation	Description
Control	Problem Orientation
Strategy	Spontaneity
Neutrality	Empathy
Superiority	Equality
Certainty	Provisionalism

Most of us have difficulty separating the pairs as neatly as Gibb has done, and few situations are wholly defensive or wholly supportive. Most probably include elements of both supportive and defensive climates, but a few supportive elements can be overwhelmed by defensive ones, while a few defensive behaviors can be overcome by supportive behaviors. As an aid in learning to recognize these characteristics, we shall examine each pair in turn.

---

[18] Jack Gibb, "Defensive Communication," *Journal of Communication* 11 (1961), 141–142.

Evaluation and description constitute the first pair. Anything that implies judgment will usually be taken as evaluation, and common forms include acceptance or rejection, praise or blame, like or dislike, pleasure or displeasure, and compliments or criticisms. Evaluations may be conveyed by both verbal and nonverbal signals, including questions worded to imply particular answers, facial expressions, and postures. Description is the opposite of evaluation in that it focuses attention on what has been done or what may be accomplished.

Any communication that seems intended to exercise control over the recipient is likely to trigger a defensive reaction. The tendency to defend oneself when confronted with pressure to change is an almost universal reaction. Problem orientation is its alternative, and it treats difficulties as common problems that must be solved by the superior and subordinate working together.

Behavior that appears to have been planned in advance suggests that the communicator has a hidden agenda—something to be accomplished at the expense of the person with whom he or she is talking. Prepackaged feedback and a smooth, rapid rate of speech implying a practiced presentation are very likely to produce a defensive reaction. In contrast, a spontaneous appraisal is more likely to create a supportive climate. Characteristics include relatively short statements, frequent pauses and hesitations, and a high frequency of vocalized pauses (ah, uhm, and uh, for example). The desirability of spontaneity does not mean that you should fail to prepare for appraisal sessions, but it does mean that your approach should be flexible enough to respond to the unique character of each interview.

Pretending to be personally uninvolved is an indicator of neutrality. Saying something like, "I don't care one way or the other, but . . . ." or "According to company policy . . ." is sure to trigger defensive reactions because the appearance of neutrality may be taken as evidence that the manager doesn't care for the employee. The alternative is to recognize the feelings of the employee; Gibb explains supportive communication that displays empathy as follows:

> Communication that conveys empathy for the feelings and respect for the worth of the listener . . . is particularly supportive and defense reductive. Reassurance results when a message indicates that the speaker identifies himself with the listener's problems, shares his feelings, and accepts his emotional reactions at face value. Abortive efforts to deny the legitimacy of the receiver's emotions by assuring the receiver that he need not feel bad, that he should not feel rejected, or that he is overly anxious, though often intended as support giving, may impress the listener as lack of acceptance. The combination of understanding and empathizing with the other person's emotions with no accompanying effort to change him apparently is supportive at a high level.[19]

The mere fact that one person is given a position from which to appraise the performance of another signals a difference in status between them. However, these differences need not be emphasized in the interaction between participants,

---

[19] Gibb, "Defensive Communication," p. 147.

and there is a much greater chance of providing meaningful feedback if the differences between participants can be minimized. To the extent that the appraiser feels it necessary to assert superiority and employ behaviors traditionally associated with superior status—giving orders, "telling it like it is," not listening to the other person, and giving the other little opportunity to take an active part in the feedback session—opportunities for constructive feedback are reduced. On the other hand, when the session is structured to allow both participants an equal opportunity to express their views and discuss problems of common concern, the chances of conducting a productive session are greatly enhanced.

A final cause of defensive reactions is certainty. Someone evidences certainty by reaching conclusions about an interaction and about the subject of discussion prior to the meeting. In the performance appraisal context, indicators of fixed judgment and an unwillingness to engage in open discussion include preparation of a periodic review form prior to the meeting and refusal to depart from predetermined schedules. Dogmatic, rigid managers generally state their views and beliefs as if they were matters of unquestioned fact, whereas more flexible managers state their views as opinions influenced by particular needs and situations. For example, both rigid and flexible managers might recognize a production problem, but they would describe in it different terms. Contrast the following statements about a given employee:

John isn't working out very well.
I'm not sure that John is adapting well to my system.

The difference between the two statements is recognizing that the second is an opinion, while the first is stated as if it were an unquestionable fact. The phrasing itself is of incidental importance and can be abused by someone who is willing to do so. However, the flexibility evidenced in proper use of the provisional attitude is of tremendous importance.

Conducting Appraisal Interviews

The frequency with which you conduct formal appraisal interviews is usually specified by organizational policy. In most companies, appraisals must be conducted on a yearly basis with shorter intervals for new employees or those in new positions. Remember, the stated policies specify minimum frequency and you may have the option of conducting appraisal interviews more often. In addition, you should provide your employees with ongoing feedback so that the formal interviews are seen to be extensions of regular activity rather than unusual occurrences.

Conduct the interview in private and take steps to see that you are not interrupted. The appraisal is serious business for both participants and you should act accordingly. Refuse to accept all but the most critical phone calls and make it clear that you are giving your undivided attention to the employee. One element that you might overlook is time: Be sure to schedule enough time for the interview so it can be conducted without undue pressure to finish. In most cases, an hour is sufficient, but it is a good idea to schedule the interview at a time of day that allows you to go beyond the specified period if necessary. Avoid scheduling appraisal interviews immediately before lunch, at the end of the day, or when you can expect other anticipated interruptions.

The appraisal inteview differs from a formal presentation in that you want to provide abundant opportunities for the employee to react and discuss the materials covered. However, you can use a modified speech format with an introduction, body, and conclusion.

The primary purpose of the *introduction* is to set the employee at ease. Begin with a pleasant, personal greeting, explain the purpose of the interview, and describe the procedure you will use. In explaining the purpose of the interview, avoid anything that would seem to reduce its importance. Some managers try to make the employee feel more comfortable by minimizing the importance of the interview, but they only create an atmosphere of greater tension—the employee knows that the interview is important and efforts to say that it isn't may be taken as a threat. "He's just trying to soften the blow" is the common reaction to statements that imply a casual attitude. A better approach is to briefly describe company policy and summarize the conclusions of your last interview with the employee. Your preview should enumerate the topics you want to discuss and indicate the amount of input you would like from the employee on each. Some employees may be reluctant to speak up, so it is important for you to set the ground rules at the start. For example, you might prepare the employee for a high level of participation by saying, "I'd like you to provide much of the information on these topics and I'll let you do most of the talking." If you have never witnessed an appraisal interview this may seem to be an unnecessarily rigid approach. However, you will learn that most employees feel considerable tension during the early stages of the interview and will remain quiet until they know precisely what is expected of them.

The *body* of the interview is the portion during which the employee should do at least half of the talking, and it is important to allow the subordinate frequent opportunities for comment. It may be necessary to change the order in which you discuss individual topics to suit the interests of the employee, but the interview should always include five major concerns:

1. The employee's duties
2. The employee's past performance
3. The employee's needs
4. Targets for the following year
5. The employee's future prospects

Discussing the employee's duties is a crucial step to insure that you both have a common understanding of the job. Consider not only the specific duties, but also the relative importance and amount of initiative the employee is expected to display in each. This portion is potentially the most rewarding because it provides an opportunity to clarify any misconceptions and to ensure that you have established common ground for discussion of the remaining topics. Marked disagreement is unlikely, but you may want to have a copy of the individual's job description at hand. Be sure to note the individual's reasons for emphasizing parts of the job and discuss any differences between your interpretations.

Discussion of the employee's past performance is the point at which conflict is most likely. If possible, allow the person to take the lead or use the targets established at the previous year's appraisal to guide discussion. In addition, it is important for you to share any reports you have received concerning the individual's performance. Since there may be conflict here, you should have substantial documentation and be willing to share the supporting materials with the employee. There is great diversity in measures of performance used in different occupations, but most can be interpreted in terms of the types of supporting material that prove or disprove and clarify. Detailed illustrations are particularly helpful because they allow the employee to see clearly how you measure performance and on what specific behaviors you base your evaluation.

The third topic to be considered is the employee's needs. This follows logically from discussion of past performance because employees may be anxious to point out circumstances that make it difficult for them to fulfill their assignments. Some employees use this step to avoid responsibility, but it remains vitally important. It helps the employee to cope with feelings about the job, and it gives management an opportunity to identify needed changes in the work environment. At this point you may encounter one subject that gives managers particular difficulty: indications of personal shortcomings. If you have established a climate of trust, some employees will point out things you do that make it more difficult for them to perform as expected. At this time, you may become defensive and miss a vital opportunity to learn. Remember, the reactions of your immediate subordinates are one of the best sources of feedback concerning your work as a manager. If you find yourself becoming defensive, try to avoid the reaction by using the active listening skills previously discussed. Paraphrasing to ensure you understand the employee's point of view is extremely important, and the attention required often short-circuits the defensive reaction.

Establishing targets for the next appraisal period helps shift attention from evaluation to problem orientation. Working with the employee, try to establish four or five specific work related behaviors to be improved during the following period. These behaviors should be described precisely and both of you should agree on their importance. In addition to listing and defining the behaviors, decide how they will be measured and establish dates by which improvement should be evident. Merely saying that an employee is expected to ''improve relationships with coworkers'' does not identify a specific behavior and is not a suitable target. The same concern could be addressed by focusing attention on volunteering to help coworkers. Adding a means of measurement and setting target dates results in the following goal.

> John will increase the frequency with which he volunteers to help coworkers. This will be measured by his own reports and should reach an average of five times a week by the end of January.

Some people object, believing that not all behavior can be measured so precisely. However, it is impossible to fairly evaluate individuals on criteria that cannot be described, and real improvement can be made when both the supervisor and employee know precisely what is expected.

The final topic to be considered is the employee's future prospects. This discussion may duplicate information available elsewhere (newsletters and public announcements), but it should focus on things affecting the particular individual. Employees are always anxious to know how changes in company policy will affect them, what recent economic developments mean for them, when new hiring policies will apply to their task group, and so forth. Topics of continuing interest are future assignments and the likelihood of promotion. These should be discussed candidly, even if there are limited opportunities for the future. Honesty in discussing these concerns will help establish a trusting relationship and an open climate.

The *conclusion* should summarize all points on which you agree and list any remaining points of disagreement. Immediately following the summary, use a clearinghouse probe, "Have I missed anything?" to ensure a complete list. Some companies ask that you have the employee initial the list of recommendations made to guarantee that the person has seen them and to avoid future legal complications. The final appeal can be nothing more than a cordial parting, "Good bye," but you may also include directions for future contact. "I look forward to seeing you next week (month)," will work, and you can be even more specific by establishing a definite appointment. The important thing is that the employee should know that you are available for further consultations and that you would like to meet whenever there is more to discuss.

SUMMARY

This chapter describes three formal types of dyadic communication: selection interviews, informational interviews, and appraisal interviews. Preparing for a selection interview involves preparing a resume and developing answers to typical questions, while participating in the interview involves avoiding negative factors and adapting to the interviewer's style. Informational interviews are intended to keep the boss informed and you should consider factors related to earning your superior's trust, deciding what to report, and timing your report. Appraisal interviews always present the danger of defensive reactions, and the final section of this chapter describes the characteristics of effective feedback, elements of defensive communications, and the conduct of the appraisal interview.

LEARNING ACTIVITIES

1. Preparing for selection interviews is one of the most important activities at the beginning of one's career. Review a job description from the want ads or your placement service and begin preparing yourself to be interviewed. In addition to preparing a resume and composing answers to probable questions, learn as much as you can about the organization offering the position. Use files prepared by your college or university placement service and look up the organization in *Everybody's Business: The Irreverent Guide to Corporate America*[20] and by reading recent articles about the company referenced by the *Business Periodicals Index.*

2. Planning an informational interview always requires thinking about the needs of the potential audience. Think of your classroom audience as if it were the superior to whom you report and select an article from a professional journal in your field. Try to identify features of the article that could interest the audience and determine what portions of the information contained would be appropriate for an oral report. Outline the report and ask your instructor or another student to comment on your plan.

3. Put yourself in the position of a university administrator charged with evaluating the performance of faculty members. Select a faculty member with whom you have worked and prepare to conduct an appraisal interview with that person. What are his or her duties? By what criteria is performance of these duties evaluated? How well has this person performed? How can you get the faculty member to talk about personal needs? What kinds of targets can you establish for the next academic year? How can you assess the instructor's future prospects? Armed with answers to these questions, consider the problems you are likely to encounter in conducting the interview. How can you establish a supportive climate? What negative information must be conveyed? How can you encourage subordinate participation? How will you cope with emotional or defensive reactions to the situation?

4. Put yourself in the position of an employer who needs to hire someone from your professional area. Begin by listing the technical qualifications or skills the employee must have in order to perform the duties of the position. Then, list the ways in which an interviewee might have acquired the skills or might be able to demonstrate professional ability. How many of the qualifications do you possess? Can you show that you have the necessary skills? Does your resume show that you have the skills and qualifications? How can you change your resume to emphasize necessary skills and qualifications?

[20] Eds. Milton Moskowitz, Michael Katz, and Robert Levering (San Francisco: Harper & Row, Pub. 1980).

CHAPTER FOURTEEN
PRESENTATIONAL
ACTIVITIES
IN TASK GROUPS

Most professionals find that meetings of both regular and special groups occupy large portions of managerial time. David R. Seibold summarizes some recent literature on the subject of meetings as follows:

> A study sponsored by the 3M company revealed that the number of meetings and conferences in industry alone nearly doubled during the past ten years and their cost tripled. Estimates suggest that most organizations devote between 7 and 15 percent of their personnel budgets to meetings. One large California-based corporation figures that almost $30 million of its $350 million personnel budget is spent on meetings. At the individual level, middle managers in industry may spend as much as 35 percent of their work week in meetings. That figure can be as high as 50 percent for top management.[1]

Before we go much further, we should note that many different activities are called "meetings." Distinguishing between them is important because behaviors that are appropriate in one are unnoticed or unrewarded in others, and inappropriate at still others. The most important characteristic of the various types is the number of participants. Differences in what constitutes appropriate behavior depend on the number of people present.

[1] David R. Seibold, "Making Meetings More Successful: Plans, Formats, and Procedures for Group Problem-Solving," *The Journal of Business Communication*, 16 (1979), 4.

The largest activity called a ''meeting'' is a convention or conference. Conventions may include several thousand people, and they are usually divided into smaller units attending formal presentations. Assemblies with 100 or more members and councils with 20 or more participants also have ''meetings.'' Their size limits the amount of interaction between participants, and the audience is usually gathered for the purpose of hearing a series of speakers. When people attending conventions and members of assemblies or councils are called upon to make decisions, formal parliamentary procedures are used to ensure that all points of view are heard. Presentations are generally very formal, and members of the audience have few opportunities to interact with speakers or to develop additional ideas.

The smallest and probably the most frequent type of meeting is one conducted by a task group or committee. Task groups are limited to fifteen members and seem to function most effectively with as few as seven or nine participants. Formal presentations are generally considered inappropriate, and there is a high degree of interaction between the participants. Parliamentary procedures are rarely used, and the group generally tries to make decisions by considering all available information and reaching a consensus, a decision that satisfies all members.

Although task group meetings are only one type of activity commonly called ''meetings,'' they are extremely important. As the work environment has become increasingly complex, more and more organizations have turned to task groups as their primary problem-solving and decision-making units. Task group meetings often are the only way to gather together people with the necessary expertise to solve a problem, and the relatively informal atmosphere makes it possible to explore new ideas and develop novel approaches. Moreover, frequent meetings may be needed to make sure that coworkers with diverse backgrounds understand one another and develop a unified approach to the task. Equally important, frequent meetings develop a sense of team loyalty and commitment to getting the job done.

Conventions or conferences, assemblies, and councils all rely on formal presentations, and the skills discussed elsewhere in this book may be used without modification. However, participating in task group meetings requires special attention to the nature of the group and to the demands it makes on the speaker. In this chapter, we will explore use of presentational skills by participants in task group meetings. The next chapter discusses some special concerns that arise when you are called upon to chair a task group meeting.

PARTICIPATING IN TASK GROUP MEETINGS

Effective participation in task group meetings requires the proper attitude toward group processes. This attitude is characterized by *tentativeness,* but this does not mean that you should be modest or shy in presenting your ideas. It does mean that your proposals should be presented implicitly qualified. ''On the basis of what

I've learned so far . . . ." would be appropriate because it recognizes that under proper circumstances groups are capable of making decisions of higher quality than any individual participant. Contributing your ideas and working to see that they are understood is an important part of group discussion. However, ideas should be presented in a manner that allows other members to extend them, modify them, or even abandon them when additional information is introduced. By presenting ideas in a tentative manner, you make it possible for other members of the group to take advantage of your knowledge, background, and experiences—and for you to take advantage of theirs—without being limited to a single point of view.

Unfortunately, your pet projects may sometimes be abandoned, and the group may occasionally make errors that you would have avoided. This is part of the price for relying on the judgment of the entire group, although numerous studies have shown that groups are capable of producing better decisions than individuals acting alone. Moreover, many proposals require the support of the whole group, and an inferior solution developed by the group is more likely to be executed and will receive more support than one designed by a single individual.

A proper, tentative attitude is manifest in three specific areas: presenting your own ideas, working with the ideas of others, and helping the leader maintain group processes.

Presenting Your Own Ideas

The most frequent error made by new group members is in trying to present their ideas in a manner that no one could reject or even alter. Speakers who make this error fail to realize that the ideas presented by any one speaker are just one part of the total group process. Instead of presenting ideas in a way that invites other members of the group to work with them, these novices try to force other members to accept their predetermined approaches. Efforts to make the group accept your ideas are usually doomed to failure. Even if you succeed in dominating the group for a time, the hard feelings created are likely to remain long after the proposal itself has been forgotten.

However, failing to present your ideas clearly and with adequate support also reduces the effectiveness of the group. As a result, all the skills discussed in other sections of this text may be used in presenting ideas to a task group meeting. That is, your presentations to the group should be clearly stated, well organized, supported by appropriate materials (both verbal and visual), delivered with care, and so forth. A formal speech is seldom appropriate in a task group meeting, but all of your skills may be applied in the preparation of messages that are brief, specific, relevant, timely, and informal.

Effective messages are brief   Whereas formal presentations may be thirty minutes or more in length, presentations to a task group should seldom be longer than five minutes. The five-minute rule is arbitrary, but it is well founded on the nature of group processes. Lengthy presentations reduce opportunities for other members to participate and reduce the effectiveness of the group as a whole in developing and processing material. The principal exception to this rule arises when you have been asked to make a formal report to the group on some particular matter. Other than that, long presentations may be taken as efforts to dominate the group and usually reduce attention while generating hostility.

Occasionally, adequate presentation of your ideas requires more than five minutes. This generally happens when the materials are highly detailed or complex and thus not suited to oral presentation. When you encounter this situation, you are wise to compose a memorandum with all pertinent data and distribute copies two or three days prior to the meeting. Include a brief cover note explaining that you will refer to the data during the meeting, and ask participants to examine the material and bring their copies to the meeting. Incidentally, if you distribute the material more than three days prior to the meeting, many people will set it aside and forget to either review it or bring it to the meeting.

One further caution should be noted. If you intend to introduce matters requiring lengthy discussion, you should check with the chairperson before you distribute materials. Remember, this person is responsible for conducting orderly meetings, and the unexpected introduction of major items may make it impossible to schedule appropriate amounts of time for each item on the agenda.

Effective messages are specific   Presentations to task groups can be much shorter than formal briefings because they are more specific. Task groups are smaller than other audiences, and you need not appeal to such a broad spectrum of backgrounds and abilities. As you come to know the other members of the group, you can speak directly to their interests, omitting background information that might be necessary for other audiences. You can also rely on the common knowledge and shared experiences of the group members. As a result, the amount of developing material necessary to present your ideas is greatly reduced. A single piece is often sufficient, while presentations to other audiences might require three or more. In addition, the common experiences of the group make it possible to rely on specific instances and brief references, while a formal presentation would require use of illustrations and examples.

In terms of the speech format that is explained in Chapter 4, your message to the group can be made more specific through the following adaptations. First, most of the introduction can be eliminated because you can generally depend on having the group's attention, and the orientation material will probably be unnecessary if the group is already versed in the topic. You may state your purpose, but it will probably be apparent to other members of the group, and the brevity of your presentation will render a preview unnecessary. Second, the body of the message will generally be reduced to a single main idea or contribution. Even if you would like to comment on several aspects of the subject being discussed, limiting yourself to one at a time allows other members to participate. Finally, the conclusion may be almost nonexistent. No summary will be needed and the final appeal can be reduced to a mere statement of what you would like to see done next.

Effective messages are relevant   Subjects that may be discussed at a meeting are generally defined by the specific charge or task of the group and by the agenda. Subjects beyond the scope of the group may be interesting to you and other members, but they are certain to be time killers. Since they are beyond the scope of the group, it is unlikely that anything can be done by the group. Of course, individual members of the group may have positions outside of the group that make it possible for them to do something while the group as a whole can do nothing. In these cases, particular individuals should be approached in a setting other than the task group meeting. Such private appeals are more likely to be effective and spare the other members of the group.

The second factor limiting subjects to be discussed at a task group meeting is the agenda. Agendas are used to keep a meeting "on track," and experienced chairpersons routinely prepare and distribute one prior to meetings. Some are little more than lists of topic areas to be discussed, while others specify actions to be considered and the time available for each. (Agendas will be discussed in Chapter 15.) Whichever type you receive, subjects that do not contribute to the orderly progression through the agenda should not be introduced. In rare cases when something that appears urgent is not on the agenda, you should mention it to the chairperson prior to the meeting. The decision to include it or not should be the chairperson's—not yours! The chairperson will find room for it on the agenda if he or she shares your view of its importance. If not, you will need to find some other means of dealing with it. Also, many agendas include a catchall heading, "Other Business." This is a good point at which to introduce new items, but don't expect too much to result from the initial discussion. Other members of the group may be unprepared to discuss a new item, so don't plan on resolving important issues. The best you should hope for is making other members aware of your concern and securing a spot on the agenda at the next meeting.

Effective messages are timely   Saying that a presentation is timely means that it is consistent with the problem-solving activity of the group at the time it is made. Like individuals, groups are most effective in solving problems that are broken down into clearly marked steps. One of the most popular sequences used in group problem solving parallels the steps in creative thinking originally outlined by John Dewey. A group employing this sequence breaks the discussion into six distinct steps and tackles them one at a time. The six steps are:

1. *Characterizing the problem.* In this step, the group decides how the problem should be described: What are its principal characteristics? How is it related to other problems? How serious is the problem?

2. *Identifying the cause of the problem.* The group assembles historical and other background information that will help it to assess the cause of the problem. When did it first come into being? What special conditions existed at that time? Are these conditions logically sufficient causes?

3. *Determining criteria by which potential solutions can be evaluated.* The group decides what

qualities it would like the solution to have: How long should it take to implement? How much money can be spent? What other resources can be employed?

4. *Enumeration of possible solutions.* The group should attempt to list all of the possible solutions to the problem. Care should be taken to describe each possible solution as fully as possible and to list data supporting each. Questions asked about each solution include: How does it work? What resources are required for its implementation? How long does it take to become effective? Will it reach all of the people affected?

5. *Selection of the best solution.* Here the group compares the possible solutions listed in step 4 and determines which best meets the criteria elaborated in step 3. Ultimately, the group must decide which solution does most to solve the problem with the resources available. The group may also consider which has the greatest advantages in addition to solving the principal problem.

6. *Preparing to answer objections and implement the solution.* The group should compile a list of objections that may be raised and of difficulties that may be encountered in implementing the solution. To avoid additional problems, the group should develop answers to the objections and solutions for the difficulties.

Sequences like the one above may be imposed by problem-solving groups, but even those that do not impose a predetermined sequence follow a natural order. B. Aubrey Fisher has identified four distinct phases in group decision-making.[2] The phases are characterized by the communicative behaviors of the participants and occur in the following order:

1. The *orientation phase* is marked by the initial discussion of the problem. This phase is characterized by uncertainty because the participants are unsure of their own preferences concerning the problem and of other participants' reactions to their ideas. The uncertainty is reflected in cautious, timid, and ambiguous statements about the problem and in frequent efforts to reinforce other participants. Throughout the orientation phase, even ambiguous statements may be reinforced as the group members struggle to establish a harmonious working relationship and tentatively enumerate possible approaches to the problem.

2. The end of the orientation phase is signalled by substantial disagreement and emergence of the *conflict phase.* During this phase there is marked dispute over proposals, and members may divide into rival subgroups, each supporting a particular proposal. Polarization is evident as members introduce evidence and argument to develop their points of view. Tentativeness and ambiguity are suppressed, and efforts to reduce controversy inhibit the normal group process.

3. During the *emergence phase,* conflict declines and polarization is reduced. Increasing numbers of ambiguous statements signal the willingness of members to consider proposals other than those for which they argued during the conflict phase. Rival subgroups break down and a group consensus may develop. By the end of this phase, a solution preferred by the majority has been developed and dissent has been replaced by ambiguity.

4. The final phase is the *reinforcement phase* during which all members of the group are expected to "pull together." Disagreement is no longer appropriate, and members of the group join in a common effort to ensure that the chosen solution is successful.

[2] From *Small Group Decision Making,* 2nd ed., by B. Aubrey Fisher, pp. 144–49. Copyright © 1980 by McGraw-Hill Book Company. Used with the permission of McGraw-Hill Book Company.

Conflict has been replaced by high levels of social reinforcement as group members display unity on the chosen solution.

Timely presentations are those that are consistent with both the subject matter order suggested by Dewey and the communicative behaviors observed in natural groups. Introduction of materials inconsistent with the problem-solving sequence distracts the group from the step at hand, and behaviors inconsistent with the interaction phases may isolate you from the other group members.

Effective messages are informal   The exchange of ideas in a meeting is usually facilitated by an informal atmosphere that invites all members to participate. The chairperson is usually responsible for determining the degree to which a meeting follows formal procedures, but each participant is responsible for trying to maintain an appropriate climate. This climate should be as informal as possible to facilitate participation by all members. Presentational behaviors that reduce opportunities for discussion should be avoided, and some specific behaviors should be noted. First, resist the temptation to stand or otherwise set yourself apart from the group while speaking. Unless physical arrangements or use of visual aids require you to stand, remain seated with the other members. Second, your delivery should include more pauses than in a formal presentation. Such pauses signal a willingness to allow interruptions and provide opportunities for others to ask questions. Third, maintain eye contact with as many members of the group as possible. This is more difficult than it may seem because the natural tendency is to maintain eye contact only with supporters or to lock eyes with expected antagonists. Both extremes exclude other participants and may generate or exaggerate a hostile climate. Finally, avoid sweeping, dramatic gestures. Gesture as you normally would in casual conversation, but avoid movements that make those seated near you uncomfortable. Broad gestures may force others to back off or move away from you and isolate you from the group by increasing spatial differences.

Working with the Ideas of Other Participants

The presentation of your own ideas should occupy a relatively small portion of your effort at a meeting. The activity that is likely to claim the greatest share of your attention and effort is helping others to present and develop their ideas. Remember, many of the people with whom you work in the future may have difficulty making effective presentations to task groups. Even when their proposals have merit, the group may not give them a full hearing because the presentation is lacking something. In these cases, you can enhance the functioning of the whole group by contributing to the development of ideas initially presented by others. Specialized presentational activities in this context include clarifying ideas, volunteering supporting materials, suggesting applications, and correcting errors.

Clarifying ideas   Many promising ideas are unclear when they are first presented to the group. This happens because specialists often have difficulty translating technical proposals into terms other participants can appreciate, and because a person who has developed a proposal may be so involved in it that he or she fails to recognize the difficulty others have in understanding it. When a proposal or suggestion produces little comment from others at a meeting, it is possible that at least some did not understand it.

When an idea needs clarification, your primary tool to ensure that you understand it is the paraphrase. Preface the paraphrase by saying something like "Let me see if I understand you correctly," or "Do you mean that . . . ," and restate the idea in your own words. If you are correct, the other person will probably acknowledge that fact. If your interpretation is incorrect or excludes major items, the other person will have an opportunity to further explain the proposal. Care must be taken in forming the paraphrase to avoid sounding as if you blame the other person for making an initially inadequate presentation.

Once you are sure that you understand the proposal correctly, you may help other participants to understand it by using any of the forms of developing material that have clarification as their primary function. These forms include examples and illustrations, restatements, comparisons and contrasts, and definitions (see Chapter 2). Any one of them might help other members of the group understand the proposal. For example, if someone in the group said that "Groupthink results in inferior decisions," you could clarify the statement by defining "groupthink" and presenting an example. Your comment might look like this:

> "Groupthink" is the tendency for members of a group to ignore information that might produce disagreement. It happened to us last year when we decided to market the new switch mechanism. Remember, the engineering department warned us that it would be difficult to get enough material to fill the orders, but we didn't listen and launched the advertising campaign. We're still getting flack from upstairs for that.

Volunteering supporting materials   Even when a proposal is clearly understood, other members of the group may be reluctant to accept it, and, the person who introduced the idea may not be able to argue for it effectively. This situation arises when the initial presenter lacks skill in oral presentation or wants to avoid the appearance of dominating the group. Potentially valuable suggestions may be lost because they have not been supported by developing materials that prove they have merit.

When an idea is presented, but the original presenter is not able to argue for it effectively, you may assist the group by providing support for the ideas that appear to you to have merit. The kinds of material that you may use include all forms that have the capacity to prove a statement. These are real instances, examples, illustrations, statistics, and quotations (see Chapter 2). A unique feature of this situation is that simply stating your support for an idea may function as a quotation because it shows that someone other than the originator supports the proposal. The following comment displays the use of several techniques for developing an idea presented by another person:

> I agree with Mary's proposal for adding a portable unit to our line. Some statistics in the last business survey show that many of our regular customers would like the versatility of a portable model, and our major competitor sold more than 300 portables last month alone.

Suggesting applications   Occasionally, valuable suggestions will fail to earn the support of the group because they are stated too abstractly. This may happen even though the group understands the suggestion and recognizes its potential value. Such suggestions may be greeted with a "Ho-hum" or "So what?" response, and the person making the suggestion may be too frustrated to pursue the matter further. In such instances, you can help the group by suggesting concrete applications for the proposal. The applications should be phrased tentatively and need not be fully developed, but they should be specific enough to invite further discussion. For example, university administrators are fond of talking about the "quality of education" and the means of improving the "educational environment." Both of the quoted phrases represent worthwhile goals, but they are stated so abstractly that it is difficult to see what needs to be done and who should do it. At one meeting, a dean made a lengthy plea on behalf of these goals, but his remarks failed to produce any reaction from the departmental planning committee. One faculty member suggested a series of applications, which paved the way for further discussion. His remark was, "I guess we could improve the quality of education by reducing the size of our classes, using more supplementary materials, and doing more to prepare teaching assistants for their classroom responsibilities." Even these applications could be made more concrete by identifying "supplementary materials" and indicating the kinds of preparation graduate students could receive. However, the list of possible applications was a necessary means of directing attention to specific proposals, and the rest of the meeting focused on developing these applications.

Correcting errors   Correcting errors without creating hard feelings is one of the most difficult tasks you will ever face as a group participant. Whether it be good or bad, participants in a discussion often feel a strong urge to support or defend their ideas. Moreover, the fact is that most people feel a strong tie between themselves and their statements. As a result, even well-intentioned efforts to correct an error may be taken as a personal attack. However, correcting errors is an essential part of the discussion process, and every member of the group should accept responsibility for listening critically and correcting errors.

Organizing your thoughts on the spur of the moment can be difficult, and other participants may have difficulty determining the relationship between your correction and the ongoing discussion. The *rebuttal format* commonly employed by debaters can help to solve both problems. The format has four parts. First, begin by identifying the statement or idea that you intend to correct. Be as specific as possible and indicate precisely what part of the statement you believe to be incorrect; don't disagree with everything a person says. In identifying the statement to be corrected, take special care to separate the idea from the person who introduced it. Remember, your obligation is to correct the error, not to attack the person. The act of correcting an error makes it necessary for you to identify the point at which correction is necessary, but you should be able to identify the error without calling attention to the person who made it. Compare the following references:

WRONG	RIGHT
John said	It has been suggested . . . .
Steve favors	One view is . . . .
Margaret argues	It is argued that . . . .

The second step is to indicate precisely what you think is wrong with the statement. Simply saying that it is "untrue" or "incorrect" does little to enhance the discussion, and use of loaded words such as "lie" or other derogatory expressions only fuel personal resentments. Simultaneously, you should try to phrase your point in a manner that gives the other person an "out" or plausible reason for the error. For example, you might say that information is dated or that it depends on a particular perspective. For example:

1. At one time it was believed that . . . , but more recent studies show that . . . .
2. From a marketing perspective that may be true, but from a broader point of view . . . .

Third, provide any materials that support your position. Be as specific as possible and provide as much information as is readily available. This step is critical for both task and social reasons. From the task point of view, this step is critical because it adds to the total amount of information available to the group. Socially, it is important because it gives the other group members a basis for decisions unrelated to the personalities involved.

Finally, indicate how the group can proceed on the basis of the information you have added to the discussion. Remember that your purpose in correcting an error is to direct the group to the best decision possible, and take care to show how your correction should affect the decision-making process. Some examples follow:

1. Before going too much further, we should see what the people in R&D have discovered.
2. We probably should try to identify some other possible approaches.
3. This builds an even stronger case for the program.
4. Rather than trying to eliminate interference, maybe we can concentrate on developing the fine tuning system.

In an actual discussion, the complete format could be used like this.

> I'm worried about the part of the plan that calls for disposal of our older machines. I don't think it's a good idea because we might need to use them if one of the new ones breaks down. Remember last year when Number 15 broke down? It took us six months to get parts and we had to use all of the old machines just to keep up. Maybe we can find a way of putting the old machines in storage so they won't take up space; in this way they can still be made available if needed.

A word of caution should be mentioned. Even if you use the rebuttal format and are careful to separate incorrect statements from the people who make them, you need to be sensitive to the norms of the group and to the feelings of individual participants. Some groups try to avoid disagreement and apply pressure to control dissent. This is not a healthy situation because it reduces the effectiveness of the group, and your ability to change it is limited. The best approach is to make a correction or two and see if other members follow suit. If none do, continued efforts on your part may alienate other members and isolate you. If you encounter such a situation, it would be wise to discuss it privately with the group leader. If the leader shares your concern, then he or she can take the lead in changing the group norms. Otherwise, you may have to learn to live with the existing norms.

Reactions of people whose statements are corrected can also be a problem. Unfortunately, many are not skilled in group work and resent corrections, even when they benefit the group as a whole. There is very little you can do in dealing with such people, but you need to prepare yourself for their reactions. The most common reaction is an effort to defend their initial statement coupled with a personal attack on the person correcting them. In extreme cases, the personal attack far outweighs the defense. When you are the object of the attack, you must avoid responding in kind. In fact, the safest course is to avoid any response at all. Let the other members of the group resolve the dispute while you retain your composure. When someone else is the object of the attack, direct your own comments to the substance of the disagreement and disregard comments about the personalities. Focus attention on the legitimate needs of the group and let personal attacks die for lack of attention.

Assisting the Chairperson

Your final responsibility as a member of a task group is helping the chairperson maintain group processes. This does not mean that you should try to assume the formal role of chairperson, but you can focus your attention on activities that will complement the leader's strengths. Some chairpeople are remarkably good at maintaining the social relationships between group members; others are particularly good at focusing attention on the group task; some are good at handling particular social issues and are blind to others; and, some chairpeople are good at handling part of the task, but have difficulty with other elements. The possible variations are almost endless, but you can help yourself and the group as a whole by helping the chairperson deal with any weak areas. Some areas in which the leader may welcome your assistance are encouraging participation, discouraging overtalkative members, and attending to the agenda.

Encouraging participation   Drawing timid members into the group processes is often a difficult task for the chairperson. New members are likely to avoid contributing ideas because they are unsure of the ground rules and may be unfamiliar with the participants. Similarly, established members may be reluctant to speak because they fear their contributions will be rejected. Both groups can make valuable contributions, but first they must be encouraged to take an active role in the group's deliberations. You can help new members feel comfortable by introducing yourself prior to the meeting and inviting them to sit near you. Try to introduce them to other members of the group and do what you can to give them a feel for the manner in which business is normally transacted. As far as possible, explain the background of any pending business and explain terms and procedures with which they may be unfamiliar. If you have occasion to explain par-

DUNAGIN'S PEOPLE

"IT ISN'T THAT WE LACK LEADERSHIP... IT'S JUST THAT EVERYONE ELSE LACKS FOLLOWSHIP."

ticular issues or to provide background information, be sure to do so in as neutral a manner as possible. Avoid "politicizing" introductions and explanations, and avoid involving new members in ongoing disputes. Remember, your purpose is to make the new member comfortable, not to win supporters for your positions.

It may be necessary to solicit comments from both new and established group members. When a subject on which they have some expertise is raised, you may direct a question to them. Avoid loading the question to suggest an answer and give respondents enough freedom so that they can answer meaningfully on the basis of their own experiences. Any of the following might work well:

> John, you've been working on a related project, haven't you?
> Mary, how did you handle this situation when it developed in the marketing division?
> Steve, have you ever had to deal with a situation like this?
> Joann, you've worked with this in the past, haven't you?
> Jane, what do you think we should add to this?

Finally, when timid members do take part, reward their efforts. The greatest reward you can offer is your undivided attention. Look at them; ignore potential distractions; perhaps even nod and smile at them while they are speaking. A further reward is subsequent recognition. When a member has made an important contribution, acknowledge it in the minutes and in subsequent references to the discussion.

Discouraging overtalkative members   One of the most difficult situations for a chairperson to control is created by individuals who are constantly talking. Such individuals disrupt meetings by whispering while someone is speaking, and they cause unnecessary delay by speaking even when they have nothing to contribute.

The chairperson must take the lead in dealing with such an individual. However, it is essential that other members of the group support the chairperson so that the talkative member realizes that the group as a whole is unhappy with the constant babbling. Remember as well that you don't want to deny an individual an opportunity to contribute—you merely want to discourage idle chatter, which doesn't contribute to the common task. As a group member, you should not try to confront the offending individual. Any direct attack is likely to aggravate the problem and generate needless hostility. Your most effective tools are rewarding valuable contributions while discouraging irrelevant talk. The rewards used with timid members discussed above can be selectively applied to comments by idle talkers. When a member's remarks are in order and relevant to the discussion at hand, reward the person with attention. When a member speaks out of turn and begins to wander or retrace materials already discussed, withhold attention. Watch the chairperson for directions. Most chairpeople quickly learn that they can discourage excessive talk by showing signs of disinterest and agitation when an individual speaks excessively. Once the chairperson has begun to show signs of displeasure, divert your attention from the speaker and be ready to speak if called upon. Expect the leader to move the meeting ahead by interrupting the speaker with a statement like the following:

> Thank you John, you have raised a question that Marsha may be able to answer for us.

If you are prepared to provide an answer or to say something that will move the discussion ahead, let the chairperson know by nodding, smiling, or, in more formal meetings, raising your hand. But do not embarrass the chairperson by having nothing to say.

Attending to the agenda   Another area in which you may assist the chairperson is in attending to the agenda. A carefully prepared agenda is almost essential to conducting an orderly, productive meeting. However, the agenda should not be perceived solely as the tool of the leader, and many chairpeople will become discouraged if no one else acknowledges the schedule set forth. When a discussion has exhausted the time available, the chairperson will probably point out the fact and ask for directions. You can be of assistance by offering suggestions. If you think the matter has been pretty well resolved, suggest that a decision be made without further discussion; if you think that more should be said, suggest either postponing a decision to a subsequent meeting or extending the time allotted at this meeting. Whatever you suggest, phrase your remarks to show that you recognize the value of the agenda and that you support the chairperson's decision to interrupt the discussion. The following all would work well:

> Our time for this item is exhausted, but I think we've pretty well covered the subject. Maybe we can vote without more discussion.
> We don't have much time left and I think we need more. Can we put the decision off and take it up at our next meeting?
> This is so important that it deserves more time. Can we postpone the next item and spend an extra thirty minutes here?

Occasionally, a discussion will extend past the time allotted without intervention by the chairperson. This may happen because the leader hasn't noticed the time, or because he or she wants to avoid appearing to take sides. When a group is divided over an issue, extended discussion may seem to favor one faction or another, and it is essential that one of the participants calls attention to the time. Avoid putting the chairperson in an awkward position by blaming him or her for letting the discussion carry on, using the agenda to support a faction, or being timid in calling for the termination of a discussion. Of the following examples, only the final one calls attention to the agenda without reflecting an improper attitude:

> How much more time are we going to waste on this?
> Mr. Chairman! Why aren't we sticking to the agenda?

I don't think it's fair to spend so much time on this issue.
John, we've used up the time we had scheduled for this discussion.

SUMMARY

Participating in task group meetings can be enhanced by the application of presentational skills in working with your own ideas and with the ideas of other participants, and by assisting the chairperson. Effective messages used to present your own ideas should be brief, specific, relevant, timely, and informal. Your work with the ideas of other participants may include clarifying ideas, volunteering supporting materials, suggesting applications, and correcting errors. You may assist the chairperson by encouraging participation, discouraging overtalkative members, and attending to the agenda.

LEARNING ACTIVITIES

1. Observe members of a task group participating in a meeting. Use a three-column form to record the number of contributions made by each and to note any members who make longer contributions or appear to be trying to dominate group activity. List the members in the center column, use checks in the right column to mark contributions by each, and note any tendency to dominate or cut off other members in the left column. After the meeting, evaluate the quality of the discussion. Were all members given an opportunity to express their views? Did any member dominate discussion through total number or length of contributions? How did the interaction pattern affect the quality of the discussion?

2. Observe a task group meeting in which members try to solve a problem. Keep a running record of the topics discussed and see if you can identify the problem-solving sequence employed. Did the group use a predetermined sequence, beginning with characterization of the problem? Did the group follow a natural sequence, beginning with orientation? How did the sequence of discussion affect the quality of any decisions reached by the group?

3. Focus on a single member of a task group and record the kinds of contributions he or she makes during a discussion. How often did the person speak? Were his or her comments introduced in an appropriate manner? How often did the member work with the ideas of other participants? In what ways did the member assist the chairperson? Overall, how would you evaluate the individual's performance?

4. Observe members of a group trying to solve a problem. Rate each member's effectiveness in gaining support for his or her views. Use a scale from one to nine in which the following points are marked: Zero represents a wholly ineffective member who gained no support, five

represents a somewhat effective member who got support for about half of his or her ideas; and nine represents a highly effective member who got support on all issues. After the meeting, write a brief paragraph explaining your rankings. What approaches were employed by effective members? What approaches were employed by ineffective members? Were presentational skills associated with effectiveness? What other factors seemed to contribute to effectiveness?

CHAPTER FIFTEEN
CHAIRING
TASK GROUP
MEETINGS

During the early years of your career, you are likely to have few opportunities to chair task group meetings. However, as your responsibilities grow, it is probable that you will have frequent occasions to direct the activities of a group of people. You will find youself calling and chairing meetings, and you should anticipate the reactions of participants. The importance of meetings is seldom challenged, but they are the objects of recurrent criticism. The time spent in meetings is time taken away from other activities, and complaints often include the "terrible toos": there are *too* many meetings, they last *too* long, and they accomplish *too* little. When these complaints are legitimate, the chairperson is largely responsible. Numerous books explain the mechanics of conducting meetings, and you may wish to consult them for more specific directions. However, even with a working knowledge of the mechanics, you should have a clear understanding of your role as chairperson.

Chairpeople who misunderstand their role usually adopt one of two extreme behaviors. On the one hand, some chairpeople exercise tight control over the group and give the participants few opportunities for independent thought. A chairperson who acts in this manner uses a group as a staging ground for announcing decisions she or he has made and for soliciting support for personal proposals. The meeting is reduced to an arena for the chairperson's actions, and does little more than "rubber stamp" proposals that carry his or her approval. Groups

"I sentence you to 14 conventions, 10 sales pep rallies, and eight forms design committee meetings, to be served concurrently."

governed by such people are not effective decision-making entities and, at most, assume some of the responsibility when something goes wrong. Those exercising such tight control will signal their intentions through verbal cues that limit the activities of the group. Examples include, "I'm not interested in problems, just . . . ," and "Let's get this going as quickly as possible." Nonverbal cues also signal the chairperson's intent. Examples include rewarding participants who conform to the chairperson's wishes and using favored subordinates to introduce items for approval.

The other extreme is represented by chairpeople who refuse to take an active role in supporting the group process. They limit their participation to a few essentially clerical functions such as notifying members of the meeting, arranging physical facilities, and having minutes taken. Of course, these functions are essential, but they are so limited that the group is literally "on its own" as far as the critical business of making decisions is concerned. When the group fails to resolve an issue, the chairperson may use this fact as justification for inactivity; when the group reaches a decision, the chairperson carries it out in a mechanical fashion and justifies it as "the will of the majority."

The problem with both extremes is that the chairperson has failed to make it

"Miss Henderson, I'm tired of thinking. Set up a meeting."

Reprinted by permission of Tribune Company Syndicate, Inc.

possible for the group to function as effectively as it should. The domineering chairperson limits group decisions to those that he or she has made as an individual, and the docile chairperson abdicates task leadership to domineering members of the group. In contrast, effective chairpeople make it possible for the group to use all of its resources in resolving common problems and formulating decisions based on the collective wisdom of the participants. Mastering this role can be a time-consuming process, but you can get a good lead by learning to maintain a favorable climate, by selecting appropriate tasks for the group, by establishing an agenda for each meeting, and by employing appropriate decision structures. We will discuss each of these activities in turn.

MAINTAINING FAVORABLE CLIMATES

The ideal climate for a task group meeting is one that allows all members to participate equally. In fact, this is essential if the group is to function with maximum effectiveness. Many valuable contributions may come from those who otherwise might be excluded from the discussion. The characteristics of communication that generate a favorable climate are discussed in Chapter 13, and the chairperson should do everything possible to establish a supportive atmosphere. Three things a chairperson must do to maintain this climate are: avoid dominating the discussion, control the effect of status differentials, and provide an appropriate physical environment.

Avoid Dominating Discussions

The position of chairperson usually commands respect and is often assigned to those with proven ability. In business, the chairperson may also be a senior member of the staff with formal power to reward and punish group members who are also subordinates. These factors create considerable power that can become a barrier to effective group performance. There is a very real danger that the power of the chairperson will stifle effective discussion. To reduce chances of dominating the group, the chairperson should limit involvement in the actual discussion. Two specific behavior patterns may be adopted.

First, let other people do most of the talking. The chairperson has power and is free to interrupt almost all members of the group, but few members may interrupt the chairperson in return. The danger is that the chairperson will dominate the group by revealing expectations and providing few opportunities for expression of conflicting views. The chairperson should seldom speak for more than a minute or so without pausing for comments from others. The number of times a chairperson speaks should be limited to ensure that other members have the opportunity to contribute. Although limits are arbitrary, the chairperson would be wise to speak less than half as often as the average member. Of course, there are times when it may be necessary to introduce a problem to the group or to furnish background information. These are areas in which the chairperson has some flexibility, but it is generally more effective to assign these functions to a subordinate. This limits the danger of biasing the discussion and provides a convenient means of recognizing subordinates who are knowledgeable on particular issues.

Second, the chairperson should avoid voicing his or her opinion while the group is sifting information en route to a tentative decision. It is essential that the chairperson not announce a position early in the discussion. Once his or her position is known, those who disagree may withdraw, and ambitious subordinates may see supporting the "boss" as a means to advancement. This stifles discussion and unfairly loads the discussion in favor of the proposal favored by the chairperson. Remember, your position may become obvious through nonverbal as well as verbal cues and it may be necessary to leave the meeting to avoid disclosing your position prematurely. This is an extreme measure, but it may be necessary when you have strong feelings or when your feelings are known in advance.

Controlling Status Differentials

Most groups are composed of members with varying degrees of status. Differences include formal positions, years of experience, age, length of time in the group, level of education, opinion leadership functions, and perceived friendship with people in authority. These differences are a danger to the group process because they are based on factors that may be unrelated to decision-making ability and are usually incidental to the task at hand. Unfortunately, high status individuals may exercise an undue influence on the processes of the group, resulting in a less sound decision than otherwise possible.

These status differences are a serious problem for the chairperson because they are based on factors over which little direct control can be exercised. However, he or she can do much to limit their influence on the decision-making processes of the group. The chairperson must encourage participation by low status members who may have a great deal to contribute. Techniques that may be used to encourage participation include asking members who are particularly knowledgeable to make brief reports, assigning special functions to members whom the chairperson would like to encourage, and calling on participants to answer questions. Simultaneously, the chairperson should reward participation by giving full attention and recognizing contributions. Including an individual's name in the minutes and mentioning the person's contribution at subsequent meetings is a strong inducement to continued performance.

At the same time, the chairperson can discourage behaviors that do not contribute to the smooth functioning of the group. High status members frequently make longer presentations, introduce more digressions, interrupt more often, and engage in more incidental conversation than those of lower status. These behaviors can reduce the effectiveness of the group and, if unchecked, will eventually weaken the group as a decision-making entity. Moreover, only the chairperson has sufficient authority to confront those who engage in such behavior. As a starting point, you must recognize that high status members have much to contribute and their support may be essential to getting the decisions of the group implemented. As a result, the chairperson must avoid actions that reduce their level of commitment to the group, but must channel their behavior to reinforce appropriate contributions. Initially, a direct confrontation is unwise. Most problems can be solved by using nonverbal reinforcements such as attention and visible signs of agreement and interest to reward appropriate behavior while withholding rewards from inappropriate behavior. When nonverbal rewards are insufficient, the next step is to interrupt the speaker when he or she drifts off the point and quickly turn the floor over to someone who is prepared to speak on the issue. The interruption should be tactful but firm, and the following are good examples:

> Excuse me, Steve, but we need to keep remarks brief so everyone has a chance to comment.
> That's a good point, Jane. I'd like to hear what the others think of it.
> Mary, we understand that parts are scarce. What we need to hear about is the delivery schedule.
> Thank you for the background information. Can you briefly summarize the current marketing program?

Finally, if nonverbal reinforcement and interruptions do not solve the problem, the offending individual should be called aside and the specific behaviors discussed. You can think of the discussion as a performance appraisal interview, but focus on the individual's role in the group.

Selecting an Appropriate Setting

Although its effects are often overlooked, the physical setting in which a meeting takes place can exercise a real influence on the quality of the discussion. As chairperson, you should attempt to find a location that is comfortable, free from distractions, and that provides a sense of privacy. Privacy is particularly important when the participants must deal with personnel issues or with other matters affecting members of the organization who are not present at the meeting. One further item is often overlooked: The meeting room must allow seating that encourages participation by all members of the group. The ideal arrangement is a circle in which everyone faces a common focal point. (See Figure 15.1.)

Nearly as good is a rectangular-shaped or oblong table around which members are seated. Both the circle and rectangle invite high levels of participation by providing all members with more or less equal visibility. However, the rectangular arrangement may limit contributions of the members seated the greatest distance from the chairperson (see Figure 15.2). To combat this difficulty, the chairperson may select a seat on one side near the middle of the table (see Figure 15.3). This reduces the distance between the chairperson and members of the group, but it has one serious drawback: The end position is commonly associated with power and by sitting on the side the chairperson risks losing the ability to lead the group. Whenever the group lacks direction or the chairperson's authority is challenged, he or she should retain the end seat and forego higher levels of participation.

Unfortunately, many rooms are not designed for group meetings and you are likely to encounter several arrangements that work against effective discussion. Two of the most common seating arrangements that inhibit discussion are

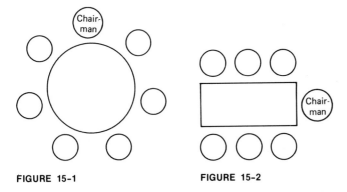

FIGURE 15-1   FIGURE 15-2

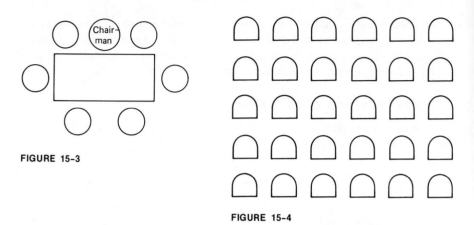

FIGURE 15-3

FIGURE 15-4

rows of seats (as in Figure 15.4) and fixed desks facing a hypothetical—or real—audience (Figure 15.5). Both of these seating patterns should be avoided whenever possible.

If someone in the group is expected to make a lengthy report requiring the use of visual aids, a separate speaking location should be provided. This should be a point six to eight feet away from the group that all members can face during the presentation. A U-shaped table is often best for gatherings of this kind. (See Figure 15.6.)

SELECTING APPROPRIATE TASKS

The second primary function of the chairperson is selecting appropriate tasks for the group. To appreciate the importance of this function, you need to know that a great deal of research had been conducted for the purpose of determining whether individuals or groups are better problem solvers. The most frequently stated conclusion is that groups make better decisions than individuals, but there are a number of qualifications. It appears that there are some situations in which reliance upon task group meetings is an inappropriate decision strategy, and the following four generalizations explain the importance of choosing between individual and group decisions:

1. Groups solve complex problems faster than individuals, but the total number of man-hours expended by the groups is far greater.

FIGURE 15-5

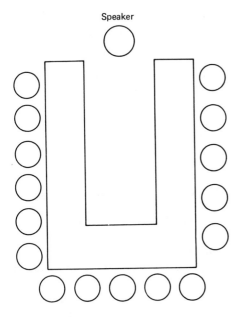

FIGURE 15-6

2. Groups are capable of processing far more information than a single individual, but they may ignore crucial data that threaten their cohesiveness.

3. Groups may reach higher quality decisions, but they are prone to take risks that individuals would avoid.

4. Groups make better decisions than their average member, but superior proposals advanced by outstanding individuals may not be given full attention.

Reviewing these generalizations, it is easy to see why the chairperson should choose carefully between tasks presented to the group and those an individual group member can handle most effectively. No single characteristic is sufficient to distinguish between tasks suited for group discussion and those that are not, and the research to date has been complex and confusing. Fortunately, Victor H. Vroom and Philip W. Yetton have integrated the conclusions of many studies into a single model that gives the chairperson ample direction. In Exhibits 15.1 and 15.2, and in Figure 15.7 the Vroom-Yetton model is applied.[1]

Whenever a task group chairperson is confronted with a decision-making situation that affects the work of his or her group, the chairperson has five possible ways of making the decision. These are listed and described in Exhibit 15.1. These five decision-making strategies are always available, but notice that only the final two involve bringing a problem to a task meeting.

[1] All three are reprinted from Victor H. Vroom and Philip W. Yetton, *Leadership and Decision-Making* by permission of the authors and the University of Pittsburgh Press. © 1973 by the University of Pittsburgh Press. An abbreviated discussion of the model is included in Vroom's article, "Can Leaders Learn to Lead?" *Organizational Dynamics* (New York: American Management Association, 1977).

EXHIBIT 15.1 *AVAILABLE DECISION STRATEGIES*

AUTOCRATIC I	(abbreviated AI) The manager makes the decision using whatever information is available to him at the time. He does not solicit information or preferences from his subordinates.
AUTOCRATIC II	(abbreviated AII) The manager obtains necessary information from his subordinates before making the decision. He requests specific pieces of information without explaining the purpose for which he will use them and without exploring his subordinates' preferences.
CONSULTATIVE I	(abbreviated CI) The manager explains the problem with selected subordinates and requests their opinions before making the decision. This differs from AII in that the manager takes time to explain the purpose of his request and secures both information and opinions.
CONSULTATIVE II	(abbreviated CII) The manager shares the problem with his subordinates in a group meeting and solicits their ideas and opinions. This differs from CI in that the manager shares the problem with all of his subordinates present at the meeting and allows the group as a whole to develop solutions and evaluate their worth.
GROUP II	(abbreviated GII) The manager shares the problem with his subordinates in a group meeting. In addition to soliciting their opinions and ideas, he agrees to abide by the decision of the group. Whereas participants in meetings conducted for CII purposes merely develop a set of recommendations, participants in GII meetings actually make the final decision.

The second step in using the Vroom-Yetton model is interpreting the problem in terms of some critical variables. Use of the model requires answering the seven questions listed in Exhibit 15.2.

The final step in using the Vroom-Yetton model is choosing between the available strategies. To simplify the process, Vroom and Yetton have developed the decision tree reproduced in Figure 15.7. To use the tree, begin at the left by stating the problem and move to the right. Each circle represents one of the seven questions answered in step two and listed at the top of the figure. Your answer to each determines which branch you should follow. Notice that some questions may be ruled out by your answers to earlier ones, and the circles mark only those whose answers are relevant to each branch of the tree. Each branch comes to an end with a list of the decision strategies that could be used. In most cases, more than one strategy could be used and the list of acceptable approaches is known as the "feasible set." To choose between the strategies included in the feasible set, the

EXHIBIT 15.2

1. Does resolution of this problem affect our ability to meet corporate goals?
2. Do I have sufficient information to make a high quality decision?
3. Is there an accepted procedure for resolving this problem?
4. Is acceptance of the decision by subordinates important for effective implementation?
5. If I were to make the decision by myself, am I reasonably certain that it would be accepted by my subordinates?
6. Do subordinates share the organizational goals to be attained in solving this problem?
7. Is there likely to be conflict among the subordinates concerning the preferred solutions?

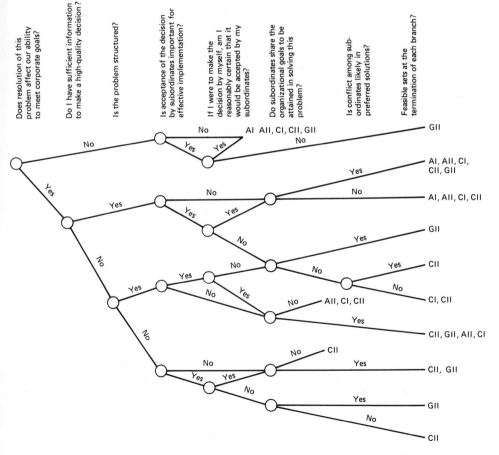

FIGURE 15-7   Decision Process Flowchart to Determine Feasible Set of Communication Behaviors

chairperson needs to consider the immediate demands of his or her work. In each set, the strategies to the extreme left are the most economical; that is, they require the fewest man-hours of work. The strategies to the extreme right are the ones that contribute most to building a cohesive group; they are time-consuming, but they help to develop the ability of the group members to work together. When groups are new or when their social relationships need to be developed, the chairpersons should prefer solutions to the right; when time is a critical concern, solutions to the left are preferable.

An Illustration

Vroom and others have found working with real examples is the best way to learn how to use the model. Try solving the following problem before reading the recommended solution.

Problem

You are the chairperson of a university department composed of five faculty members in addition to yourself. Unexpectedly heavy enrollment has forced you to add an extra section of a basic course designed for entering freshmen. You must decide who will teach the extra section. The decision should not be made hastily because one purpose of the course is to attract new majors and not all of the faculty work well with new students. You have not had to deal with this situation before, and neither the college nor the department has established procedures for changing teaching assignments. Your task is complicated by the fact that the course will be an overload, and individual faculty members have the right to refuse overload assignments. In the past, some have exercised this right, and you are not sure that they would accept your decision. The members of your department agree that the course should be used to attract new majors, but they may have research schedules that would make it difficult to put in extra time. You don't know what they have planned and you would like to avoid conflicts with other activities. Which decision strategy will you use to make the assignment?

Solution

Begin at the left of the decision tree and state the problem: deciding which faculty member will be assigned to teach the new section. The first question you must answer is "Does resolution of this problem affect our ability to meet corporate goals?" The answer is "yes" because not all faculty members work well with new students. The second question following this branch is "Do I have sufficient information to make a high quality decision?" "No," because you don't know how much research work the faculty members have scheduled for themselves. The problem is not structured ("no" to question 3), and acceptance of the solution by coworkers is important ("yes" to question 4) because they have the option of refusing the assignment. You cannot be certain that your decision would be accepted ("no" to question 5), but the faculty members agree that the course should be used to attract new majors ("yes" to question 6). This brings you to the end of the branch, and the only feasible solution is GII: You should call a meeting and let the group decide who will teach the extra section.

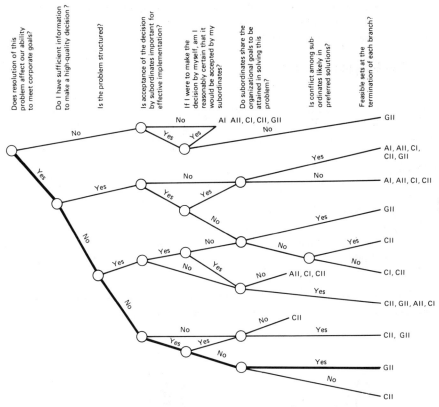

FIGURE 15-8 How do I decide who will teach the extra section?

ESTABLISHING THE AGENDA

Preparing an agenda is one of your most important jobs as chairperson. When meetings are conducted without an agenda, the resources of the group are often wasted because participants do not focus on the same concerns. Agendas focus the

efforts of participants, and they help establish a schedule to keep meetings from dragging past closing time. Agendas are often distributed at meetings, but many are incomplete or prepared without attention to important factors.

The Complete Agenda

The accompanying box displays an agenda of the type used at most meetings. It includes a list of the principal topics to be discussed and suggests the order in which they will be considered. However, it is missing two of the most important features of a complete agenda.

AGENDA

1. Current Sales
2. Research and Development Budget
3. Management Training Program
4. Communications Course
5. Data Processing Services

"As a starting point, are we all agreed that this is pathetic?"

First, it does not specify the kind of action to be taken. An item should be included in the agenda only when one of three kinds of action is expected to result from its consideration. The most limited action is informing the participants. This is the expected result of announcements and they may be included as minor parts of the meeting. Lengthy announcements and presentation of highly technical data are inappropriate, but brief announcements may call attention to the developments themselves or to documents in which they are described.

A more demanding action is developing a set of recommendations for someone else who will make the final decision. This is the decision process Vroom and Yetton label CII, and it is the expected result whenever a group is asked to consider an issue on which their expertise is valued, but on which they have no formal authority.

Finally, the group may be expected to make the final decision. This corresponds to the process Vroom and Yetton label GII, and it is the most common and proper use of a meeting.

Recognizing these possibilities, the agenda presented above might be corrected by specifying the action expected on each item. This is displayed in the accompanying box.

AGENDA

---

1. *Current Sales.* Mark Hamilton will announce the results of our promotional effort and distribute copies of the annual report.

2. *Research and Development Budget.* We have been asked to review the proposed R&D budget and recommend possible changes.

3. *Management Training Program.* Personnel has asked us to select two senior staff members to describe our marketing program to the trainees.

4. *Communications Course.* The Corporate Services Division has proposed a 21 hour course in Effective Managerial Communication. We need to decide if we are going to participate and what fraction of the expenses we are willing to pay.

5. *Data Processing Services.* Accounting has developed new procedures that require more elaborate reports. I've asked Marsha Harrington to describe the DP services available to us and summarize their uses.

In phrasing the expected action, two cautions must be observed. First, be sure to specify the expected result by identifying the end product. Saying that the purpose of an item is "to discuss" or "to consider" identifies the process rather than the result and permits pointless discussion. Second, be careful to avoid suggesting a particular decision. Remember, the chairperson's preferences may sway the group and seriously distort the end result. Phrases such as "to approve" or "to accept" suggest a particular position with regard to the substance of the issue and usually bias the discussion process.

The second feature missing from the initial sample agenda is an indication of the amount of time to be spent on each item. Discussion is potentially endless and the chairperson may be the only individual with sufficient authority to call it to a halt. Moreover, the chairperson is the only participant in a position to understand the relative importance and urgency of the items requiring attention. Therefore, advance planning should include the amount of time to be devoted to each item. The plan can be signalled to the group by placing in the left margin an indication of the time at which discussion of each item is to begin. The accompanying box shows the agenda introduced above in complete form.

AGENDA

2:00–2:15	1.	*Current Sales.* Mark Hamilton will announce the results of our promotional effort and distribute copies of the annual report.
2:15–2:45	2.	*Research and Development Budget.* We have been asked to review the proposed R&D budget and recommend possible changes.
2:45–3:15	3.	*Management Training Program.* Personnel has asked us to select two senior staff members to describe our marketing program to the trainees.
3:15–3:40	4.	*Communications Course.* The Corporate Services Division has proposed a 21 hour course in Effective Managerial Communication. We need to decide if we are going to participate and what fraction of the expenses we are willing to pay.
3:40–4:00	5.	*Data Processing Services.* Accounting has developed new procedures that require more elaborate reports. I've asked Marsha Harrington to describe the DP services available to us and summarize their uses.

In planning the time at which each item is to be introduced, two factors may require special attention. First, groups are more active and creative during the first twenty to thirty minutes of a meeting. Items dependent on creativity should be scheduled for the early part of the meeting, with more routine items planned for the latter portion. Items that require little creativity or on which immediate action is not expected may be included in the final part of the meeting. Second, latecomers may resent being excluded from discussion of items of particular interest to them. This is unfortunate, but postponing discussion of these items excuses tardiness and may be viewed as favoritism. By setting an agenda and sticking to it, the chairperson can encourage promptness and make a smooth progression from item to item.

Checklist for Composing Agendas

Executives who frequently compose agendas learn a great deal from trial and error. Few theories are rich enough to capture their accumulated wisdom, and theory is probably less important than taking advantage of experience. The following checklist is based on this author's work with executives who regularly prepare agendas, and it provides a brief summary of their recommendations:

1. Include only items whose resolution is consistent with the functions of the group: receiving information, developing recommendations, and making decisions.
2. Limit meetings to no more than two hours; longer meetings are less productive than several short ones because attention wanders and participants tire rapidly.
3. Schedule items requiring creativity for the first twenty or thirty minutes; discuss routine items during the concluding portions of the meeting.
4. If meetings often drag on, schedule them for the hour or two immediately before lunch or the end of the work day.
5. While you are preparing the agenda, solicit topics from the participants; including topics of concern to them avoids the disruptive effects of "hidden agendas."
6. Do not use the heading "other business," as the time required by unanticipated items is uncontrollable and participants may be unprepared to discuss topics not on the agenda.
7. Distribute the agenda two or three days prior to the meeting; this is enough time for participants to prepare, but not so much that the agenda is mislaid or forgotten.
8. When background reports are scheduled, include the name of the person making them so that other members can volunteer information prior to the meeting.
9. Phrase agenda items in a neutral manner so that your preferences do not influence the group.
10. Include references to source material or reports that the participants may consult prior to the meeting and bring with them.

This checklist is far from complete, but it should provide a foundation for a more elaborate one based on your own experiences. As you start adding items, remember that the function of an agenda is to provide for an orderly meeting in which each topic receives as much attention as its importance warrants. Your discoveries that are consistent with this function can be added to the list, and items that do not serve this purpose may be deleted.

EMPLOYING APPROPRIATE DECISION STRUCTURES

The final responsibility of the chairperson is employing structures that assist the group in reaching a decision. Many groups continue to discuss a question past the point at which all useful and relevant information and opinion has been introduced. When comments become repetitious, the chairperson should check to see if the group has reached consensus concerning all or part of the problem. He or she can make a statement that sounds something like this: "If I understand you correctly, we seem to agree that. . . ." The statement should be followed by a paraphrase of the items on which the group seems to agree. If consensus has not been reached on some items, discussion can focus on the remaining areas of disagreement.

If consensus has not been reached, but the time available has been exhausted, the chairperson may request a more formal vote on the question. A voice vote requires the least preparation, but it may be difficult to get an accurate count when feelings run high. A show of hands will give a more accurate tally. Finally, if members of the group have strong personal stakes in the outcome of the issue, a secret, written ballot may be used. Choosing between these voting procedures does not require strict attention to parliamentary procedure. In fact, reliance upon formal procedures is likely to be an obstacle to effective decision-making because participants may devote unnecessary attention to parliamentary maneuvering. It is important that the group understand the decision-making procedure you use, but your choices are not limited to those sanctioned by parliamentary procedure manuals designed for larger gatherings. Most chairpeople find it sufficient to begin by checking for consensus and then employing voting methods when no clear agreement has emerged.

In some cases, task groups are sharply divided over certain issues and it is impossible to reach agreement. In extreme cases, members of the group may be so personally involved that calm discussion is impossible. Issues of this type are usually signalled by unnecessary volume, visible signs of anger, and increasing numbers of personal attacks. When this situation arises, the group is unable to reach an effective decision and the ability of group members to work together is in jeopardy. This situation calls for the chairperson to limit actual discussion and impose specialized decision structures. Several are available, but the most flexible is *nominal group technique.*

Nominal Group Technique

Nominal group technique (NGT) is an effective tool for generating ideas and reaching decisions in conflict-laden situations. It also has value where participants do not feel free to speak openly. Examples include soliciting frank evaluations of company policy, recommending changes in management, and developing programs that might jeopardize the position of some group members. NGT restricts opportunities for members of a group to interact with one another and requires them to direct their questions and comments to the chairperson. It employs six steps in the following order. First, the chairperson describes the problem to be resolved. The description should be brief without indicating personal preferences for solution. Second, members of the group work independently and write all possible approaches that come to mind on sheets of colored paper provided for the purpose. Use of colored paper helps keep the lists from getting mixed in with other materials and simplifies the sorting process. Third, the group takes a brief recess while the chairperson and secretary or other assistant list all of the possible solutions on a chart. The list should be displayed for all members of the group to read and duplicates can be weeded out to simplify the next step. Step four takes place when the members return. They are asked to examine the master list and are invited to add any new ideas. After all new ideas are added to the list and items on the list have been clarified, participants are given another sheet of colored paper and asked to list their preferences in order. This preference poll is the fifth step and is the point at which group members actually record their individual decisions. If a great many items have been generated, participants can be asked to list just their top five. Again, the paper should be colored and it helps to use a different color than that used in step two. Finally, the chairperson tabulates the results. Each first place vote can be given five points, second preferences four points, and so forth.

After all ballots have been tallied, the solution with the greatest number of points is the chosen alternative. When there are few participants and the number of options is limited, the chairperson can conduct the tally and announce the results at the meeting. If there are many participants or many alternatives, the tally would be too time-consuming and it may be desirable to announce the results the following day or at the next meeting. The advantage of announcing results quickly is that the issue can be considered resolved and the group is free to move on to other business. The disadvantage of conducting the tally at the meeting is that participants may be unable to conduct other business while the count is made. After the results have been tabulated, the ballots from both steps two and four should be destroyed to preserve the anonymity of the participants.

Remember, NGT is a specialized decision technique for use when the group is unable to reach a decision through normal procedures. In those cases it is invaluable, but recurrent use weakens the ability of group members to work together. Frequent emergence of situations requiring use of NGT is a sign that issues crucial to the working of the group have not been adequately resolved or that the group is in need of restructuring. Both possibilities should be explored with training and development specialists who can suggest means of resolving underlying issues or of restructuring the group.

SUMMARY

An effective chairperson makes it possible for a group to reach its full potential by avoiding the extremes of rigid control and inactivity. The ideal chairperson maintains a favorable climate, selects appropriate tasks, establishes an agenda, and employs appropriate decision structures.

LEARNING ACTIVITIES

1. Think about the groups to which you belong. Which has the best leader? Which has the worst leader? Write a brief description of the way each conducts a meeting and try to identify the behaviors that contribute to your impressions. What does the best leader do to structure discussion and control interaction? What does the worst leader do to structure discussion and control interaction? What would happen if the leaders changed places? What strategies can you learn from the best leader? What behaviors of the worst leader should you avoid?

2. Recall a meeting in which you felt particularly uncomfortable or frustrated. What caused you to feel uncomfortable or frustrated? How did your feelings affect your conduct during the meeting? Did the behavior of the leader contribute to your feelings? What could the leader have done to make you feel more comfortable or satisfied?

3. Recall an ineffective or unsuccessful decision made by a group to which

you belong. In a brief paragraph, describe how the decision was made. Was the process consistent with that recommended by the Vroom-Yetton model? How would the process have been changed if the model were employed? Would following the model improve the quality of the decision reached?

4. Observe the meeting of a group that is open to the public. How were decisions made by the group? Did most members appear satisfied with the procedure? How were conflicts resolved? Were any special procedures employed to clarify opposing positions? What role did the leader play in shaping discussion or resolving conflicts?

INDEX

SUBJECT INDEX

Examples, as speech material (*cont.*)
  illustrations, 23–24
  real, 24, 31*t*
  specific instances, 22, 24, 31*t*
Exception, principle of, 212
Extemporaneous speech, 105–6
Eye contact
  in formal speeches, 100–101
  in task groups, 230

Familiar references, in speech introductions, 62–63
Fear appeals, in actuating speeches, 168–69
Feedback
  in appraisal interviews, 215–17
  defined, 5
  in oral vs. written styles, 79–80
  (*see also* Appraisal interviews; Listening)
Final appeals, in speech conclusions, 67, 74
Five Clocks, The (Joos), 85, 86
Flow charts, 37, 38*t*, 43 & *fig.*, 44 *fig.*
  in demonstrations, 135
Formal leaders, of audiences, 120
Formal presentations, 12–13
Formal style (Joos), 85–86
Free association questions, 202*n*
Frozen style (Joos), 85, 86*t*
Full sentence outlines
  for composing speeches, 73–74
    examples, 17–19
  for delivering speeches, 104, 106
Functional analysis, of audiences, 119–23
  formal leaders, 120
  gatekeepers, 121
  opinion leaders, 120–21
Funeral orations, 150 & *n*, 151

Gatekeepers, in communication systems, 121–22, 122 *fig.*, 123
Gestures
  in lectures, 133, 134
  in speech delivery, 102
  in task groups, 230
Goal analysis, 116
Grammar (*see also* Style)
  and frozen style, 85
  and oral style, 80
Grapevines, in organizations, 10
Graphs, for statistical data, 28, 29 (*see also* Bar graphs; Line graphs; Pictographs; Pie graphs)
Group interaction, tension in, 141–42
Groups (*see* Small group communication; Task groups)

Hierarchy, in organizations, 8–10, 11
Historical backgrounds, in introductions, 64
Historical presentations, 68–69
Humorous anecdotes
  in banquet speeches, 148, 149
  in speech introductions, 63–64
Hypothetical examples, for clarification, 30, 31*t*

Ideas, relationships between, 37, 38*t*
Illustrations, in speech writing, 23–24
  for clarification, 30, 31*t*
Image systems, of audiences, 115

Impromptu speeches, 104–5
Indexes, to publications, 20
Informal reports, to employers, 204–5
  timing of, 212–13 (*see also* Task groups)
Informational interviews, 12, 203–14
  timing of report, 212–14
  trust, employer-employee, 205–9
    accessibility, 206
    availability, 207
    confidentiality, 206–7
    loyalty, 208–9
    predictability, 207–8
    self-advertisement, 208
  what to report, 209–12
    classes of information, 209–10
    exercise of initiative, 211–12
    principle of exception, 212
    transfers of responsibility, 210–11
Information processing
  brain's rate of, 184
  information overload, 36, 204–5
Information sources, 20–21
  on employers, 194
  in speech conclusions, 67
Informative speaking, 30, 126, 127, 130–39
  demonstrations, 134–36
  lectures, 131–34
  public relations, 157–58
  reports, 136–39
Initiative, exercise of, in projects, 211–12
Intended messages, 3
Intense language, 83–84
Internal summaries, 72
Interpersonal communication, 11, 12, 179 (*see also* Dyadic communication; Interviews)
Interpersonal relationships
  and communication, 182–83, 183 *fig.*
  defined, 179
  dimensions, 180–81
Interviews, 12, 193–222
  appraisal (of employees), 214–22
    defensive communication in, 217–19
    feedback in, 215–17
    goals of, 214
    how to conduct, 219–22
    consultative style in, 86
  defined, 12
  informational (reporting to employer), 203–14
    timing of report, 212–14
    trust in, 205–9
    what to report, 209–12
  selection (employment), 193–202
    answering questions, 196, 198–99
    interviewing styles, 201–2
    negative factors, 199–201
    resumes, 194–96, 197 *fig.*
Intimate style (Joos), 86
Introductions, to speeches, 61–66
Introductory speeches, 142–44
  example, 144
  format, 142–43

Jargon
  with intimate style, 86
  precise vs. popular meanings, 89, 90*t*
  professional, 89, 182